I0819642

Grover E. Murray Studies in the American Southwest

Also in the Grover E. Murray Studies in the American Southwest

Brujerías: Stories of Witchcraft and the Supernatural in the American Southwest and Beyond

Nasario García

Cacti of the Trans-Pecos and Adjacent Areas

A. Michael Powell and
James F. Weedin

Deep Time and the Texas High Plains: History and Geology

Paul H. Carlson

From Texas to San Diego in 1851: The Overland Journal of Dr. S.W. Woodhouse, Surgeon–Naturalist of the Sitgreaves Expediton

Edited by Andrew Wallace and
Richard H. Hevly

Javelinas

Jane Manaster

PICTURING A DIFFERENT WEST

PICTURING A DIFFERENT WEST

Vision, Illustration, and the Tradition of Austin and Cather

Janis P. Stout

Texas Tech University Press

This book is typeset in Adobe Caslon. The paper used in this book meets the minimum requirements of ANSI/NISO Z39.48-1992 (R1997). ∞

Designed by Jennifer E. Holmes

Library of Congress Cataloging-in-Publication Data
Stout, Janis P.
Picturing a different West : vision, illustration, and the tradition of Cather and Austin / Janis P. Stout.
p. cm. -- (Grover E. Murray studies in the American Southwest)
Includes bibliographical references and index.
ISBN-13: 978-0-89672-610-9 (hardcover : alk. paper)
ISBN-10: 0-89672-610-X (hardcover : alk. paper)
1. Cather, Willa, 1873-1947--Illustrations. 2. Austin, Mary Hunter, 1868-1934--Illustrations. 3. Visual perception in literature. 4. Landscape in literature. 5. West (U.S.)--In literature. 6. Southwest, New--In literature. 7. Illustration of books--United States. 8. Art and literature--United States. I. Title.
PS3505.A87Z862 2007
810'.93278--dc22
2006100952

Printed in the United States of America

07 08 09 10 11 12 13 14 15 / 9 8 7 6 5 4 3 2 1

Texas Tech University Press
Box 41037
Lubbock, Texas 79409-1037 USA
800.832.4042
ttup@ttu.edu
www.ttup.ttu.edu

In memory of Susan J. Rosowski
(1942–2004)

Across the broad spaces, the limitless places,
Unfettered, unhindered, my spirit goes free.

Eliza Swift, "On the Prairie"

CONTENTS

ILLUSTRATIONS

PREFACE

The key to both Mary Austin's and Willa Cather's profound interest in the West was one of vision, or seeing. We know this from their fiction and from the record provided by their letters and descriptive writings. Their vision of the West and what it meant or might mean for American self-definition emerged largely from their own visual experience, their literal seeing of it. Both moved west in their youth, Cather from Virginia to Nebraska, and Austin from Illinois to California; both left records of their encounters with environments different from all they had known before; and both subsequently invested time and creative energy in exploring the mountainous Southwest of New Mexico and Arizona. To a great extent their ideas of the significance of these experiences, for themselves and for their society, emerged from what they saw in the course of their travels and sojourns. The nature of these experiences and the ways in which, as a result, Austin and Cather wrote about the West and Southwest are the central subject of this book.

Austin's and Cather's visual experience of the West also came to them, however, through art, that is, through the American tradition of nationalistic landscape painting and through the burgeoning—in the very years of their emergence as writers—of the practice of illustration. Like other women writers and artists at the start of the twentieth century who looked west, they found their imaginations challenged not only by the vast region itself but by this body of visual, as well as literary, representation. It was a powerfully influential tradition that was initially shaped in part by the descriptive accounts of white explorers and settlers, but in large part, too, by the work of visual artists who accompanied these explorers, and then those who came after them. Engaging the spectacle of the West's vast plains and its mountainous heights and chasms, artists as well as writers conveyed a view of the West as a rugged and forbidding place amenable to encounters only by equally rugged and daring men. The West was defined as a place of adventure and wonder, an arena in which men might prove their manhood through encounters and conflicts with the rigors of a difficult landscape inhabited by people of striking otherness. The West, in short, was gendered male.

As they engaged this regional visual tradition, Austin and Cather contested its vision of the West as an arena of rugged masculine adventure and violence, unamenable to women or receptive to them only in circumscribed ways. Some women writers and artists attempted to revise this prevailing picture of the West by feminizing it. Cather and Austin, however, proposed an inclusively androgynous vision in which women and men alike were freed of prescriptive and rigidly conventional gender roles. They went about their contesting of the insistent masculinity of western tradition not only by integrating women's experiences into their own "picture" of the West but by reordering readers' understandings of what gender can mean.

They did so in books about the West written in a highly visual prose and often (but, for reasons relating to the economics of book publishing, not always) embellished with illustrations. We know how important the art of illustration was to Cather from records of her professional engagement with its practice as an editor of *McClure's Magazine,* as well as from extensive, albeit unintended, archives of her personal letters. In Austin's case the documentary record is thinner, but not insignificant. Existing records of their direct comments on their own work also tell us how conscious and deliberate was their revision of the conventional Western. But their books themselves and the conclusions we can infer from them, as well as from the illustrations that accompanied them, are the most important evidence of how they responded to established traditions of representing the West.

These three distinct but interrelated ideas, then—the visual nature of Austin's and Cather's own experience of the West, the importance of western art and the art of illustration in the making of their books, and their revision of the gender assumptions pervading both the art and the literature of the West—are my concerns in this book. They are connected by a strong narrative thread: the founding and perpetuation of an alternative western tradition, a tradition of women's own.

The construction of this alternative vision of the West was not by any means Austin's and Cather's project alone. They built their careers alongside a number of other women writers and artists whose visions of a regendered West were strikingly similar—such as the writer and illustrator Mary Hallock Foote, the anthropologist Elsie Clews Parsons (as well as other women anthropologists working in the Southwest), the diarist and promoter of the arts Mabel Dodge Luhan, the painter Georgia O'Keeffe, and the photographer Laura Gilpin. These figures are merely glimpsed in my story. Austin and Cather are its central subjects. My contention is that they were in fact the central figures in the establishment of a new and regendered tradition of visual and literary—or indeed, visual-cum-literary—engagement with the West. They were, as Austin claims of her own books about the West, "always a little in advance" (*Earth Horizon* 320). And the tradition that they led in establishing has proved to be a sturdy one. Its continuance is demonstrated by the women of the Southwest I discuss in my closing chapter: the writer Leslie Marmon Silko, in whose vision (as represented here in her powerfully pictorial book *Storyteller*) gender and seeing are linked, the poet Margaret Randall, and the artist Barbara Byers, whose drawings accompany Randall's poems in the book *Into Another Time: Grand Canyon Reflections.*

In examining Austin's and Cather's books about the West, I will generally move from their illustrations to their highly visual prose and the complementarity between the two, and then to their conceptual visions of the West. In the writings of both, vision in the abstract sense comes out of vision in the actual, physical sense, and the structure of my study follows that ordering. I will also generally move from Austin to Cather, rather than the reverse, because I am convinced that Cather was observing and responding to Austin's work more than Austin—until very late in her writing life—was observing and responding to Cather's. At every stage, I will seek to view these two central figures within the context of the large regional tradition that has created so powerful a national mythos, most importantly the context provided by other women writers and artists of the West.

Despite the informed and persuasive argument of Judith Fetterley and Marjorie Pryse, in *Writing out of Place,* that the word "region" refers to the geopolitical condition of an area's being ruled by outside powers and forces, rather than to geographical environment per se, I use the word "region" here in the sense of a place on the map. To be sure, place entails history, and history entails politics. But for my purposes, place comes first; these other concerns are inextricable results, not causes.

This is a book of literary history. Its method is often descriptive, often analytic, but primarily narrative. Smaller narrative units are embedded within its overarching story of the development and promulgation of an alternative tradition of the West. Only rarely and tangentially is it theoretical. At times, in keeping with what I see as commonly accepted practice in art criticism, its method is more impressionistic than academic literary criticism is usually expected to be. Almost certainly, however, my comments on pictorial representations would be less impressionistic and considerably more technical if I had the benefit of formal training in art history and techniques. Alas, I have none. I can only, then, beg the reader's indulgence as I share my interest in the physical presence of these books and the regional pictorial history that comprises so important a context for both their illustrations and the texts themselves, as well as, and more importantly, my sense of why these aspects of Austin's and Cather's writing about the West matter.

This book had its genesis in my recognition of the similarity between the illustrations of Mary Austin's *The Land of Little Rain* and those of Willa Cather's *My Ántonia,* two of the most persistently tantalizing texts in which women writers contemplate the West. My interest in reading the W. T. Benda illustrations of *My Ántonia* as an integral part of the text had earlier been stimulated by Jean Schwind's 1985 article reading them as a "'Silent' Supplement to Jim Burden's Narrative." This interest intensified as I became familiar with Cather's letters to her publisher, Houghton Mifflin, in the course of my work on *Willa Cather: The Writer and Her World* (2000). It was nurtured, during those same years, by Susan J. Rosowski's work on Cather's relations with her publishers, first presented (so far as I know) in a 1995 plenary address at the Sixth International Willa Cather Seminar and subsequently published as the historical essay in the scholarly edition of *A Lost Lady* (1997). What the letters make clear and Rosowski presents so well in explaining Cather's move from Houghton Mifflin to Knopf is that Cather was closely involved not only in the selection of Benda as illustrator for *My Ántonia* but in his actual production of the drawings, now so familiar in most (sadly, not all) reprintings of the novel, and that she was involved even in the way they were presented in the design of the volume. Tracing this production history, we learn that pictures were very important to Willa Cather.

My interest in Mary Austin was steadily increasing at the same time as my interest in the pictorial dimension of *My Ántonia.* Austin and Cather knew each other; both left homes in the East and moved to the West (East and West being, of course, relative terms with shifting reference); and their lives and interests converged in the Southwest—indeed, in the living room of Mary Austin's house in Santa Fe, where Cather spent several days in 1926 working on *Death Comes for the Archbishop.* When my delight in Austin's *The Land of Little Rain* began to turn to its notable illustrations by E. Boyd Smith, and when I first realized that the Smith illustrations and the Benda illustrations to *My Ántonia* were strikingly similar, I do not remember. At any rate, that realization led to a paper presented at the Eighth International Willa Cather Seminar in 2000, published in *Cather Studies 5: Willa Cather's Ecological Imagination* as "The Observant Eye, the Art of Illustration, and Willa Cather's *My Ántonia.*" This book incorporates, then, earlier work published in *Cather Studies 5* and in a special issue of *American Literary Realism,* both edited by Susan Rosowski, but pushes considerably beyond those essays, both in textual subject matter and in frame of reference, as I move from literal to metaphorical "seeing."

The lines by Eliza Swift used as an epigraph are quoted by Joni L. Kinsey in *Plain Pictures* (114). Kinsey comments that Swift's poem was a favorite of Laura Gilpin's.

Thankful acknowledgment is owed and gladly given to more people than I will probably remember to name here. First, as indicated in the dedication, I am grateful to Susan J. Rosowski, who more than any other single person fostered Cather studies for a generation of scholars. To Dennis Berthold, who generously gave of his time and expertise to read early drafts of several chapters and whose comments helped me sharpen my thinking. To my former graduate student, now colleague in the profession, Robin Cohen, whose dissertation examined visual elements in Leslie Silko's manuscripts and printed texts. To another former student, now an accomplished writer and doctoral candidate, Susan Rushing Adams, whose undergraduate honors thesis on Cather remains more suggestive and stimulating than anyone could ever expect undergraduate work to be. To Richard Archuleta, Office of the Governor, Taos Pueblo, for information about traditional attire. To Timothy Bintrim, who shares my interest in Cather and illustrations (and Cather as illustrator), and whose expertise about the archival record of Cather's early years is unsurpassed—thanks, Tim, for calling my attention to Cather's column in *National Stockman and Farmer.* To Zao Liu, Kristen Smith, and Carolina De Leon at Evans Library, Texas A&M University, who tirelessly supplied me with the materials I needed and steadfastly resisted what must have been a strong urge to cry "Hold! Enough!" To Audrey S. Kauders, Director of the Museum of Nebraska Art, for information about Marion Canfield Smith. To the Harry Ransom Humanities Research Center of the University of Texas, and in particular to Rachel Hertz, for assistance with the letters of Mary Austin to Alice Corbin Henderson and for the dust jackets of *My Ántonia* and *Death Comes for the Archbishop.* To Kelly Wolfe Bachli and others in the Special Collections department of the Honnold/Mudd Library, Claremont University Consortium, for access to rare copies of books by Mary Austin. To Samantha Rippner, Assistant Curator, Department of Prints and Drawings, the Metropolitan Museum of Art, New York, and to Virginia O'Hara, Curator at the Brandywine Valley Museum, Chadds Ford, Pennsylvania, for sharing their expertise on illustration practices in the early twentieth century. To Callie Vincent, of the Amon Carter Museum, Leslie Green, of the Smithsonian Institution, Kate Bergeron, of the Autry Center for the American West, and Aimee Marshall, of the Art Institute of Chicago, for assistance with reproductions of art works held in those collections. To Marjorie Pryse, of the State University of New York at Albany, and to Mary Beth Dunhouse, Coordinator of Special Projects and Collections, Boston Public Library, for information about early editions of *The Land of Little Rain.* To Elizabeth S. Burke, Charles Mignon, Andrew Jewell, and Kari Ronning at the Cather Project, University of Nebraska, for helping me through many quandaries. To Jim Sullenberger for bringing to my attention Margaret Randall's and Barbara Byers's *Into Another Time.* To Margaret and Barbara themselves for being tolerant of my words about their work and for providing answers to direct questions. To Diane Quantic for sharing her work on Cather, Keith Jacobshagen, and other Great Plains artists. To J. Lawrence Mitchell at Texas A&M University for helping me locate information about the history of printing and for cheering me on. To the two scholars who anonymously read the manuscript for Texas Tech University Press, whose comments and suggestions opened doors in my mind (and to one of them especially for the phrase "reordering readers' understandings of what gender can mean"), and to Judith Keeling, Editor-in-Chief, for her unflagging encouragement. And always and most to Loren Lutes for laughing at me when I say I've written my last, for tolerating my obsessiveness when I get going on a project, and this time for providing technical help with illustrations.

PICTURING A DIFFERENT WEST

1

WHITE AMERICA'S GENDERED VISION OF THE WEST

Westward the star of empire takes its way, in the whiteness of innocence.

John Quincy Adams, commenting on the Louisiana Purchase, 1803, quoted by Drinnon, vii

I'm afraid the West is a man's world.

Mabel Dodge Luhan
Letter to Carl Van Vechten, 1913

If we think of the national context into which Mary Austin and Willa Cather were born, an obvious historical marker is the Civil War. Austin's life began in Illinois in 1868, three years after the war's end, and Cather's in Virginia in 1873, when it was eight years past but still very present in the minds of Virginians. Continentally speaking, such a marker draws our view of these two writers toward the east. But if we instead turn westward in trying to imagine the world in which Austin and Cather came to consciousness, we find a different historical marker, one of at least equal importance to their conception of their culture and American nationhood: white Americans' burgeoning fascination with the West and especially what we now call the Southwest.[1] In the last two decades of the nineteenth century, the decades in which Austin came to young adulthood and migrated west and Cather migrated west before coming to young adulthood, that fascination both produced and was fueled by a great surge of visual images. A lively and expanding visual culture of the West joined the well-established (and now well-recognized) tradition of American landscape writing in which they came to their literary vocations.

We have not often recognized the extent to which Austin and Cather experienced the West, and wrote of it, in visual terms, as well as in ways that contested prevailing conventions. They came to artistic maturity within the context of a visual culture of the West that emphasized masculinity and violent action. Only if we understand the nature and prevalence of those conventions can we appreciate the significance of the visual aspects of their own books about the West and Southwest—that is, both their highly visual language and the visual dimension of their books constituted by illustrations. Austin and Cather offered an alternative way of seeing western spaces and peoples. From a grasp of how they saw the West—literally *saw* it—and how the total physical presence of their books leads readers to see it, we can better proceed to the question of how they "saw" the West conceptually and how the regional visual tradition in which they participated continues today.

The year of Mary Austin's birth, 1868, also saw the death of an artist whose huge (twenty-by-thirty-foot) painting *Westward the Course of Empire Takes Its Way* was emblematic of the nation's commitment to a white triumphalist vision of the West. Emanuel Leutze's celebration of Anglo westering had been commissioned in 1861 for the west stairway of the U.S. Capitol (figure 1.01). Its passive and genteel women at the left center being ushered west by a larger-than-life protective male would scarcely accord with the views of women in the West that Austin would develop as she matured.

By 1868, too, Albert Bierstadt (1830–1902) had completed several of his monumental paintings of the mountain West—*Storm in the Rocky Mountains* probably in 1866, and *The Domes of the Yellowstone* in 1867. Bierstadt followed an earlier generation of painters—including George Catlin, Karl Bodmer, and Alfred Jacob Miller—who traveled the West and produced paintings of the Native peoples, Anglo mountain men, and open or romantically rugged landscapes they saw there (Etulain xxv–xxvi). But Bierstadt, together with Thomas Moran (1837–1926), influenced by the rugged Hudson River School and Thomas Cole's "negotiations of a national style" (Daniels 169), raised to new heights of grandeur a monumentality readily associated with national identity.

At the same time, a more bucolic artistic view of the West was developing, reflecting the aspirations of settlers attracted to the West by the Homestead Act of 1862, with its promise of land settlers could not have hoped to purchase back east. Junius Sloan's 1866 painting *Cool Morning on*

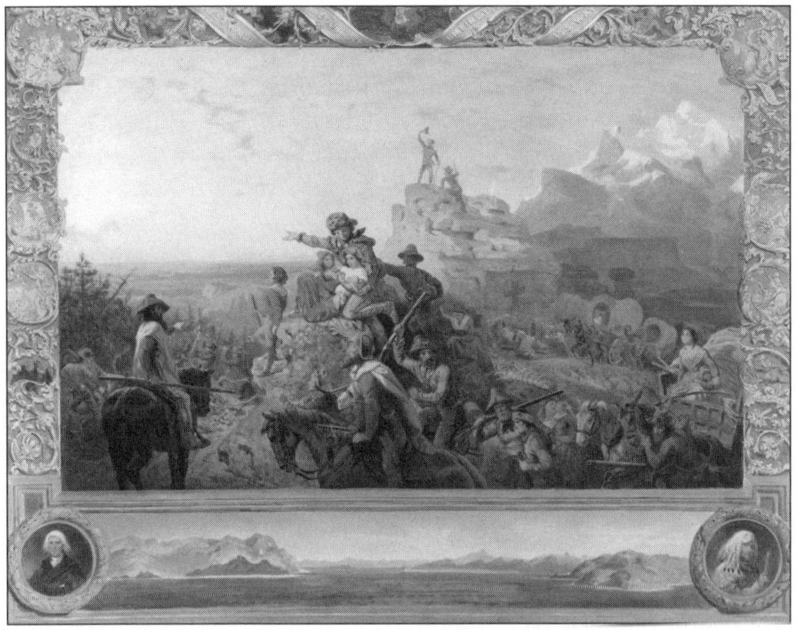

1.01 Emanuel Leutze, *Westward the Course of Empire Takes Its Way,* mural study, U.S. Capitol, 1861 (Smithsonian American Art Museum, bequest of Sara Carr Upton)

the Prairie, depicting the environment so many settlers would find dauntingly harsh as instead a scene of tranquility, invoked a landscape vocabulary of questionable appropriateness, one of humid mists and wooden fence posts (Kinsey 79). It is an example of the promotional imaging of the West that would be an important aspect of Austin's and Cather's professional world and one in which they would sometimes participate. In 1867, however, the year before Austin's birth, Theodore Kaufmann's *Westward the Star of Empire* took the opposite tack of showing the plains as a place of peril awaiting Anglo settlers, with Indians lurking in the dark to derail an oncoming train. Pictorial representations, along with the "tremendously popular" written accounts of explorers such as John C. Frémont (Kinsey 57), were providing Americans a range of conceptions of the West.

In 1873, the year of Cather's birth, artist Jules Tavernier toured the West making sketches that were published in the leading illustrated magazine of the day, *Harper's.* That same year, Thomas Moran went to the Grand

Canyon and the West Coast on commission by *Appleton's Magazine* to produce illustrations for what would become the most popular parlor table book in 1870s America, *Picturesque America* (Rainey xiii). Only the year before, Congress had purchased Moran's seven-by-twelve–foot painting *The Chasm of the Yellowstone* for $10,000, making him the "rising star of Western landscape art" (Rainey 168), and Yellowstone had become the nation's first national park. Bierstadt's luminist canvas *Sunrise, Yosemite Valley* (ca. 1870), a result of a trip he made to see the wonders of Yosemite after seeing photographs at an exhibit in New York in 1862, has been said to convey the idea of "a land of gold" (museum notes, Amon Carter Museum). With the "westward trajectory of national identity" facilitated by the completion of the transcontinental railroad in 1869, artistic interest shifted from the Hudson River Valley to the "fresher" and "more magnificent" scenery of the Rockies and the Sierra Nevada (Daniels 169)—jumping over, for the time being at least, the Great Plains. In 1874, the year following Cather's birth, Moran painted *Cliffs of Green River* (figure 1.02), showing a majestic, mountainous landscape empty of any sign of human habitation except a small party of explorers following along the river and wondering at what they see. The painting glorifies the bold project of exploration along with the wonders of North America.

In July 1876, less than three years after Cather's birth, Mary Hallock Foote, who would become a notably successful writer as well as illustrator of western scenes, first went west with her engineer-developer husband. Foote's stories and drawings would be widely distributed in the 1880s in the pages of *Century*, a leading magazine purchased and preserved by the Cather family in Nebraska.[2]

But the Cathers had their own source of visual images of the West even before they left Virginia for the Great Plains in the spring of 1883. Before his marriage to Willa's mother, Charles F. Cather had made a trip to the Mountain West and sent back reports of what he saw. In an 1870 letter to his sister Jennie, he described his ramblings in Wyoming, Colorado, and New Mexico in adventurous terms, saying that he had seen bears, wolves, and desperadoes, and pronouncing it all "splendid country." Pronghorn antelopes on the high plains, he said, were "the most beautiful things you can imagine."[3] We can well believe that Cather heard her father reminisce about this trip during her childhood and that she also heard her aunt Franc and uncle

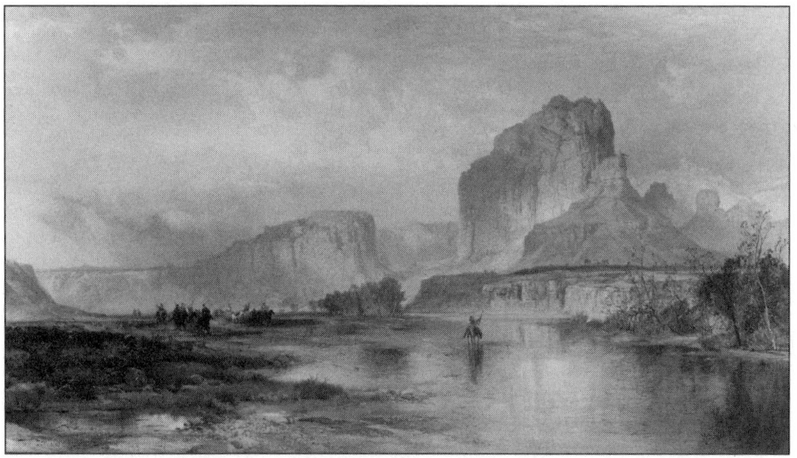

1.02 Thomas Moran, *Cliffs of Green River,* 1874, oil on canvas (accession number 1975.28, Amon Carter Museum, Fort Worth, Texas)

George's accounts of life on the plains in the years before her own family joined them there. We glimpse these latter in George's report to (again) Jennie Cather Ayre on March 17, 1876, that "about 200 Omaha Indians passed in sight of our place last week."[4] Both the implied threat and the perceived vanishing of the Native American, along with the beauties of western landscape, were a part of the family lore.

Austin and Cather not only grew up in a period of burgeoning painting (as well as photography) of the West, but in the years of the emergence and rapid expansion of illustrated periodicals. From mid-century on, large-circulation newspapers and magazines, the "mass media of the day," began to feature prints made from woodblocks (Rainey xiii, 6–7). The use of such illustrations greatly expanded in the 1860s with the development and spread of the electrotyping process, which afforded economies of scale in producing "exact duplicates of woodcuts as well as of letterpress type" (Rainey 13; also Larson 19). *Harper's Weekly,* launched in the 1850s, was the first of these successful illustrated magazines, followed by *Scribner's and Century* in the 1870s and 1880s (Larson 20).

Although changes in technology made the pictured West more readily available to large numbers of interested Americans in the latter part of the century, visual representations had in fact accompanied verbal accounts from the early days of western exploration. Throughout the nineteenth century, cartographers and painters regularly accompanied explorers' expeditions in the West.[5] By 1865 or 1870, their maps, drawings, and paintings had gained some limited circulation from the published reports that resulted, such as John C. Frémont's *Report of an Exploration* . . . in 1843.[6] In his book *Indian Country,* Martin Padget underscores the partnership of word and image by speaking of explorers' reports and travelers' writings as a verbal "mapping." Such mappings, he argues, constituted a kind of "colonizing" by Anglos such as Frémont who wished to "possess the terrain [they] surveyed" (4, 14).

After the 1860s, as improved technology made it feasible for publishers to satisfy public demand for pictorial information about the West, newspapers and magazines also began to send artists and illustrators on extended western tours (Taft 149). It was *Harper's Weekly,* for instance, that commissioned Tavernier's trip in 1873, the year Cather was born. But the most significant of these commissioned projects was the series of artistic excursions sponsored by Oliver Bunce at *Appleton's,* resulting in the lavish two-volume publication *Picturesque America.*

Topical articles about notable American sites, always with illustrations, were published in *Appleton's* beginning November 12, 1870. These were subsequently issued in fascicles that could be bound together by subscribers who received them as they came out between 1872 and 1874, and then in a generally available two-volume set. Sue Rainey's *Creating Picturesque America* provides a definitive study of the production and significance of this extended project. The year 1870, Rainey writes, brought "intensifying rivalry" among illustrated periodicals, with the number and quality of illustrations a featured point in the competition (22). American artists, writers, and their public had for decades been "keenly aware of the lack of historic architecture" in their own country, as compared to Europe, and now they looked to natural scenery as an alternative site of national glory. During the years when *Picturesque America* was appearing, the West—not so much the Great Plains as the Mountain West—became "the primary locus of sublime natural scenery" in the awareness of Americans (Rainey 93–94, 215).

Drawing on William Cullen Bryant's wide reputation as a poet and patriot of the American natural world who had long since celebrated the midcontinental prairies as a "region of the American imagination" (Buell 78; Bryant's poem "The Prairies" was published in 1833), Appleton showed

Bryant as the nominal editor of the book version of *Picturesque America,* although the actual editor was Oliver Bunce, who had commissioned the enterprise. Bryant did supply a two-page preface that strikes the nationalistic tone pervading the entire project. "Our country abounds," he proclaimed, "with scenery new to the artist's pencil, of a varied character, whether beautiful or grand." Probably few of us now would make the distinction between the beautiful and the grand, but it was still a time of studied vocabularies of landscape description. "In the Old World," Bryant continued, "every spot remarkable in these respects has been visited by the artist [and] Art sighs to carry her conquests into new realms" (iii). Thus the very lack of a long tradition became a national distinction, since visual representations of American scenery, especially in the "remarkable" West, could be fresh, in contrast to the implied staleness of European landscape art. The first volume featured "Our Great National Park," Yellowstone. The second, despite a more urban character signaled by its frontispiece of New York City, featured "The Rocky Mountains," with illustrations by Thomas Moran. In both volumes, text and pictures alike tended to emphasize "untrodden wilds" and a "savage and tremendous" quality of America's natural scenes (*Picturesque America* II 377). Most of the nonurban illustrations either included no human figures or showed them as diminutive, thereby emphasizing the vastness of the natural setting.

In considering painterly responses to the West, it is important to distinguish between the Mountain West, which readily lends itself to a gorgeous vastness and ruggedness in artistic representations, and the Great Plains, whose treelessness or seeming emptiness was daunting to early visitors and settlers as well as artists.[7] Until the passage of the Homestead Act made the Great Plains "available" for settlement by Euro-Americans and made it desirable in the minds of investors and nationalistic expansionists to attract such settlers (Kinsey 37), the plains were frequently known as the Great Desert, a term attached to these relatively dry expanses by Major Stephen Long, who explored the terrain from the prairies to the Rocky Mountains in 1819–1820.[8] Few Americans had possessed even rudimentary information about the plains at the opening of the nineteenth century, and even after the reports of government explorers began to be known, there was no "single, universally accepted view" of the region (J. Allen 209). Lewis and Clark, for example, depicted a more arboreal West because they mostly followed rivers, and French explorers, too, glimpsed the vast central spaces of the continent from watercourses, and therefore did not have what might be called a true prairie experience (Kinsey 34). Cross-country explorers like Major Long judged the plains by comparison to previously known environments; they "encountered what their forest backgrounds led them to believe were arid conditions" and for that reason described what they saw in terms suggestive of a desert (J. Allen 210). Europeans coming to the plains were, as Robert Thacker puts it, "historically ill-equipped to view and understand the prairie landscape," to the point that the European experience of the plains, beginning with Coronado's incursion in 1540, demanded "the creation of landmarks in a region that seemed . . . without them" (Thacker 2).

In the mid-nineteenth–century heyday of landscape appreciation, artists were not only conditioned to be responsive to outdoor scenery but were accustomed to using trees as framing devices for the composition of landscape paintings, and elevated outcroppings or hills as vantage points. Such framing devices and elevations were rarely available on the plains, and artists such as George Catlin who sought to paint the Great Plains in the earlier decades of the nineteenth century had trouble conveying perspective and depth.[9] Catlin was best able to solve the challenge of the plains' openness and flatness when he could devise ways of interrupting the level horizon, as he did (with billows of smoke) in *Prairie Meadows Burning* (1832). Yet the bareness and openness of the plains and the looming hugeness of the prairie skies were in themselves an aesthetic that Catlin adopted in a number of paintings (such as in figure 1.03) whose bareness of clutter makes them seem far ahead of their time, as if he were anticipating a modernist such as Georgia O'Keeffe.

Despite inherent difficulties of perspective, the flatness and openness of the Great Plains could present "artistic opportunities" when an artist adopted an imagined elevation to depict great distance (Kinsey 19, 24). Such an imagined elevation is seen, for instance, in John Gast's frequently noted *American Progress* (1872) (figure 1.04). In this painting, the vantage point is perhaps that of History, which is not limited to actual terrain. The distance shown is also, by implication, a promise of the extent and endurance of the nation's greatness. The march of white Americans across the plains, especially the striding allegorical figure stringing telegraph lines as she goes, clearly represents the idea of Progress. It was in a similar vein of idealization that

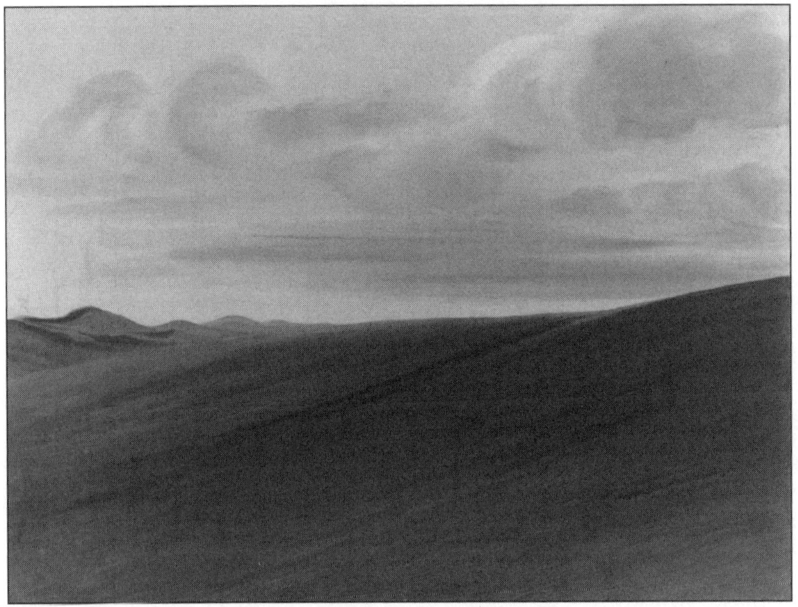

1.03 George Catlin, *Nishnabottana Bluffs, Upper Missouri,* 1832
(Smithsonian American Art Museum, gift of Mrs. Joseph Harrison, Jr.)

John Quincy Adams cast the march westward, in the statement quoted in the first epigraph to this chapter, as taking place "in the whiteness of innocence." In view of subsequent history, we may question whether whiteness was indeed innocent, or innocence white. Adams's statement has accumulated multiple ironies.

If the designation "West" reflects a racialized and politicized Anglo perspective, so does the elevated perspective commonly employed by Gast and others in depicting these exciting "new" reaches of the continent. Painters of the Western Luminist school flocking to produce images of the Mountain West often either adopted or simply imagined physical eminences affording a panoramic breadth of view. This "trac[ing]" of a "visual trajectory from the uplands to a scenic panorama below" is well designated by Albert Boime as the "magisterial gaze" and by Mary Louise Pratt as a "master of all he surveys" view. In Boime's words, the "structural paradigm" of the elevated view shared the "ideology of expansionist [and we might add, racist] thought" that we identify as the notion of Manifest Destiny (3–5).[10]

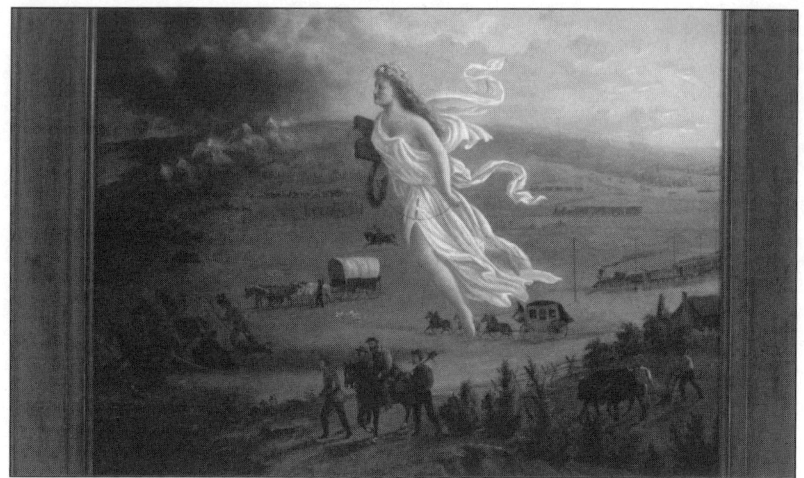

1.04 John Gast, *American Progress,* 1872 (Museum of the American West collection, Autry National Center, Los Angeles)

The Grand Canyon, providing unparalleled opportunities for such panoramic views, quickly became a favorite site for landscape artists. But the great number of paintings of the Canyon can be attributed not only to its inherent majesty but also to purposeful promotion by the Santa Fe Railway (more properly, after 1896, the Atchison, Topeka & Santa Fe Railway). Determinedly expansionist, the Santa Fe promoted the Grand Canyon as "a tourist attraction of sublime natural wonders, prehistoric and colonial historic significance, and colorful, [but significantly] tamed, native peoples" from 1882 to World War II (Weigle, "From Desert to Disney World" 115). In 1895 the passenger division of the Santa Fe formulated a policy of using art of the Southwest for advertising purposes and accordingly provided the already well-known Moran free transportation to the Grand Canyon in return for the right to choose one of the resulting paintings for use in its advertising (Schwarz 32; also, see D'Emilio and Campbell 7–38).

Like Niagara Falls, the Grand Canyon was regarded as an emblem of a mighty America—which in the nineteenth century the United States still only aspired to be—because of its extraordinary size and drama. This emblematic significance was soon extended to other scenes that potential passengers on the Santa Fe could readily associate with the Southwest.

William Haskell Simpson, who took charge of passenger division advertising in 1900, continued and expanded the practice of providing free trips for artists. The resulting paintings, frequently including Santa Fe trains and Harvey House hotels such as El Tovar, at the south rim of the canyon, were widely distributed in magazines, framed reproductions, and calendars. Originals hung in stations and ticket offices. Simpson's promotional plan, which centered on "portraits of Indians, landscapes, and genre scenes" of the region, capitalized on the happy fact that the city whose name the company shared was coming to epitomize the Southwest (D'Emilio and Campbell 17; Chris Wilson 80–84). Beginning in 1903, Simpson spearheaded the outright purchase of paintings, in preference to paying use fees that might at times be subject to artists' contrary wishes. For instance, Moran's *Grand Canyon,* one of his many spectacular paintings of the Canyon, was purchased by the railway in 1912. Simpson thus launched a collection that eventually grew to about six hundred canvases, many of them characterized by the nationalistic monumentality associated with Moran and Bierstadt. By century's end, even Bierstadt's "grand canvases" lost favor and were "sold at knock-down prices" as plein-air impressionistic landscapes gained ascendancy (Daniels 169).[11] But these, in fact, served the railway's aims even better.

Vastness and ruggedness in the natural setting, along with the strangeness—to Anglo eyes—of local inhabitants, were also emphasized by early photographers in the West. Skilled photographers came to the West in the 1860s, when freedom from the cumbersome equipment required by daguerreotype processes first allowed them to work outdoors in any "persistent" way (Naef and Wood 12). The period in which photographic views of the West began to be generally known—the decades immediately after mid-century—coincided with the great surge of landscape sensibility that had fueled the reception of Bierstadt and Moran, and landscape photographs of the West quickly began to show an aesthetic rather than purely documentary impulse. Pictures of the majestic beauties of Yosemite were being made by the mid-1860s.[12] The emphasis in these early landscape photographs of Yosemite and in others of waterfalls, mountains, and canyons in the West was regularly on ruggedness and hugeness—that is, on monumentality.

During the 1880s photographers concentrating on the beauties of the land and the charm of the Spanish (and Mexican) heritage made pictures, especially stereographs, for sale as mementoes and for the enlightenment of easterners who might not travel to the West but were curious (Coke 1).[13] Nineteenth-century photographers of New Mexico, in particular, often seem to emphasize an idea of the area's Native inhabitants as curious vestiges of the past. Many posed Indians against artificial backgrounds or in highly contrived arrangements, in a soft-focus style that readily implies the vanishing-Indian idea. Some of William Henry Jackson's photographs of Native Americans taken around 1880 are exceptional in according their subjects a stark dignity, untainted by quaintness. At times these seem to anticipate the austere, factual, and dignified pictures Laura Gilpin would later take of the Navajo. In most of his work, however, Jackson, who accompanied the Ferdinand Hayden survey teams to Yellowstone, falls into the group that Martha Sandweiss characterizes as being "always outsiders, cataloging the natural wonders of the terrain for their employers" (71). Survey photographers, Sandweiss writes, "brought back views of an empty landscape ripe for commercial exploitation" (63). Susan Hegeman concurs that popular photographs such as Jackson's "did much to stimulate western tourism" (51). To borrow Elizabeth Hutchinson's notably understated phrasing, photography of the West "primarily served the needs of the dominant culture" (335).

Portraits of Native Americans constituted a major subgenre of western photography. Probably the most significant of these and surely the best known in our own time were Edward Curtis's extensive documentation, in pictures and text, of the faces, costumes, and activities of Native peoples. Curtis (1868–1952) worked as a photographer in Seattle and Alaska before formulating the goal of documenting the remaining Native tribes in North America in about 1903 or 1904 (Adam 12). His vast project would consume more than thirty years, during which time he traveled the continent seeking to build a comprehensive record of (so he believed) the "last living traditions of North America Indian tribes" (Adam 6). That is, Curtis's photographic project was largely motivated by his acceptance of the theory of the Indians' imminent vanishing—an idea that would enter into Austin's and Cather's writing of the West in various ways. When Curtis began his work, he was not well schooled in Indian cultures and practices, but in the course of the project he not only assembled scientific information never before available and descriptions of some seventy-five languages (sometimes doing the research and writing himself, sometimes coordinating the work of a team of assistants) but also gained a respect for Native religious beliefs, ritual practices, and social patterns—a respect that Austin emphatically shared. To be sure, Curtis is often criticized for sentimentality and staginess. Yet he maintained a keen awareness that as members of an "alien race" he and his staff should refrain from passing quasiauthoritative judgment on Native ways—especially since, as he put it, the Indians found "some of our [Anglo] customs highly objectionable" (quoted in Adam 25).

The place, or sometimes nonplace, of Indians in western photographs is complex and even contradictory. On the one hand, the western landscape was usually shown as empty space, "stripped of the Indian presence and made symbolically hospitable to settlement from the East" (Hegeman 59). But at the same time, and for a range of unformulated purposes, Indians were being photographed and their images sold as collectors' items. In part, these simply served motives of curiosity, but they were also a gesture of control, especially when "wild" Indians were "captured" in interior scenes. When they showed Natives in outdoor landscapes they demonstrated that humans could, after all, live in such inhospitable places and thus implied that Anglo humans could do so, especially since the Indians were "vanishing." In the photographs of this "subgenre," Hegeman writes, Indians join immigrants, the poor, and the "criminal classes" (as in the exposés of Jacob Riis) as "objects of study, quantification, and control" (61).

Mary Austin's respect for Native Americans in California and in New Mexico, although sometimes manipulative, would be at a polar opposite from such attitudes.[14] And both Austin and Cather, as they embarked on their literary careers at the turn of the century, would contest the implication, conveyed by images of ruggedness and vastness in both late nineteenth-century landscape photographs and paintings, that the West was a terrain hospitable only to adventurous males. The aesthetic of ruggedness, with its associated ethic that in Jane Tompkins's words "vindicates conflict, violence, and vengeance" (73), was exclusive in its implications for gender. Austin's and Cather's ethic would be inclusive.

In the western genre paintings of Frederic Remington and C. M. Russell, the rugged masculinity implicit in Bierstadt's and Moran's landscapes became explicit. While "deemphasizing" the monumentality of Bierstadt's and Moran's "gigantic spaces," Russell and Remington fixated nostalgically on adventure and cowboying (Etulain 56). The centrality of these activities in their canvases implied even more clearly that the West was unsuitable for women.

Remington traveled the West in the 1880s, including a jaunt to war-torn Arizona in 1885–1886 on assignment from *Harper's Weekly.* In these early years as a magazine illustrator, he generally limited himself to painting in black, gray, and white, since full-color paintings were difficult to reproduce. Yet even in these subdued tones he succeeded in conveying a sense of action, excitement, and drama—as in *Crow Indians Firing into the Agency,* published in *Harper's Weekly* in 1887 and based on an actual event that very year (collection notes, Amon Carter Museum). Later reprinted in Hamlin Garland's *Book of the American Indian,* the picture furthered a popular image of the Wild West that had been developing since the days of the dime novel. Only two years later, in 1889, Remington's career as a serious artist, not merely an illustrator, was launched by his large, colorful painting *A Dash for the Timber,* in which, in a scene of furious action, Anglo males, one of them wounded, fire their guns at a pursuing group of Indians. In masterly "cinematic" composition (the term used in the collection notes, Amon Carter Museum), the horses run directly toward the viewer.

If action is central to this celebrated painting, setting is also important, with a yellow-toned desert ground, a few scrub trees, mountains in the background, and strong light. Indeed, continued attention to a splendid ruggedness of scenery in both Remington's and Russell's canvases calls into question the idea of a sequence of sharply discrete "phases" of nineteenth-century western art, each lasting "roughly a generation," proposed by Peter Hassrick. Hassrick's scheme has first the art of exploration, then the art of frontier experience, then the art of landscape grandeur associated with national identity, and last an art conveying "the demise of native cultures and indigenous animals" (27). But Remington's and Russell's canvases centering on such staples of frontier experience as hunting and trapping, Indian fighting, and cowboying did not precede, but followed, Bierstadt and Moran. In the work of painters favored by the Santa Fe Railway collection, a sense of the Vanishing American combines with an art of monumental landscape, and a somber and recollective spirit frequently hangs over depictions of Native Americans. In Russell's and Remington's, there is more nostalgia for the adventure of it all. But in both these related bodies of art the land itself is celebrated in images of ruggedness and splendor. Hassrick is clearly correct in identifying "progress, Eden, and masculinity" as pervasive "mythic themes" (27 and ff.).

A Dash for the Timber was exhibited at the National Academy of Design in New York in 1890, the same year that the U.S. superintendent of the census essentially declared the frontier closed. Three years later Frederick Jackson Turner published his essay, "The Significance of the Frontier in American History," with its now-familiar thesis that the advance of American settlement into so-called free land—meaning land not inhabited by other whites, only by Indians—had shaped the national character. Instinctively grasping the essence of this idea, Remington devoted his career to producing canvases conveying a vivid sense of wildness and open space for adventure. Celebrating the Wild West in an enormous number of painted and sculpted works, he perpetuated a vision of the desert Southwest as "a stage across which humans moved" with a "sense of heroism" (Teague 58, 63–64). We see this emphasis on violent masculine action, along with an equal interest in color tones and sense of place, in *His First Lesson* (1903), where, in a scene of furious action, men try to hold and mount a wild-eyed horse against a background suggestive of Mexico, New Mexico, or southern Arizona (figure 1.05).

If Remington's visual world was masculinist, it was also indisputably Anglocentrist. He did frequently depict Indians, but with an emphasis generally on violence and curiosity value. His pictures of Indians, most of them done for the various Harper's publishing interests, can be sampled in Hamlin Garland's *The Book of the American Indian* (1923). Keith Newlin has demonstrated in an introduction to a recent reprinting of the book that Harper's insisted on using these illustrations over Garland's objections, in order to boost sales (xli–xlii). Garland saw Remington's vision of Native life as being radically opposed to his own reformist urge toward justice for a people he regarded as dignified and fully human albeit less "evolved" than whites. He later wrote that Remington painted Indians with a conventionalized "contempt," showing them as "gross of feature" and "cruel" (quoted in Newlin xliii). In the great abundance of Remington's work, it is possible to find exceptions to almost any generalization, but for the most part his interest in Indians as a subject followed the stereotyping and sensationalist patterns that Garland perceived, in fact, as "help[ing] to make the English-speaking peoples the most ruthless conquerors the world has ever seen" (quoted in Newlin xlvi).[15] Except for Indians, Remington's pictured world is almost exclusively

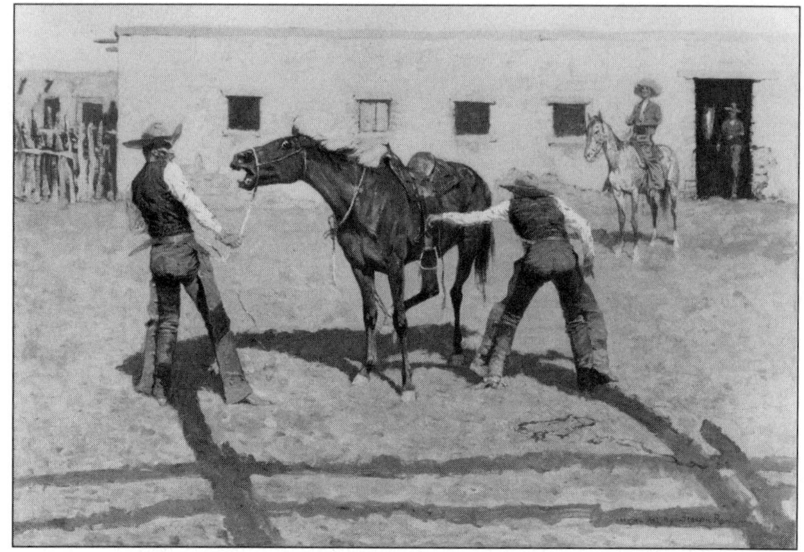

1.05 Frederic Remington, *His First Lesson,* 1903, oil on canvas (accession number 1961.231, Amon Carter Museum, Fort Worth, Texas)

white. His letters reveal, indeed, a pronounced racism against, as he himself wrote, "Jews, Injuns, Chinamen, Italians, Huns—the rubbish of the Earth" (quoted in Etulain 57).

In the latter years of his career, Remington's artistic ambitions moved toward neoimpressionistic work suitable for the best museums and his vision increasingly turned toward quieter themes of the ending of an era. *The Death of the Cowboy* (1895), with its somber grays and its arrested motion as cowboys have to dismount to open a gate in the newly fenced range, was an early herald of what would be an increasing bent toward solemnity and environmental determinism. Another fine and sumptuously beautiful example of this darkened mood is *The Grass Fire* (1908), with its night sky and the intense color on Indians' skin and the coats of their horses as they set a backfire (figure 1.06). Although dominated by human figures, it is a quiet scene free from aggression or conflict. The Indians' bodies, reflecting the light of the fire, are shown as beautiful and their actions thoughtful and protective. A strong sense of environmental threat and potential destruction of a way of life pervades the whole.[16] But this is an uncharacteristic grouping for Remington, who more characteristically showed the West as a locus of rough-and-ready white males at work, at play, and in conflict. That he exaggerated and even at times fabricated episodes of physical excitement in a deliberate effort to "perpetuate" a Wild West idea has been demonstrated by comparing one of his written accounts with a local newspaper from the same place on the same day (Taft 201). In that instance, the action-packed West he wrote about was one he constructed.

Much the same could be said of Charlie Russell, whose highly narrative canvases continue to attract a devoted following just as Remington's do.[17] Russell went west to Montana in 1880 when he was not quite sixteen and worked as a cowboy for eleven years while developing his abilities as a painter. His work reflects a thorough knowledge of cowboy gear linked to a vision that insistently turned backward to the kind of Wild West adventures that actually occurred in Montana before his arrival. Russell created a West of harsh environments whose Indian population seemingly existed mainly for the purpose of providing adversaries for violence-prone white males. His paintings combine a certain realism with the romanticism of heightened adventure and nostalgia for a past time. Both nostalgia and an interest in the doings of rambunctious males are seen, for example, in the familiar *In Without Knocking* (1909), showing a group of cowboys riding across the porch and in through the door of a saloon. The event it depicts occurred twenty-eight years earlier.[18] Another demonstration of Russell's vision of the West as a site of masculine adventure that also, and instructively, depicts an actual event is *Loops and Swift Horses Are Surer than Lead* (1916). It was in 1904 that the Montana cowboys shown in figure 1.07 came upon a bear and roped it. But in Russell's recollective imagination, which treasured the "reckless, adventure-seeking spirit" (Cristy 154) of the frontier years before the West was, as he saw it, spoiled by modernity, its facts have been greatly enlarged. As museum notes point out, the bear was not a grizzly, as shown, but a smaller brown bear, and none of the cowboys carried guns, as they do in the painting.

Virtually all of Russell's paintings emphasize ruggedness and splendor in the Montana setting. If foregrounded action is not occurring on rocky, uneven terrain, craggy and majestic mountains appear in the background. The natural setting matches the ruggedness of the sinewy white males whose violent activity is the focus of interest. It is as if nature itself, the world in

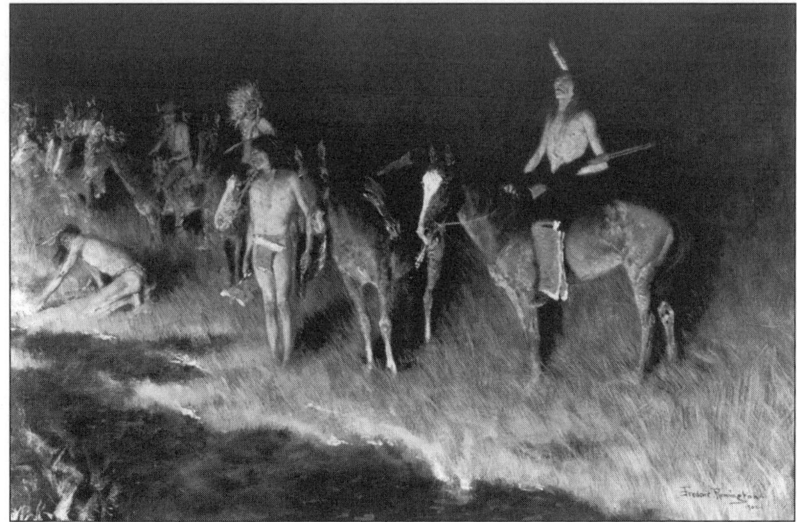

1.06 Frederic Remington, *The Grass Fire,* 1908, oil on canvas (accession number 1961.228, Amon Carter Museum, Fort Worth, Texas)

which these muscular men operate, were masculine—beautiful but never gentled. And women are almost never shown in the paintings of either Russell or Remington.

In contrast, the paintings collected by the Santa Fe Railway frequently sought to gentle the West while maintaining its allure as an exciting place to visit. Dennis Berthold has observed, in a paper presented at the American Literature Association in 1990, that the picturesque mode of the nineteenth century "provided a method of appreciating the American landscape that invited women to partake of its sublimity." Berthold's reference is primarily to the illustrations in *Picturesque America,* which sometimes show women in mountainous terrain, perhaps "not quite as adventurous as their male companions" but nevertheless "comfortable" in the wilderness scene. Such a compromise is evident in Louis Akin's famous *El Tovar Hotel, Grand Canyon,* purchased by the Santa Fe Railway in 1907. Rugged rocks in the distance are rendered mauve and blue by the quality of light and air, and in the nearer midground an Anglo woman on horseback encounters two Native women afoot, with El Tovar behind them looming over the drop-off to the canyon. The Mountain West is seen as a place suitable for white women to visit, if

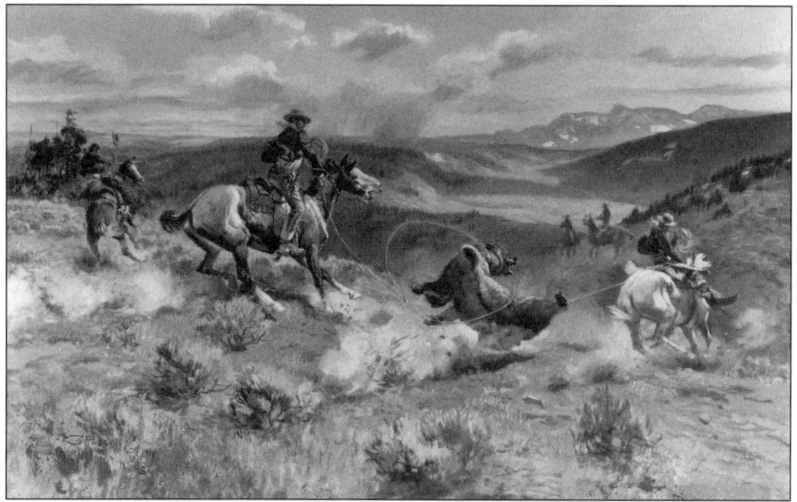

1.07 C. M. Russell, *Loops and Swift Horses Are Surer than Lead,* 1916, oil on canvas (accession number 1961.180, Amon Carter Museum, Fort Worth, Texas)

perhaps not a good place to make a home. True, the female visitor is shown riding on a clear, smooth road, wearing genteel riding clothes, not struggling down or up the rugged sides of the canyon, but still, she is there. In Oscar Berninghaus's painting *A Showery Day, Grand Canyon* acquired by the Santa Fe Railway in 1915, elaborately dressed women, along with men genteelly carrying walking sticks, are yet more emphatically separated from the ruggedness of the canyon; they stand looking at its crags from behind a breast-high masonry wall. In both paintings, the rugged West is made amenable to the female presence, within limits.

Despite depicting the West as a world of violent and heroic action by tough white males, both Russell and Remington participated in the nostalgic idea of the Vanishing American—a version of what has been called imperialist nostalgia, or regret for the changes or destruction that the white imperialist has himself wrought. I am dubious, then, when Alfred Runte asserts that their paintings "made a distinct contribution to a preservation consciousness" (34). They seem, instead, to celebrate conquest. Their nostalgia seems to have been at least as much for violence itself as for pristine land. We might contrast the emotional tone of Remington's and Russell's characteristic work with the more subdued or inward nostalgia evident in Thomas Eakins's celebrated *Frank Hamilton Cushing* (1895), a portrait of the noted anthropologist who lived for years among the Zunis in New Mexico and published retellings of their sacred texts and folk tales.[19] Cushing is seen standing among relics that he has brought back east, looking solemn, weary, and perhaps regretful, or perhaps only wishful that he could go back.

Imperialist nostalgia is abundant in paintings from the end of the nineteenth and the early twentieth centuries. Portraits of Pueblo Indians by Robert Henri in the 1910s and 1920s, for example, combine realism with romantic heightening.[20] Wistfulness for a vanished time and a supposedly vanishing people was cultivated by the Santa Fe Railway in its patronage of artists who painted the Southwest. Sheer otherness was also cultivated—a sense of the exotic or of a quality of life that could be experienced only by visiting the Southwest, perhaps by taking the Santa Fe and one of the "Indian Detours" organized by the Fred Harvey enterprise. Accordingly, the Indians of New Mexico were at least as frequent a subject as the landscape. The stark beauty of Taos Pueblo, which would soon prove so compelling to Austin and Cather's friend Mabel Dodge Luhan, was a favorite of artists of the Taos and Santa Fe schools in the 1910–1919 period, such as Walter Ufer and Ernest Blumenschein. Blumenschein's *Evening at Pueblo of Taos* (1913) shows golden highlights and mauve shadows on the adobe walls of the multistory pueblo structure, with quiet, rather stately Taoseños standing or sitting on their horses, apparently sharing a few words at the end of the day, against the natural background of blue mountains.[21] We can be certain that Cather was at least somewhat familiar with Blumenschein's work, since several illustrations by him were published in *McClure's* during her years as editor, including the color illustration of her own story "The Namesake" in March 1907.

The style of paintings such as Blumenschein's *Evening at Pueblo of Taos* (and, to judge from published samplings, most of the Santa Fe collection) is what might best be called romantic realism. A real effort seems to have been made to depict both the landscape and its human inhabitants and their social practices with accuracy, even as the artists, whether by preference or because of the incentive of their corporate patron's wishes, colored their southwestern subjects with a romanticized glow.[22] The almost fantastic ruggedness of Bierstadt and Moran and the muscularity of Remington and Russell have been gentled to an appealing, yet still mysterious, beauty. Native Americans emerge as a primary interest, but with only rare hints of the frightening savagery of their portrayals in nineteenth-century painting. Prominent among these twentieth-century southwestern artists favored by the Santa Fe was E. Irving Couse, several of whose paintings were used on the annual calendar. In painting after painting Couse shows Pueblo Indian people of quiet dignity engaged in activities such as basket making, hunting small game (a far less violent activity than the Plains Indians' hunting of buffalo), shepherding flocks, making jewelry, playing musical instruments, or meditating. Couse especially liked rendering profile views of minimally clad subjects that emphasize their long, glossy, bronze flanks (as in *Good Medicine,* 1912). The peaceful and beautiful, yet still exotic, image of the Southwest delineated by Couse and others represented in the Santa Fe collection is clearly one that would be favored by interests seeking to promote tourism.

In visual works such as these, the Southwest is rendered as a locus of enchantment (a word that would later be incorporated into the New Mexico state motto) much as, during the same years, it was exoticized and rendered quaint in the writings of Mary Austin's sometime mentor, Charles Lummis. Beginning in the 1880s, writers such as Lummis, as well as painters and photographers, tended to "idealize cultural differences" and to employ "discourses of loss . . . imperialist nostalgia, regionalism, [and] ecocriticism" by imagining the Southwest in terms of "sublime landscapes and empty spaces, images of picturesque and eroticized natives, and assertions of communal harmony" (Goodman xiv–xxviii). Not so elevated in his rhetoric as others to whom Goodman is referring, Lummis was not only an enthusiast but a promoter. During his years as editor of the magazines *The Land of Sunshine* and *Out West* (1895–1909), he hammered home the message of economic opportunity in southern California, publishing article after article about agricultural prodigies, notable buildings, and the newly burgeoning oil industry. In his "Lion's Den" column he trumpeted the growth of Los Angeles. At the same time, he never tired of showcasing quaint or curious features of the Southwest, particularly its pueblos, or ancient Native villages.

Especially after World War I, as they recoiled from the effeteness and spiritual bankruptcy of Europe with its collection of old grievances, Americans were eager to embrace such images. The frontier had been declared closed, creating a sense of loss of the pristine continent. Postwar disaffection from "capitalist civilization" spurred an interest in "folk cultures, agrarian communities, and peasant life" (Pells 101). The Southwest was a site of such otherness within the nation's own boundaries, amid landscapes not yet spoiled by capitalist expansion.[23] Austin and Cather, in their own ways, participated in that hegira. Yet the very industrial dynamo from which they were disaffected was itself driving the turn to the Southwest. By 1900 "regional mythmaking" was "under the control of the railroad, the tourist industry, and the Anglo elite" (Goodman 84).[24]

After about 1900, a countertradition emerging in a powerful current of female response to the western environment made it clear that the male dominance in imaging the West that I have been surveying was far from total. This alternative to the prevailing version of the West, with its emphasis on masculine adventure, violence, and sharply defined gender roles, and Austin's and Cather's centrality in forming this tradition of their own, will be my primary concern in the remainder of this chapter and the chapters that follow. Among their contemporaries who participated in the establishment of a countertradition of the West were the diarist and promoter of the arts Mabel Dodge Luhan, the anthropologist Elsie Clews Parsons, the painter Georgia O'Keeffe, and the photographer Laura Gilpin. These minimalist artists and writers developed what Martha Banta calls an "aesthetic of absent things" or of "refusal" (256–57). Visual experience and images were, as I have indicated, enormously important to Austin and Cather and to the western tradition generally. But the images of the West rendered by O'Keeffe and Gilpin, as well as the verbal images found in the texts to be considered here, are of a very different nature than those of a Russell or a Remington. It is as if these women opened a window, pointed through it, and said, "Look! This is the West, not what you thought."

The form this emerging tradition sometimes took was an assertion that women, too, could participate in western ruggedness, but more often it proposed a different vision altogether. O'Keeffe and Gilpin, most clearly, emphasize a spaciousness in landscape that bespeaks inner tranquility, a freedom from clutter and distraction and posing, and a quiet if stark peacefulness. When Gilpin and Austin, in particular, provide populated scenes, they are scenes of community rather than conflict. As Patricia Trenton writes, by their very existence as well as their range and variety, women artists of the West "call into question the veracity of our picture of an overwhelmingly masculine American West" (xi). The presence, personal comments, and artistic works of these women artists of the West provide not so much an influence, since for the most part it is unclear whether Austin and Cather were even aware of these female colleagues and exemplars, as another significant context within which to understand their revisionist writings—Cather's about the Great Plains and the Southwest, and Austin's about the Southwest and California.

When women came to the Great Plains in significant numbers after the Civil War, they—like the male explorers who preceded them—found a landscape that in Julie Jeffrey's words "lacked many of the visual qualities conventionally associated with natural beauty in the nineteenth century" (69). By recovering and studying the diaries of these pioneering women, the work of Annette Kolodny, among others, has greatly increased our awareness of dissenting voices among them that challenged prevailing masculine ideas of the West. It has been well established, for example, that white women who visited or settled in the West tended to see its vast spaces as a potential garden rather than as a wilderness for adventure and conquest. One, writing in her diary in 1865, called the plains "tedious and monotonous." Once they were settled and no longer moving through the seemingly endless expanse, many expressed a yearning for perspective, some elevation that would let them "see where they were" in their surroundings. Having brought with them a conception of what a home should be, many wanted greater "definition" through variety and landmarks (Jeffrey 71). Their envisioning of the plains as a potential garden, then, and their planting of actual gardens were not only acts of necessity, if they were to put food on their families' tables, but expressions of optimism and ways of affirming the new place's similarity to a remembered home—socially as well as visually, since the sharing of flowers and seeds was a familiar ritual of friendship among women.

Yet it is a mistake to assume that the rhetoric or aesthetic of women in the West was all of a kind. As Vera Norwood writes, women did not respond "one-dimensionally." Many saw their new environment, not after the model of a home they had left and wished to replicate or as a potential garden, but as "an opportunity to expand their knowledge of nature" or as a place of freedom and release from the constraints of eastern gentility (Norwood, "Crazy-Quilt Lives" 77, 84). If some found the plains landscape "visually tedious and psychologically overwhelming" (Jeffrey 73) and struggled to make gardens and fenced enclosures that would give their lives definition within the encompassing space, as well as similarity to remembered homes, others were able to appreciate the prairie on its own terms. The more economically deprived could regard it with zest in the hope of improving their lot in life, thanks to the Homestead Act. Some, despite the discomforts of extreme weather and inadequate housing, found the storms and sudden changes of weather exhilarating. Jeffrey quotes numerous comments by women settlers about the beauty and greenness of the prairies, the pleasant breezes afforded by living on a swell of ground without trees all around, the soughing grasses, and the big skies. The big sky, in particular, evoked many comments by women who saw in its brilliant spaciousness or dramatic clouds an emblem of release from earthbound monotony. The relation of earth and sky generated a new way of seeing beauty despite the starkness of the plains (Evernden 1, 6–7). Women, then, as well as men, although motivated perhaps by different impulses and invoking dissimilar terms, might depict the West as a place of freedom and adventure.[25] Even Kolodny, who has championed the idea of women's having perceived the West as a potential garden, concedes that the "postbellum Eve" of the high plains and the farther West "soon spoke in the voice of *both* adventurer *and* domesticator" (*Land* 240–41).

Among women artists we see a similar variety. Some perpetuated the prevailing view. Frances (Fanny) Palmer, for example, who worked for Nathaniel Currier and James Ives for some thirty years, produced images such as *Across the Continent—Westward the Course of Empire Takes Its Way* (1868), which fully participates in a visual rhetoric of heroism and Manifest Destiny (Daniels 175, 184–85). In one corner of the picture smoke from a train blows into the faces of observing Indians. Dawn Glanz comments astutely that this detail "signifies how the white race has outstripped the Indian in progress" and is also "perhaps an unintentional but also an accurate prefiguration of industrial pollution" (84).[26] The works of landscape painter Edith Hamlin (1902–1992) have been judged as monumental and austere as any man's (Moore 149), and Bertha Menzler Dressler's *San Francisco Peaks,* which was in fact the first painting purchased by William Haskell Simpson as he launched the Santa Fe Railway collection in 1903, presents the West as a site of exciting (and implicitly masculine) action. With a snow-capped peak in the background, it shows a stagecoach rushing through, with a gun in evidence in the guard's hand (D'Emilio and Campbell 40–41). The very fact that a woman should paint a scene usually associated with masculine adventure can be interpreted as resistance, of a kind, to gender stereotyping.

It is scarcely surprising that women competing in a male artistic world might adopt a prevailing idiom. Moreover, for women painters to challenge the masculine dominance of visual art as an endeavor and a profession meant also challenging a set of social norms of Anglo gentility, some of which were brought to bear on the practice of art. One such norm was that women who painted should paint floral arrangements and portraits, preferably of children. Plein-air landscape painting was generally regarded as unfeminine, in that it required exertion and free movement.[27] Sue Rainey observes that there are no women among the artists who produced the numerous pictures in *Picturesque America* since the "working conditions" unavoidably entailed in plein air drawing and painting were regarded as "'obviously impossible for a woman,' especially an unmarried woman" (Rainey 105, quoting *Godey's Lady's Book*). For reasons of distance, absence of town conveniences, and ruggedness of terrain (the very ruggedness being depicted by established artists), these strictures were especially forbidding for women who might have wished to paint western scenes.

Nevertheless, by 1893, the year in which Turner enunciated his frontier thesis, more than half the exhibitors at the art gallery of the California pavilion at the World's Columbian Exposition in Chicago were women (Scharff 2). It is not clear how many of these women artists were in fact painting the West, as opposed to still-lifes and interiors. Certainly the artists documented in Trenton's *Independent Spirits: Women Painters of the American West, 1890–1945* are women of the West who painted, not necessarily women who painted the West. But while acknowledging that many of the women artists of California were "traditionalists" who eschewed plein-air landscape painting, Trenton does identify a few who began to emerge as landscapists early in the twentieth century (41–73). Kate Cory (1861–1958) has been noted for photographs as well as paintings documenting Hopi life and ceremonials (Moore 131), and Marjorie Helen Thomas's *Navajo Indians at Desert Water Hole,* acquired for the Santa Fe Railway collection in 1910, shows its often feared subjects in a moment of peacefulness with the sheen (literally, a sheen of reflective water) characteristic of romantic realism.

Women painters were probably more numerous and influential in the Great Plains than in the Mountain West. For several decades women made up the majority of the art faculty at the University of Nebraska, among them Alice Cleaver (1878–1944), who traveled to New Mexico and Arizona to paint Pueblo people and exchanged paintings for rail fare on the Santa Fe (Kinsey 247). Marion Canfield Smith (1873–1970) studied at the universities of Nebraska and Minnesota and at the Art Institute of Chicago and the Pennsylvania Academy before becoming the founding chair of the art department at Kearney State College in Nebraska (249). Mary Bartlett Pillsbury Weston (1815–1895?) exhibited a painting at the World's Columbian Exposition in 1893 called *The Spirit of Kansas* in which, in a gentled or (one might say) feminized color palette, Kansas is shown as an allegorical female figure on a racing white horse holding up a dove of peace. Since the University of Nebraska was a center of considerable activity by women artists during the very years when Willa Cather was a student there, and given the ample evidence of her interest in visual art, it seems likely that she would have been aware of some of these painters—especially Marion Canfield Smith, who was a niece of James Canfield, then chancellor of the university and the father of Cather's close friend (then and intermittently for the rest of her life) Dorothy Canfield Fisher. Cather was an intimate of the Canfield family during her student years.[28]

Perhaps the most important of the women artists of the West in the generation preceding Austin's and Cather's was Mary Hallock Foote (1847–1938). It does not stretch credibility to imagine that Hallock Foote, who was both a writer and an illustrator, may have directly influenced both of them as writers given to word pictures who significantly incorporated illustrations into their books about the West.

Mary Hallock Foote's illustrations had been published in magazines and books even before she became "an 'exile' in the West" in 1876, following her engineer husband (Miller 3, 30). Soon her work would be appearing regularly in *Century*. The Footes lived variously in California, Idaho, and Colorado, as Arthur Foote sought the success in mining and irrigation that continually eluded him. Throughout these years of her increasingly unhappy marriage, Hallock Foote responded to life in the West in complex and conflicting ways that by no means replicate those of her male contemporaries. A "reluctant westerner" who felt "isolated" both as a woman and as an artist (Miller 4, 61), she drew on her feelings of displacement in establishing her major subject matter in numerous stories and novels as well as illustrations of her own and others' works. A genteel traditionalist, she consciously departed from tradition in her depictions of the West, avowing to her editor and friend Richard Gilder that she wished to work "in a different line" than the "plains wagon and settlers cabin story of the Great West" (quoted in Miller 142). A believer in traditional self-effacing roles for women, she nevertheless took over the financial support of her family and pursued her ambitions to the point of becoming "the best-known woman writer and illustrator of the American West" (Miller 93). She was a realist in her depictions of work gear and landscape but cast a romantic glow over her scenes of domestic life. At the same time, she also incorporated into her writing "naturalistic impulses" showing how women's choices in their lives are circumscribed both by gender and by environment (Gruber 364–65). Deploring the quality of life afforded by the West, she still exulted in the "'glory and wild grandeur'" of its scenery (Miller 76, 71).

Hallock Foote's views of the West can be described as revisionist primarily in their emphasis on feminine and familial subjects. However disappointed she was in her own life, she depicted the West as a place for living, an incipient home and garden in which peaceful women and children, rather than contentious males, are the central presences. Probably her two best-known illustrations are "The Coming of Winter," which shows a man holding a gun and a woman holding a baby, standing outside a rough-hewn dwelling whose walls are hung with tools of domesticity: mop, washboard, and washtub; and the more idyllic "The Irrigating Ditch" (figure 1.08), which reduces the male of the family to a distant laboring figure while giving centrality to two images of fertility: a stream of life-giving water and a life-giving woman with baby in arms.

Hallock Foote's two best-known drawings appeared in a series called "Pictures of the Far West" that ran from November 1888 to November 1889. Since we know that the Cathers read *Century,* it seems fairly likely that the fifteen-year-old Willa would have been aware of the series and of Hallock Foote's writing and visual art more generally. If so, we can be certain that she would have found them striking in their feminized presentations of the "wild" West; the evidence lies in her own woman-centered books. Indeed, the first drawing in Hallock Foote's "Pictures of the Far West" series, "Looking for Camp" (figure 1.09), with its gentle tribute to the dignity of the slim central figure, may well have remained in Cather's mind and reemerged in W. T. Benda's drawing of Mr. Shimerda in *My Ántonia* (see figure 4.08).

Anglo women pursuing their own purposes, as distinct from women settlers accompanying their husbands, began coming into the West and Southwest in the late nineteenth and early twentieth centuries.[29] These included painters, photographers, writers, and, significantly, anthropologists—"daughters of the desert," as Barbara Babcock styles them. The first woman anthropologist in the Southwest was apparently Matilda Coxe Stevenson, who came with her husband to conduct research in 1879. In the early decades of the twentieth century, a great many others followed, most of them students of Franz Boas.[30] Among these was Elsie Clews Parsons.

When Clews Parsons made her first trip to New Mexico in the summer of 1910, she was already well established as a sociologist with a keen interest in familial and social constraints on women. It was, in fact, largely because such constraints were being brought to bear on her own freedom of movement that she made this first trip. Having desired to accompany her congressman husband, Herbert Parsons, on a trip related to the Congressional Committee on Public Lands, she found herself shunted aside because the forestry official with whom he would be traveling did not approve of taking wives along (Deacon 84). As a result, she decided to see the New Mexico cliff dwellings alone, before meeting Herbert at the Grand Canyon. Further offended by Department of the Interior officials in Santa Fe, who in essence told her this was no place for a woman, she caught a train to Española and chanced to meet on board a woman named Clara True who had already demonstrated her adequacy to life in the Southwest as a rancher (Deacon 84). Staying at True's ranch, Clews Parsons rode horseback, camped, and explored the area with the help of a Pueblo Indian guide.[31] As her biographer writes, she was immediately "captivated," both aesthetically and intellectually, by what she saw. Largely because of her guide's reluctance to discuss artifacts they found in ruins at Puyé, she was seized by an interest in Pueblo ceremonial life (Deacon 85). She found the southwestern landscape around Española beautiful and compelling and her activities there zestfully adventurous.

Adventure and freedom are important elements in the response of women to the Southwest, just as they are primary values in the traditional Western. But the freedom women found there was not the adventure of danger, violence, or conquest, but rather the unaccustomed degree of autonomy

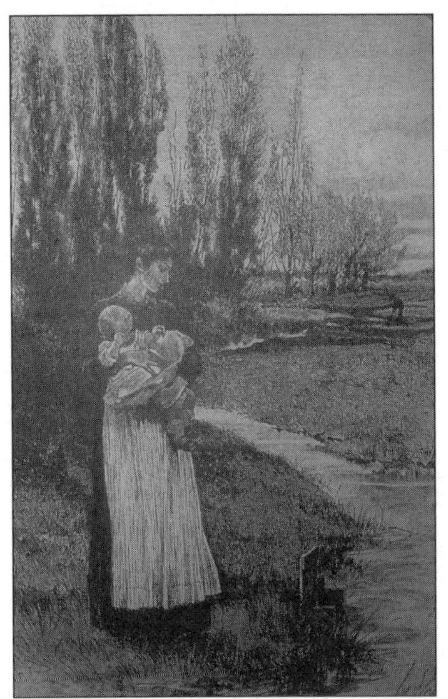

1.08 Mary Hallock Foote, "The Irrigating Ditch," *Century Magazine,* June 1889

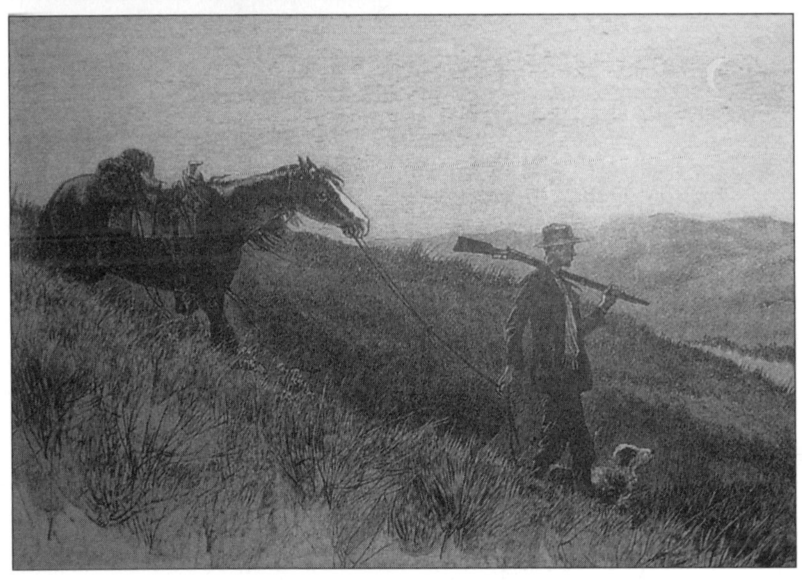

1.09 Mary Hallock Foote, "Looking for Camp," *Century Magazine,* November 1888

and physical activity in a strange new place. They came to New Mexico and Arizona for the adventure of living vigorously (Norwood, "Crazy-Quilt Lives" 84). Seeking, as Barbara Babcock puts it, "freedom from their stays," they found "not only topographical and psychological space, but an otherness that intrigued and nurtured" (*Daughters* 1). We see Cather's enjoyment of such freedom in snapshots of her on horseback and in her accounts, as well as Austin's, of long rides and hikes.

Clews Parsons returned to New Mexico in September 1912, three months after Cather completed her mind-opening first visit to Arizona and New Mexico. This time she went specifically for research purposes, possibly on commission from the American Museum of Natural History. Riding long distances on horseback with Clara True, she reveled in the "glory" of the place and her studies. Her excitement is evident in her glowing language in writing to her husband on September 12, 1912:

> We had about 1 1/2 days (all told) stretch of monotonous sage brush desert country; but the rest was very beautiful, varying mountain outlooks, cliffs, tablelands, river courses. Plenty of water, but only one swim in the Chama. North of Abiquii [*sic*] the country was pretty wild. Clara True saw a mountain lion, I, a coyote, & one night the coyotes barked & laughed around us. (Quoted in Deacon 91)

In the fall of 1913, Clews Parsons again returned for a week's ride through the Rio Grande pueblos, and in August 1915 "fled" to the Southwest for work at Zuni, to escape conflicts with her husband (Deacon 145, 154). In February 1918 she again fled from the war mania she felt all around her, including her husband's, and continued her research into Pueblo ceremonialism at Laguna and at Zuni. All of this was part of an effort she had enunciated to Herbert, to "strip herself of the whole language of Anglo-American life—the paraphernalia of unconscious understandings, theories, conventions, catchwords, and ideals that made up the intellectual equipment of the modern American" (Deacon 194). Over the next two decades, Clews Parsons continued to make research trips to the Southwest for ethnographic work among various Pueblo peoples. In addition to ceremonial observances, she had a strong interest in the lives of women, especially their family relationships. That is, very much like Mary Hallock Foote and Mary Austin, Elsie Clews Parsons saw the Southwest not only as a rugged place and not only as a beautiful place but as a place for human living and social practice.

We can feel confident, I think, that Austin and Clews Parsons were acquainted. Clews Parsons was one of the original members of New York's Heterodoxy discussion group, and Austin seems to have attended Heterodoxy gatherings intermittently. Certainly she knew women who did. It would seem that Cather, too, *should* have known Clews Parsons, from the number of parallels between their lives and interests. Both resided in New York off and on during the same years; both turned to the Southwest for relief and regeneration at about the same time and went back and forth between New York and New Mexico with some frequency; and Cather repeatedly visited the American Museum of Natural History, poring over the very collections that Parsons was helping to develop. They knew many of the same people, notably Franz and Marie Boas and Mabel Dodge Luhan, who went to the Southwest in 1917, five years after Cather. Elsie visited Mabel and her husband Tony Luhan at their home or compound near Taos in 1922, and subsequently stayed there "often" (Deacon 230). Cather and her companion Edith Lewis stayed there in 1925 and 1926. Yet I have been unable to find real evidence that Cather and Clews Parsons were acquainted or even that their paths ever crossed. They would have disagreed on America's entry into World War I, and almost certainly on Clews Parsons's advocacy of looser social conventions related to sex, but would have shared a passionate interest in the Southwest and its people.[32]

Their mutual acquaintance Mabel Dodge Luhan spoke of her 1917 move to the Southwest in *Edge of Taos Desert,* in terms of her life breaking into two parts—terms very similar to those Cather had famously used in a more general sense a year earlier in her preface to *Not Under Forty:* "The world broke in two in 1922 or thereabouts." But while Cather's point was that her sensibility belonged with the world before the break, Luhan's was that her real or authentic self emerged after the break, with her discovery of a new landscape and what was to her a new way of living. That way of living was taught her, she said, by the husband she took in Taos, Tony Luhan, a very traditional member of Taos Pueblo. We may want to take Mabel's assertion about her new life with a grain of salt; she continued to cast herself, as she had in New York, as the presiding doyenne of a salon, summoning to her compound near the pueblo a number of artists and writers, notably including D. H. Lawrence. Virginia Scharff notes that she "created a Taos arts community . . . by force of will" (5)—scarcely a characteristic of the accepting, nonmanipulative ethos Mabel attributed to Taoseños.[33] Even so, Mabel saw New Mexico in terms of clarity (resulting from the clear, dry air and the absence of visual clutter), authenticity, and spiritual renewal—terms radically revisionary of the traditional masculine images.

Georgia O'Keeffe, too, was an acquaintance of Mabel Dodge Luhan. Barbara Babcock writes that women drawn to the "light and space" of the Southwest found its seeming "emptiness" a "geography of possibility" (*Daughters* 1–4). It is that very combination of light and space, that emptiness, that we see in O'Keeffe's southwestern canvases. Both she and Laura Gilpin practiced an art stripped to essentials, an art that directs us to forget the visual density and clutter of other places and whatever incidentals may distract us even here in order to focus our eyes and our minds on what is most important in this stark place. It is a stripping to essentials that we also see in significant ways in Willa Cather's prose and sometimes in Mary Austin's—perhaps the stylistic equivalent of that personal stripping to essentials that enabled Cather, Austin, and Luhan to find more authentic selves in the Southwest.

O'Keeffe was painting minimalist pictures of the plains as early as 1917 (at the same time as Cather was hard at work on *My Ántonia*), before she began to paint New Mexico. Her *Light Coming on the Plains II* (1917) (figure 1.10), a wonderfully stark watercolor with a glow at the center of blue darkness, is part of a series "inspired by the minimalism of the plains and the light that suffused it" (Kinset 114).

After New Mexico became her "private world" when she visited Taos in 1929 as a guest of Luhan, as well as during her later residence at Abiquiu, O'Keeffe continued to produce landscapes of a similar minimalism (Broder, *Modern Vision* 163). She found New Mexico "even finer" than she had remembered from a previous visit and "felt exhilarated by the crystalline air" whose "clarity . . . sculpted" the mountains (Eisler 385). In Scharff's words, O'Keeffe more than any other twentieth-century artist defined the western landscape in terms of "lonely breadth and clarity" (Scharff 6) in, for example, *Black Cross, New Mexico* (1929) (figure 1.11), where sense of place is con-

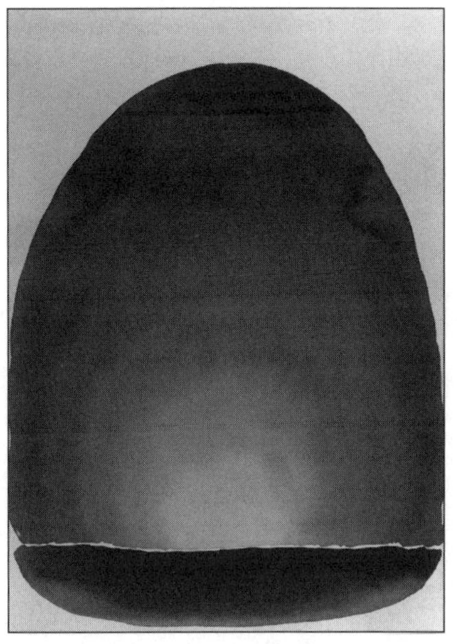

1.10 Georgia O'Keeffe, *Light Coming on the Plains II,* 1917, watercolor on newsprint (accession number 1966.32, Amon Carter Museum, Fort Worth, Texas)

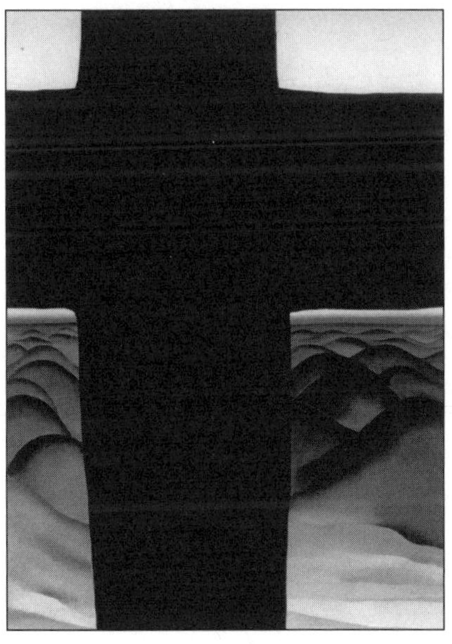

1.11 Georgia O'Keeffe, American, 1887–1986, *Black Cross, New Mexico,* 1929, oil on canvas, 99.1 x 76.2 cm (Art Institute Purchase Fund, 1943.95. Reproduction, The Art Institute of Chicago. Photography copyright © The Art Institute of Chicago)

veyed by stylized shapes of hills and a massive assertion of a regional cultural symbol, the rugged cross associated with the devout Penitentes of northern New Mexico, whose harsh devotional practices centered on Good Friday observances.

The Penitentes compelled Cather's attention at about the same time as they did O'Keeffe's; *Death Comes for the Archbishop* was published two years earlier, in 1927. No more than Cather in her novel of religious practice and hegemony in New Mexico does O'Keeffe seek to render a full or realistic depiction of either the southwestern landscape or regional social practices, but to assert a vision of the West as a place of quiet strength, rather than the riotous action of a Russell or Remington or the gaudy monumentality of a Bierstadt or Moran.

O'Keeffe's later work in New Mexico took on even more strongly the visionary quality that has become familiar to admirers of her art while maintaining its characteristic minimalism—a starkness implying penetration to essence and a muscular strength entirely unlike masculine adventurousness. A notable example is *Ranchos Church, New Mexico* (1930–1931) (figure 1.12), with its emphasis on bulk, overall shape, and desert colors. Painting the back of the church rather than its frequently depicted front, so that not even the cross is in evidence, O'Keeffe emphasizes (with color and with the way the structure spills past the edge of the canvas) the unity of the building with the ground on which it stands, implying the unity of a culture with its geographic place. Interestingly, Laura Gilpin also chose to photograph the back of the church (*West View, Ranchos de Taos Church, New Mexico—1972)*, to very similar effect.

O'Keeffe's *From the Faraway Nearby* (1937) also demonstrates her combination of minimalist simplification with visionary significance, in this case the theme of "the continuity of life and death" (Broder, *Modern Vision* 153). A deer skull and antlers are superimposed on a starkly bare landscape. Here is no "garden," the image of the West commonly attributed to women, but a West of geographic harshness emblematic of inward, rather than aggressively outward, meanings. As Eric Anderson observes, O'Keeffe perceives the "sublime" and alluring sense of vast emptiness of such spaces and "empties them further by abstracting bare images of death and vitality" (81). Death and vitality are of course never far apart in the desert—thus the sense of encountering there the utterly real.[34]

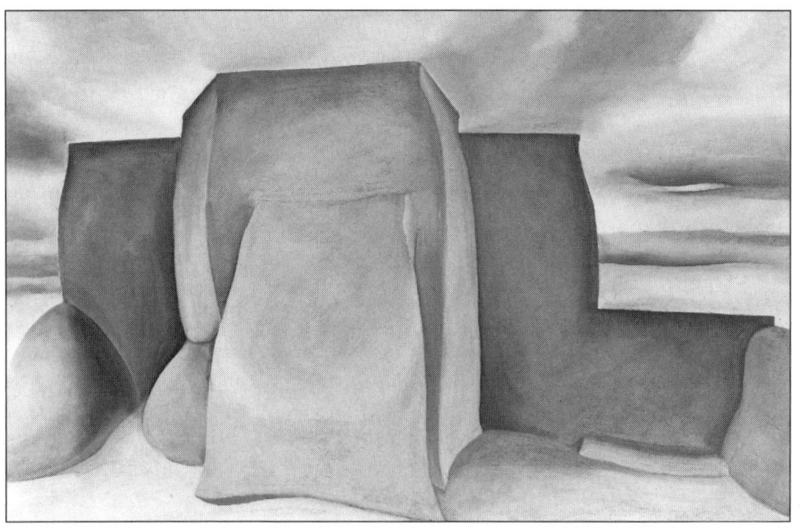

1.12 Georgia O'Keeffe, *Ranchos Church, New Mexico,* 1930–1931, oil on canvas (accession number 1971–16, Amon Carter Museum, Fort Worth, Texas)

We can see tantalizing parallels between O'Keeffe and Cather not only stylistically, in their avoidance of any level of plenitude and their emphasis on landscape and on chosen emblems, but (as we can between Cather and Elsie Clews Parsons) biographically. Both the bisexual O'Keeffe and the ambiguously lesbian Cather came to New Mexico in the 1920s when the state provided "psychological space and sexual freedom" to a "growing colony of lesbian women" (Eisler 458). Both stayed at Mabel Dodge Luhan's compound near Taos. It is scarcely to be imagined that Mabel would not have spoken of each to the other. Yet again, as with Parsons, there is a striking lack of evidence of any mutual awareness. The qualities we see in common between Cather's southwestern writing, especially in *Archbishop,* and O'Keeffe's southwestern paintings are a matter of shared attraction to the region, shared modernist predilections, and a shared impulse to revise the prevailing masculinity of regional visual tradition. We see such a revision most startlingly in O'Keeffe's paintings of hillsides with folded slopes like female genitalia—as fully a gynecological vision of the West, despite her denials of painting female anatomy in the guise of flowers or landscapes, as the canyon country in Cather's *The Song of the Lark,* famously discussed by Ellen Moers.

A similar sweep of spaciousness and light characterizes Gilpin's photographs of the Southwest. *Big and Little Shiprock* (1951) is characteristic (figure 1.13). As Martha Sandweiss writes, Gilpin (and Cather is comparable in this) "preferred wide, all-encompassing vistas that better suggested the sweep of human history" to the "extreme close-ups of . . . [n]atural subjects" often favored by contemporaries such as Eliot Porter and Ansel Adams (66). Sandweiss's explanation is that "emblematic details could never suggest the intricacies of the interrelationship between people and nature that made the landscape a compelling subject" (71–72). We might question whether vastness necessarily conveys such intricacies better than the mystery of being that is conveyed in intensive views of isolated details—a question that will become pertinent as we compare Mary Austin's achievements in *The Land of Little Rain* and *The Land of Journeys' Ending.* And Gilpin did at times make emblematic close-ups. But it is true, as Sandweiss argues, that her photographs more often convey not only "enormous scale" but a "broad, emotional response" to regional landscapes.

Early in her career Gilpin followed the prevailing soft-focus style that was seen as conveying affective quality. Her 1917 *Prairie* (figure 1.14) shows, however, that she followed it in her own way, joining an emphasis on starkness and expanse to an insistence on a female perspective, represented here by the ecstatic figure at the left. This photograph has aptly been called a "balance between modernity and traditionalism" (Kinsey 114). Some, viewing it, may be reminded of Alexandra in Cather's *O Pioneers!* But even in the sharply focused black-and-white photographs of place that Gilpin made after she abandoned the soft-focus style, she continued to convey a "romantic fascination" and "intuitive affection" for the region (Sandweiss 65).

That same affection, or what might better be called respect, characterizes Gilpin's photographs of people within these huge and simplified spaces. In Solnit's words, she made "explorations of the desert as a cultural space" (67). Notably in her major project, *The Enduring Navajo,* in both color and black-and-white photographs of people in their own environment, she conveyed vastness of time as well as space, and a sense of long-standing adaptation to the landscape (Sandweiss 70–71). A fine example is "Timothy's mother, who lives near Lukachukai" (figure 1.15). Woman and child, standing beside the supports of a brush arbor, are seen as the centers of the Navajo world. Although a degree of anxiety is evident in the child's eyes and posture,

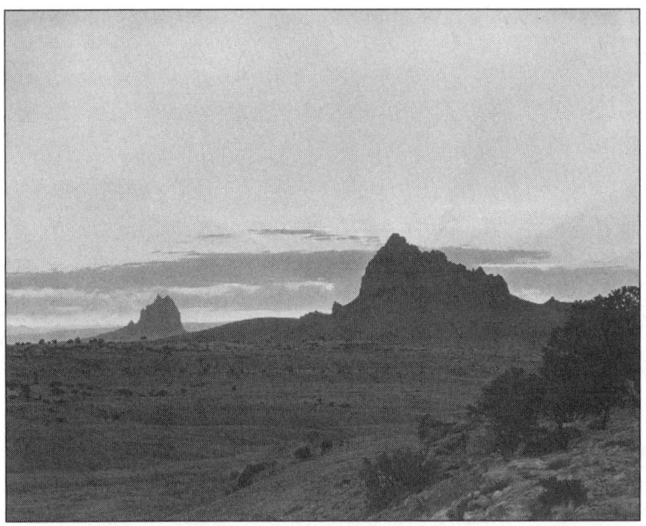

1.13 Laura Gilpin, *Big and Little Shiprock,* 1951, gelatin silver print (accession number P1979.95.10, copyright © 1979, Amon Carter Museum, Fort Worth, Texas, gift of the artist)

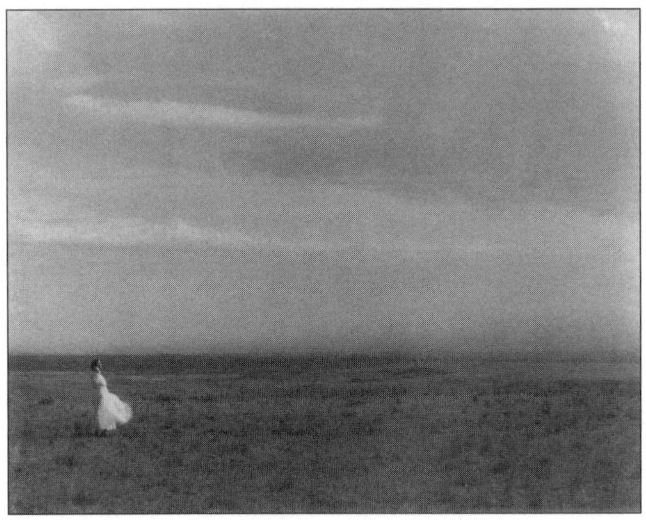

1.14 Laura Gilpin, *The Prairie,* 1917, gelatin silver print (accession number P1979.128.251, copyright © 1979, Amon Carter Museum, Fort Worth, Texas, bequest of the artist)

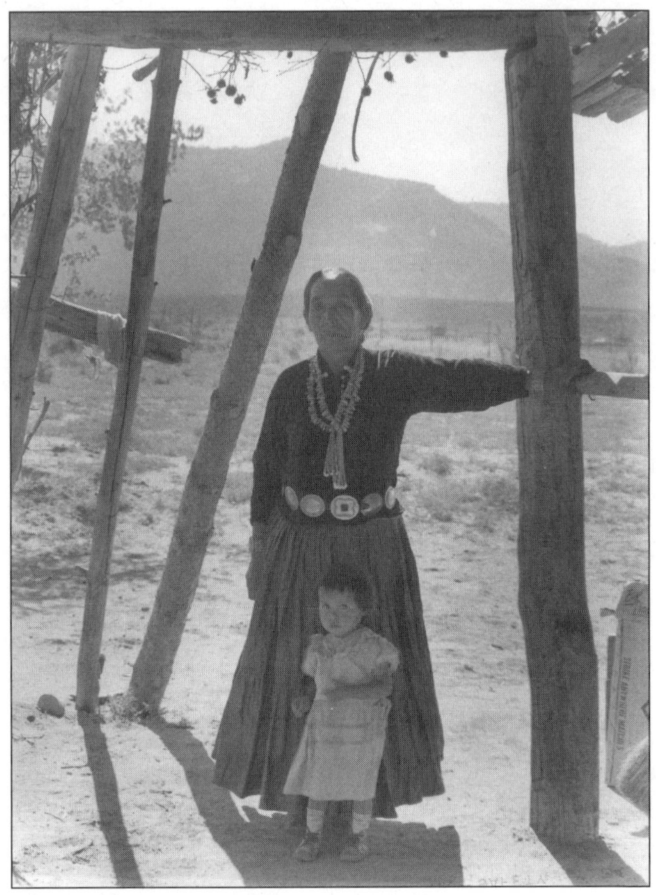

1.15 Laura Gilpin, [Kellywood, "Timothy's Mother and Child"], September 18, 1951, captioned in Laura Gilpin, *The Enduring Navajo* (p. 75), "Timothy's mother, who lives near Lukachukai" (accession number P1979.128.251, copyright © 1979, Amon Carter Museum, Fort Worth, Texas, bequest of the artist)

both face the camera unflinching. The woman, imparting her evident strength to the child who cowers against her skirt, is accorded her full measure of dignity. Fully vertical, she is juxtaposed and thus made analogous to the mountain directly behind her, with its strong upward thrust. Both are visually rooted in the dry earth. This, the Navajo woman seems to say, is our life; it is ours; we do and will maintain it. In Vera Norwood's persuasive judgment, Gilpin found in such women's lives "a culture which supported women's attempts to live a domestic life that respected the primacy of the land" and "provided these women . . . strength in the face of great hardship" ("Photographer" 24).

Europeans (Anglos) encountering the desert, coming out of their preestablished notions of what a hospitable world should look like, with trees and water and farms, may usually have seen it in terms of its lack of these expected attributes, "in terms of what it was not" (Solnit 67). In movie Westerns beyond number, the desert has served as a test of masculine toughness and as a stage cleared for the assertion of the hero's will (Tompkins 71, 72). But the desert was seen by Gilpin and O'Keeffe, as well as by other modernist artists, not in terms of lack but of unclutteredness and integrity of structure, as a space for habitation that not only demands but enforces continuity between place, plant and animal life, and human existence. In both O'Keeffe's and Gilpin's representations of the Southwest we see a modernist vision immersed in a powerful geographic vision, and a vision equally rejecting of both a stereotypically masculine and a stereotypically feminine aesthetic.

That is very much what we also see in Austin's and Cather's writing. Both would become leading voices in reconceptualizing the West and Southwest in ways usually thought of as feminizing what had been a strongly masculine—and masculinist—view. My own reading is that it was not so much a feminizing as a dual gendering of the West. They developed an aesthetic that incorporated and perhaps balanced what we are accustomed to thinking of as the masculine and the feminine.

2

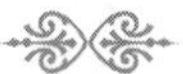

MARY AUSTIN: ILLUSTRATION AND TEXT

Seeing comes before words.

John Berger
Ways of Seeing

Her country was the West. Even today, long after she is dead, her impress lies across the whole Southwest. Whosoever travels there will find her moving before him—will see a hill move suddenly into the shape of the words she gave it.

Nancy Newhall
"Mary Austin's Country," Arizona Highways

Mary Austin emerged as a professional writer during what is often called the golden age of illustration, extending from near the end of the nineteenth century to (in the case of books) around 1920.[1] Accordingly, her very first book, *The Land of Little Rain,* published in 1903, was abundantly and finely illustrated—indeed, a paragon of the art of book design and an all-too-rare example of how illustrations can support and enhance literary text. The illustrations of *The Land of Little Rain,* underscoring as they do the visual nature of Austin's writing, contribute importantly to the new vision of the West that she was establishing.

The importance of illustrations in the early years of Mary Austin's and Willa Cather's careers evolved from the flourishing of mass-circulation illustrated magazines in the 1870s, 1880s, and 1890s, publishing short, light fiction that readily lent itself to illustration. It was because of the prevalence of illustrated magazines that readers increasingly expected illustrations in books, which in turn led to an increase of trained artists, often from art programs that specifically taught illustration (Larson 20).[2] The prestige gained by illustrators in the closing years of the nineteenth century was registered in 1895 by a historian of the art of illustration, Joseph Pennell, who judged

American illustration to be "more interesting than that of any other country" and attributed that to its having been fostered by the great magazines' willingness to pay well (113, 116). But another reason for the increased prestige of illustrators was their increased freedom of discretion as the customary division of labor in magazine and book publishing houses shifted. Before 1900 art editors not only assigned stories or articles to particular artists for illustration (illustrators usually worked by the job, on a piecework basis, not as staff members), but told them what scenes to illustrate. By the turn of the century this choice was "almost always" left to the illustrator (Larson 25). Until about 1920, the illustrator also usually designed the page format—a practice that could produce notable effects, as in *The Land of Little Rain*—but that function gradually shifted to an art editor.

In illustrated books, text normally takes precedence.[3] When illustrations are done well, however, looking at the pictures is not only a pleasant way of entering a book but one that helps us focus our attention as readers on the images created by the text and on the total visual quality of the book as object. Illustrations become an important part of what Jerome McGann terms the "reading field." Observing the interaction of pictures and text helps us think more effectively not only about the nature of such books and the visions they convey, but about ways in which readers experience books in general. Ideally, illustrations achieve a state of complementarity, or as Philip Beidler terms it (177), "supplementarity," with text in style, in mood, and in emphasis. As it happens, whether by great good fortune or as a result of some process of design to which we do not have access, Austin's *The Land of Little Rain* was a singularly fine example of such complementarity.[4]

We know that Cather was well aware of how magazines if not book publishers worked with illustrators and designers, from her editorial role at *McClure's Magazine* from 1906 to 1912. It is less clear that Austin had such an awareness. Although she was on the fringe of the writing and publishing world in California by 1892, and by 1899 had become acquainted with Charles Lummis, former city editor of the *Los Angeles Times* and founder and editor of the magazine *Land of Sunshine*, later retitled *Out West*, she was never a regular staff member with any major publishing enterprise. It is difficult, then, to assess her initial expectations for illustrations. Nor do we know whether she collaborated directly with the illustrator of *The Land of Little Rain*, E. Boyd Smith (1860–1943). The various archives of their papers that

I have been able to locate do not include any letters between them and, indeed, do not address any aspect of their combined work on this beautiful book. We do know that they collaborated when Smith illustrated Austin's *The Flock* three years later. Such collaboration was not the usual practice—for the most part, illustrators dealt with publishers—but neither was it unknown. It is clear from Austin's 1929 letter to Ansel Adams (see n. 3) that she did not assume close collaboration was likely; the best an author could usually do, she told Adams, was to try to exert persuasive influence on the publisher.[5] On the other hand, Helen Hunt Jackson had direct influence, if not control, over the illustrations of her articles on California published in *Century*.[6]

This chapter will primarily consider text and illustration, and the complementarity of the two, in *The Land of Little Rain* and three other books by Austin about California and the Southwest: *The Flock* (1906), *The Land of Journeys' Ending* (1924), and *The Lands of the Sun* (1927).

Mary Hunter, later to be Austin, migrated from Illinois to California's Tejon region—a corner of hilly Kern County, north of Los Angeles, on dry land west of the Mojave Desert—in 1888, having been dragged west by an uncaring mother to rejoin the son who had gone to California to take up free land.[7] She was twenty years old and just out of college, and had lived her entire life until that point in Illinois, reveling in its green grass and trees. Indeed, she believed she had met what she could only designate as God—a sense of the totality of all life—at the age of five under a walnut tree (*Earth Horizon* 51–52). Now she confronted a drastically different environment—barren, inhospitable, and offering only flimsy hovels for the family's housing. She would achieve not just reconciliation but communion with the desert that was her new home through an act of will: her determination to get out and explore it on her own.

Austin's experience of the West was from its outset intensely visual. Although she may have suffered a "nervous collapse" on the way (Fink 35), she later recalled becoming "happily absorbed" in the "vast space and silence" of the Great American Desert (*EH* 182)—that is, the plains—as she gazed from the train window. When she and her mother and younger brother finally reached Pasadena, after weeks of visiting relatives along the way, and set out by horseback and horse-drawn wagon for the land her brother Jim had selected for homesteading, she initially encountered a "lush, Edenic" place (Lanigan Stineman 25–26). Her first publication, "One Hundred Miles on Horseback," which appeared in 1889 in her college magazine, the *Blackburnian,* gives an account of this journey. Reading the language in which Austin conveys her ecstatic delight in the landscape, one thinks of Emerson's "transparent eyeball."[8] She thrilled to traveling "in the fast deepening twilight through these narrow gorges where the mountains close in upon us so silently and mysteriously that one unfamiliar with such scenes would declare there is no outlet in either direction." Traversing lushly vegetated slopes, she gloried in "magnificent" live oaks and "heavy garlands of mistletoe" hanging from "the branches of oak and sycamore" ("One Hundred Miles" 29–30).

All the more shocking, then, was her arrival at the desert place that was to be the family home. Confounded by what she first saw as its barren ugliness, resenting her mother's dictatorial control and continual criticisms, and feeling a profound sense of displacement, she fell into deep depression accentuated by malnutrition due to her refusal to eat the limited food, mostly canned, that was available. Her biographer conjectures that she suffered from anorexia nervosa and points out that separation from the sufferer's family is sometimes recommended as a therapy (Lanigan Stineman 35). And Mary did return to flourishing good health after she moved away from her family. But she herself attributed her cure to a different act of self-healing: her discovery of wild grapes when she was out on a solitary ramble.

Austin learned about local flora and fauna, including wild grapes, both through independent close observation during lone tramps in the desert that her family considered unwomanly and by benefiting from talking to other denizens of the area who took an interest in their surroundings, especially General Edward F. Beale, a nearby rancher.[9] In the spring of 1890 she moved to a nearby dairy to teach as the sole teacher at a small school. Still near her family but far enough to afford separation from her mother and older brother, she continued her naturalist observation and note-taking under the tutelage of Beale and his employees (Evers xi). Turning away from the proprieties of her midwestern, conservative Christian upbringing, she sought out the friendship not only of these ranch hands but of such marginalized people as sheepherders and Indians, whose company and talk she found authentic and liberating. After her 1891 marriage to Wallace Austin, a man who at the time was attempting to make his living in the cultivation of grapes but who later made it, or failed to, as a school supervisor and in various endeavors relating to water supply, she lived in various small towns in Inyo County (Lone Tree, Independence) situated between mountain ranges about a hundred miles north of Bakersfield, where her mother was now established, and west of the present Death Valley National Monument. When she wrote about "paths that wild creatures use going down to the Lone Tree Spring," Austin was drawing on her own experience and on the habit of outdoor living and close observation that she had first developed at the Beale ranch.[10]

Although Austin draws a wry analogy between the wild creatures' trails to water and the footpaths men wear to the doors of saloons, her own paths did not lead to such populous haunts but rather to isolated spots where she could observe what was blooming or what the animals were up to. In years of walking and camping, she followed her own advice that "for seeing and understanding, the best time is when you have the longest leave to stay" (*LLR* 117). *The Land of Little Rain* clearly reflects this long preparation in the closeness of its descriptions. She writes of plants with an especially keen eye, as in the following example from the chapter "The Streets of the Mountains":

> First, near the cañon mouth you get the low-heading full-branched, one-leaf pines. That is the sort of tree to know at sight, for the globose, resin-dripping cones have palatable, nourishing kernels, the main harvest of the Paiutes. That perhaps accounts for their growing accommodatingly below the limit of deep snows, grouped sombrely on the valleyward slopes. The real procession of the pines begins in the rifts with the long-leafed *Pinus jeffreyi*, sighing its soul away upon the wind. And it ought not to sigh in such good company. Here begins the manzanita, adjusting its tortuous stiff stems to the sharp waste of boulders, its pale olive leaves twisting edgewise to the sleek, ruddy, chestnut stems; begins also the meadowsweet, burnished laurel, and the million unregarded trumpets of the coral-red pentstemon. (*LLR* 117)

In this admirable passage we see the evidence of Austin's keenness of sight both in little things (the leaves "twisting edgewise") and in large (the "valleyward slopes" with their grouping of different varieties of pines). We see as well that her vision of the West was not of landscape only, but included the human inhabitants—here, the Paiutes—and their communion with place.

The Land of Little Rain is a book of sketches, a form often employed by female regional writers and one that has frequently contributed to such writers' marginalization (Fetterley and Pryse 169) even when they have, as Austin's do, a strong and artful thematic coherence. The *Little Rain* sketches—some more like essays, some more like stories—are a close scrutiny of the land, plants, animals, and few people of the central California desert and mountains—primarily the land itself and its shaping of life-forms. The pieces were initially published in *Atlantic Monthly,* which at that time did not carry illustrations. When Houghton Mifflin decided to bring them out as a book, it was natural to add pictures, given the demand for illustrated books at the time and the visual quality of both Austin's subject matter and her style, readily lending themselves to visual embellishment. Indeed, this embellishment was done on such a scale as to make *The Land of Little Rain* what we would call a coffee table book. It was released in both a larger and a smaller format. In the larger, Smith's striking line drawings were supplemented by halftone illustrations. The question of which is the definitive version remains, in my mind at least, unresolved. Since it is the smaller version (without the frontispiece that Houghton Mifflin sometimes but not always included) that is followed in both an attractive reprint issued in 1974 by the University of New Mexico Press and a composite volume (with *Lost Borders*) issued by Rutgers University Press in 1987 (under the title *Stories from the Country of Lost Borders,* edited by Marjorie Pryse), I take it as having become standard. My comments here are keyed to the 1974 text.

One wonders who selected E. Boyd Smith as illustrator and whether Austin played a role in his selection.[11] Certainly he was a reasonable choice, a successful although not star-caliber illustrator who specialized in western material. Since Smith was also doing the illustrations for Andy Adams's *The Log of a Cowboy,* published by Houghton Mifflin the same year as *Little Rain* (and indeed had done other work for the company), we can guess that it was an editor with the press who thought of using him for Austin's book as well. One wishes even more to know whether Austin worked with Smith directly in developing his illustrations, which are very different in style from his usual work. For *The Log of a Cowboy,* for example, he produced six densely shaded pictures, including frontispiece, all heavily encumbered with details and primarily emphasizing action scenes—the stampede of the herd, swimming the herd across the Platte River, a meeting with Indians, and the cowboys' celebration in Dodge. For *Little Rain* he produced drawings of an altogether different nature, both in style and in subject matter. Showing, for the most part, the plants or animals that Austin writes about, they emphasize landscape and the life-forms that accommodate themselves to that landscape, including in a few cases the human figures who form a part of Austin's literary ecosystem. They are spare, clean, minimal line drawings that make superb use of white space.

In *The Illustrated Book* (1938), Frank Weitenkampf concurred with earlier historians of book publication in judging that line drawings (such as Smith's in *Little Rain* and *The Flock*) were preferable to the halftones that came into use in the late 1800s because, like the line of type, they use white space on the page as "an integral part of the composition" (10).[12] That is, he based his preference for line drawings (which he rejoiced to see coming back into use) on a principle of complementarity with type, the visual manifestation of text. His standard for judging the artistic quality of illustrations was similar: their substantive and stylistic harmony with text. Such complementarity with text, he judged, ought always to be the illustrator's goal, although the book that attained a "perfect union of the elements involved" was "excessively rare" (257). Weitenkampf cited, as an example of perfect union, the John Tenniel illustrations to Lewis Carroll's *Alice in Wonderland,* with their "precision of line" (162). He might equally well have cited *The Land of Little Rain.*

We can appreciate the difference between Smith's illustrations for *The Log of a Cowboy* and *The Land of Little Rain* by considering a drawing that in fact appears in different versions in both. In *The Log of a Cowboy,* the first illustration after the frontispiece is captioned "Heat and Thirst" (figure 2.01). Depicting situation more than action (unlike most of the illustrations in the book), it shows the longhorns of the herd with heads low and tongues hanging out. Two specific animals at the front are emphasized, with the herd strung out behind them to a full horizon line interrupted by a cloud of dust. A similar drawing of cattle suffering from thirst in *The Land of Little Rain* appears in figure 2.02. The lead animal in the *Little Rain* picture is recognizable as the second animal in the *Log of a Cowboy* illustration. The lead animal in the *Log* illustration is recognizable as an animal slightly farther back (about fourth) in the *Little Rain* illustration. The composition is similar, and the cloud of dust on the horizon looks very much the same in both, but in the *Little Rain* drawing the horizon line is only minimally indicated and the drawing is placed low on the page, in contrast to its high placement in *Log,* with the result that an abundance of white space is left above the image. Again and again in Smith's illustrations for *Little Rain,* white space is used in this way to convey the sense of a big sky. Another difference is that cowboys visible toward the back of the herd in the *Log* illustration are not present in the *Little Rain* illustration at all; there are only animals. Buzzards have been added, but on the whole the effect is of simplification, or elimination of details.

Was it solely Smith's own reading of Austin's spare text that led him to switch from the one style to the other? Or did Austin herself have a vision of how she wanted her book illustrated and persuade him to produce line drawings of such elegant spareness? No answer is presently available. But we do have a hint: Barney Nelson has demonstrated that when Houghton Mifflin hired Smith to illustrate Austin's *The Flock,* another book of nature sketches, she provided drawings she had made herself in order to ensure that details such as work gear would be done accurately. Nelson observes that Smith incorporated some of Austin's drawings "almost line for line" (Afterword 272). Whether Austin's involvement in the illustrations of *The Flock* indicates a similar involvement in those of *Little Rain* is impossible to say, but it at least indicates that she attached considerable importance to the visual accompaniments to her verbal text.

Throughout *The Land of Little Rain* words and pictures sustain a lively but always harmonious conversation. This is most obvious (and for that very reason least remarkable) when objects, plants, or animals mentioned in the text immediately appear in small inserted drawings, as when Austin concisely describes (in words that give a wonderfully clear picture of how the bird really looks as it moves) a roadrunner "go[ing] tilting and balancing down the gully" and the bird, appearing to be doing just that, is seen at the end of the sentence (*LLR* 26). Or again, she describes glyphs used by the Native people to convey information, and drawings are provided showing

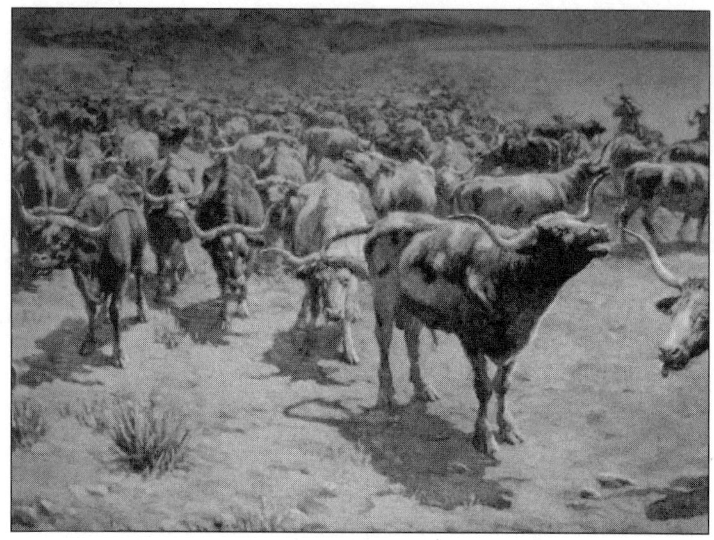

2.01 E. Boyd Smith, "Heat and Thirst," from Andy Adams, *The Log of a Cowboy* (p. 60)

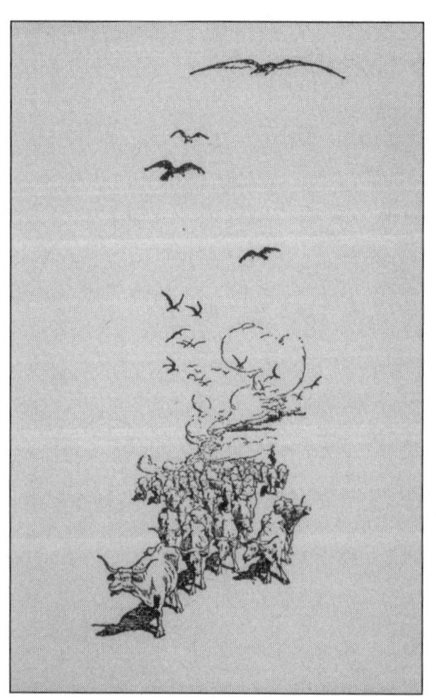

2.02 E. Boyd Smith, full-page drawing of thirsty herd, from Mary Austin, *The Land of Little Rain* (p. 32)

precisely what her words have described (*LLR* 26–27). But in addition to this kind of resonance of subject matter, with the artist showing us the visual essence of an object or animal or a sequence of events given in the text, there is also a more subtle resonance of style. Smith's clean, restrained, uncluttered line drawings perfectly approximate Austin's concise prose style (concise here, although not always). Her writing in the *Little Rain* sketches is precise, warm, and personal; direct in its second-person address to the reader; often humorous; evincing close observation of her environment; and sometimes chatty but never prolix. Smith's drawings have an equivalent simplicity, directness, and sympathy with their subjects. The result is a paragon of bookmaking.[13]

The elegance and discipline of E. Boyd Smith's line drawings is announced on the half-title page of the first chapter, in a stylized drawing of the sun, the central fact of life in hot, arid regions.[14] Equally precise head-pieces precede each subsequent chapter, on half-title pages where the only words are the name of the chapter, with white space all around. The one for "The Mesa Trail" (figure 2.03) demonstrates how these head-pieces focus attention on essential features of the text.

As Melody Graulich comments in her afterword to *Earth Horizon,* Austin's autobiography, her work is "filled with imagery of walking and trails" (376). Precisely visualized trails wind through *Little Rain* from the minute "mouse trail[s] . . . faint to man-sight" by which the smallest "furred and feathered folk" go to water, mere "ribbon[s] in the leaning grass" (*LLR* 17), to the foot trails and stagecoach trails of humans and even the mountains' own "streets," the "river cañons of the Sierras of the Snows" that are "better worth while than most Broadways" (*LLR* 115–16). In the "Mesa Trail" chapter, they wind from the opening sentence to the last word. Along the way their significance broadens from the literal to the figurative in a reference to "trail-weary" travelers who may be so fortunate as to "fall in with" Petite Pete, the sheepherder who spends his year on the mesa trail (*LLR* 99).

Besides head-pieces, the illustrations vary from full-page pictures to small drawings inserted between or within paragraphs, such as those of the roadrunner or the glyphs that I have referred to. A howling coyote looks as if it could trot off the page yet is actually quite stylized, made up of discrete lines (figure 2.04).

It is in the full-page illustrations, though, such as the one of the thirsty

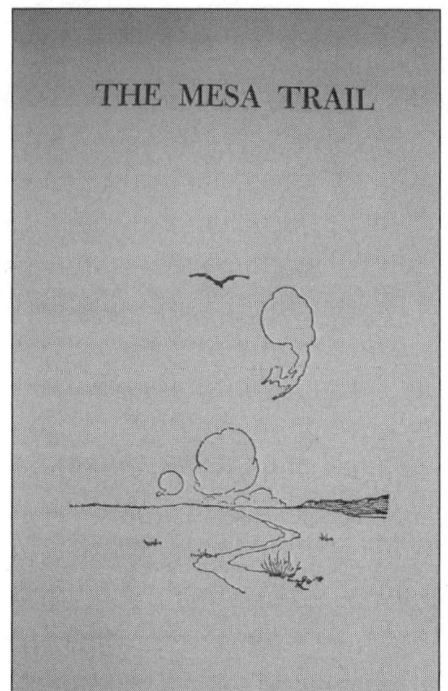

2.03 E. Boyd Smith, half-title page drawing for "The Mesa Trail," from Mary Austin, *The Land of Little Rain* (p. 89)

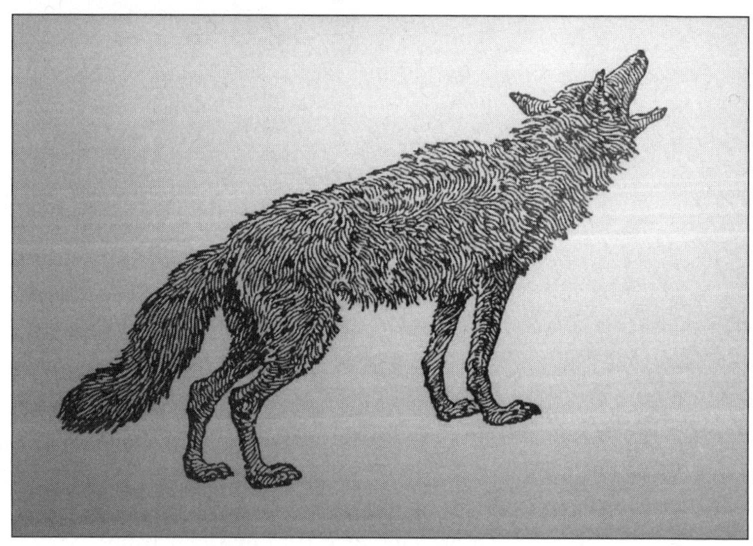

2.04 E. Boyd Smith, drawing of coyote, from Mary Austin, *The Land of Little Rain* (p. 13)

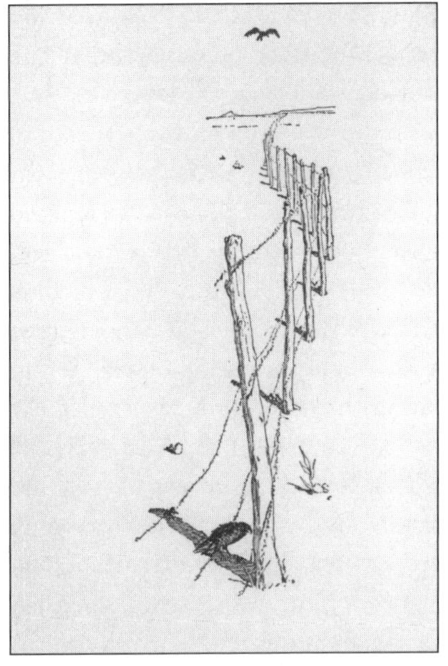

2.05 E. Boyd Smith, drawing of bird resting in shade of fence post, from Mary Austin, *The Land of Little Rain* (p. 10)

herd shown above, that we best see how Smith utilizes white space, that notable advantage of line drawings. Among the most remarkable of these is the opening chapter's drawing of a single crow or raven sitting in the narrow shade of a fence post (figure 2.05). A couple of weeds appear nearby and the wavering line of the fence diminishes into the distance, but whatever is off to the sides simply drops away. A single bird in the sky seems to be looking for a similar bit of shade to light in. The distant horizon is indicated by only a couple of lines. Here, white space conveys the empty distance of the desert floor and also the sense of a big sky that is so important a visual element of *Little Rain.* As we will see with the W. T. Benda drawings for Cather's *My Ántonia* that also emphasize a big sky—one of the primary features of an aesthetic of the Great Plains and the Far West as developed both by pioneer observers and by early painters in the West—this illustration is placed relatively low on the page, allowing it to open up into white space above.[15] The chapter in which this drawing of the crow in the shade of the fence post appears—the opening chapter of the book—is devoted to the dryness of the region and its effect on small animals. The drawing itself refers specifically to the sentence, "There was a fence in that country shutting in a cattle range, and along its fifteen miles of posts one could be sure of finding a bird or two in every strip of shadow" (11). Austin states the situation economically and visually, but Smith economizes even further, reducing the several distinct birds of the text to a single one.

Not that this is the only bird seen so clearly and precisely. Even earlier in the opening chapter a two-thirds page illustration shows a single raven perched on a dry cow skull, with a few puffs of dust devils lightly indicated, a few widely spaced squiggles showing weeds or low brush, and two lines showing the horizon. An entire landscape is reduced to one bird, the remains of a dead animal, a hint of dry grass, and a slight turbulence of air. The big sky is again indicated by low placement on the page. Birds reappear in the second chapter, with two nicely personalized owls and the previously noted roadrunner. The head-piece for the third chapter, "The Scavengers" (i.e., the head-piece on the page where text begins, as distinct from the decoration on the half-title page), shows buzzards lined up on a fence, the first and second seen with great precision, the rest disappearing into blankness. Four pages later the nearest of a group of crows or ravens is drawn with clarity to the point of a distinct bright eye. The sequence of birds continues three pages on with a marvelous drawing of a Clark's crow, "that scavenger and plunderer of mountain camps" (*LLR* 39). The drawing refers specifically to two separate passages, a paragraph on the behavior of the Clark's crow and, a half page later, a shorter one on humans' "disfigurement" of the environment. Smith combines the two by showing an example of such litter (three cans, one of them having held sardines, and the remains of a small campfire with a thin ribbon of smoke rising from it) alongside a single disgusted-looking bird (figure 2.06). Again he eliminates the extraneous through sharp focus on a small number of central objects set off by white space. Similarly, in the full-page illustration at the end of "The Pocket Hunter," we see the man himself seated at his campfire, with two cooking implements and two burros, and nothing else (figure 2.07). In neither of these two drawings is there any horizon line at all. This is true bareness, a true minimalist style.

In writing of wild creatures and their paths to water, Austin frequently uses a language of "little people" to refer to the rodents and other small four-footed inhabitants of the desert, as well as to birds. Such a language can readily be criticized as a sentimentalization of animal life. She has been taken to task by William Scheick, for example, for her "tendency to anthropomor-

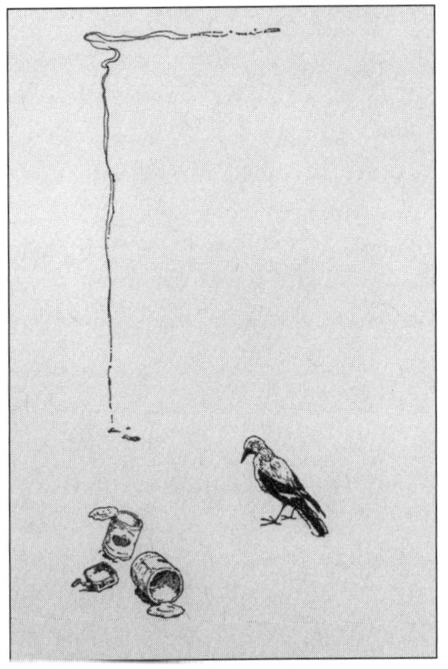

2.06 E. Boyd Smith, full-page drawing of bird objecting to human litter, from Mary Austin, *The Land of Little Rain* (p. 38)

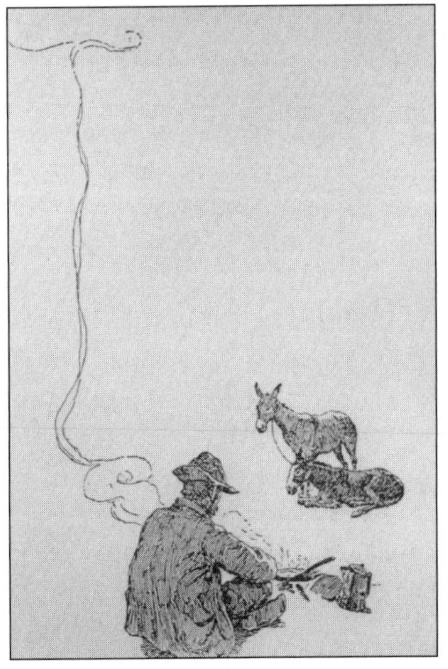

2.07 E. Boyd Smith, drawing of pocket hunter, from Mary Austin, *The Land of Little Rain* (p. 53)

phize her descriptions," a practice he regards as "a form of colonization of the land." Scheick also sees Austin's humanizing language as evidence of a failure to achieve either mystical oneness with the eternal as revealed through nature ("transcendental encounter") or the discipline of accurate, impersonal reportage (which he judges to be the proper discipline of a "documentary artist") (37, 42). But it seems to me that in making this argument Scheick imposes his own goals on Austin. Her language of "little people" is but one figure of speech in an overall strategy of accommodating human life and nonhuman nature to each other as parts of a single whole. She presents the harsh landscape of central California's arid mountains and valleys as a fact to which all living things who occupy these spaces, human and nonhuman alike, must conform. Accordingly, she presents the lives of the lower animals (lower, as they are usually conceived) as reflecting needs and impulses shared by humans.

In doing so, Austin does indeed take up a shaky position that threatens to tip her over into bathos. Ascribing qualities like happiness to nonhuman animals, for instance, oversteps literal accuracy. We don't know whether the "crested quail that troop in the Ceriso are the happiest frequenters of the water trails" (*LLR* 25); we don't know if they can be said to be happy at all. We only know that they *seem* happiest to the human observer. Attributing "pride" to young birds first leaving the nest (*LLR* 34) or judging that a coyote "seemed ashamed of the company" of carrion birds (*LLR* 36) does indubitably humanize these creatures. But it serves the purpose of showing a continuum of the human and the animal—as when, describing cows dying of thirst, she conjectures that they "know nearly as much of death as do their betters, who have only the more imagination" (*LLR* 33). Often she makes this point with a whimsicalness of language that disperses any gathering clouds of sentimentality—as when she characterizes buzzards and hawks gathering to watch coyotes bring down an antelope as "trooping like small boys to a street fight" (*LLR* 37). In every such instance her humanizing language adds visual clarity to a verbal image. Conversely, her humans are implicitly animalized when they "run footpaths drawing down to the Silver Dollar saloon" just as small rodents run footpaths to the few water sources (*LLR* 72). Barney Nelson is on firm ground in judging that Austin's world is finally "more animistic than anthropomorphic" (*Wild and Domestic* 41).

Water, watercourses, and the need for water are always the central facts of *Little Rain.* Lawrence Buell correctly observes that "her protagonist is the land, more particularly the geography of its watercourses and the patterns of life created by water scarcity" (80). Frequently her prose merges the hidden sources of life-giving water with her interest in a life-giving female principle, as Judith Fryer observes by implication in her essay "Desert, Rock": "Following the deep groove that runs from the sheltering fold in the rock, one would come to the life-giving source itself: water" (34).

For Austin, visual acuity does not preclude whimsical touches. The *Pinus jeffreyi* "sigh[s] its soul away" (*LLR* 117). Plant life in the chapter "Water Borders" is like human life in its (attributed) discomforts and preferences:

> Every handful of loose gravel not wholly water leached affords a plant footing, and even in such unpromising surroundings there is a choice of locations. There is never going to be any communism of mountain herbage, their affinities are too sure. Full in the runnels of snow water on gravelly, open spaces in the shadow of a drift, one looks to find but tercups, frozen knee-deep by night, and owning no desire but to ripen their fruit above the icy bath. Soppy little plants of the portulaca and small, fine ferns shiver under the drip of falls and in dribbling crevices. The bleaker the situation, so it is near a streamborder, the better the cassiope loves it. (*LLR* 129)

Smith captures the quality of Austin's prose in this passage about mountain flora with a precise little drawing of a single stem with its bloom, on an otherwise empty half page. Yet even in the context of these keen but friendly observations of individual blossoms, Austin reminds us of the harshness of natural life in the mountains:

> On a little spit of land running into Windy Lake we found one summer the evidence of a tragedy; a pair of sheep's horns not fully grown caught in the crotch of a pine where the living sheep must have lodged them. The trunk of the tree had quite closed over them, and the skull

> bones crumbled away from the weathered horn cases. We hoped it was not too far out of the running of night prowlers to have put a speedy end to the long agony, but we could not be sure. (*LLR* 132)

Again and again we see this note of interdependence, the insistence that all are bound up together: life and death, the least and the strongest, animal and human, place and life-form.

Considering the nature of Smith's illustrations, we may well wonder what Austin would have thought of the 1950 edition of *Little Rain* with visual embellishments entirely different from those in the original—photographs by Ansel Adams.[16] Unlike Smith's drawings, and contrary to Adams's own description of the volume as "an amalgam of Mary Austin's writing and my photographs" (109), his pictures are not distributed throughout the text but grouped in a separate section in back, each photograph accompanied by a sentence excerpted from the text. Austin's words have become, in effect, merely captions for the pictures. One would not want to call the photographs cluttered—Adams was too fine an artist for that—but it is hard to imagine visual images more dissimilar to the original illustrations by Smith and indeed more dissimilar to Austin's prose style. In his characteristically romantic, soft-focus manner, they depart as sharply from the precision and wittiness of Smith's line drawings as if he had deliberately eschewed such qualities. Adams gives tribute to Austin's success in conveying "so much the spirit of earth and sky, of plants and people, of storm and the desolation of majestic wastes, of tender, intimate beauty" (109), but does not mention E. Boyd Smith at all.

I am especially brought up short by Ansel Adams's words "tender" and "intimate"; I question their accuracy as descriptors of Austin's writing of place in *The Land of Little Rain.* Intimate, yes, if one means taking an up-close view and providing an empathetic account of the patterns of life of animals and birds that to most of us might seem insignificant. The trails she speaks of in "Water Trails of the Ceriso" are not only the trails of deer and coyotes but the far narrower, far less obvious ones of "gopher and ground rat and squirrel" (*LLR* 17). In order to observe these, she recommends "getting down to the eye level" of such animals, essentially adopting their perspective on things. If we do so, she tells us, we will see that to these "little people" their ribbon-like routes to water are like "wide and winding roads" marked by "scents" as obvious as "signboards" are to us. Yes, then, "intimate" in this sense, although the connotations remain dubious. But the word "tender" is truly problematic. However affectionate Austin was toward the "little people" of the desert and the land itself, she was always tough-minded as well, particularly in recognizing the desert's harshness. An example is her flat statement of the danger of thirst in the desert: "To underestimate one's thirst, to pass a given landmark to the right or left, to find a dry spring where one looked for running water—there is no help for any of these things" (*LLR* 6). Or again, her account of the destiny of small rodents: "At the spring the bobcat drops down upon them from the black rock, and the red fox picks them up returning in the dark. By day the hawk and eagle overshadow them, and the coyote has all times and seasons for his own" (*LLR* 22).

The omnipresent coyote is the subject of two of Smith's finest drawings. We have seen the scraggly, skinny-legged beast shown "howling and howling" in the first chapter—fully convincing in its coyote-ness to anyone who has ever observed one. A second line drawing of a coyote is actually interwoven with the text so that the two, picture and text, demonstrably assist each other (figure 2.08). The block of type becomes the landscape separating the coyote from the rising moon that he looks at apprehensively over his shoulder—a remarkable instance of complementarity of text and illustration.[17] Smith was surely functioning as page designer here, as well as illustrator. Indeed, design is a significant element in the total artistry of *The Land of Little Rain* as a physical object. Visual elements, by which I mean primarily illustrations but also layout, might well be called, as Jean Schwind calls the Benda illustrations of Cather's *My Ántonia,* a "silent supplement" to the text.

But Austin's text is also, in a sense, silent. The argument that it makes about its own place vis-à-vis the prevailing tradition of literary and artistic representation of the West is a tacit one. What matters about the West, it argues implicitly but never in so many words, is not derring-do but natural presence, not conquest but harmony with a frequently stern natural order.

Three years after *The Land of Little Rain,* another book of Austin's, *The Flock,* appeared with illustrations again by E. Boyd Smith. In later years, Smith would also provide a frontispiece for her problem novel about water rights

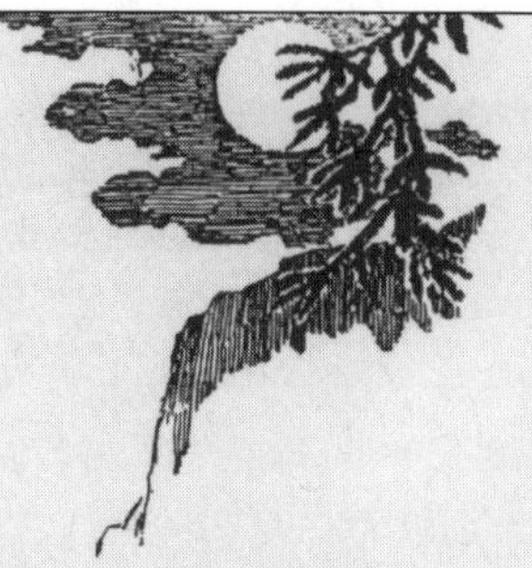

surprised by its sudden rising from behind the mountain wall, slink in its increasing glow, watch it furtively from the cover of near-by brush, unprepared and half uncertain of its identity until it rode clear of the peaks, and finally make off with all the air of one caught napping by an ancient joke. The moon in its wanderings must be a sort of exasperation to cunning beasts, likely to spoil by untimely risings some fore-planned mischief.

But to take the trail again; the coyotes that are astir in the Ceriso of late afternoons, harrying the rabbits from their shallow forms, and the hawks that sweep and swing above them, are not there from any mechanical promptings of instinct, but because they know of old experience that the small fry are about to take to seed gathering and the water trails. The rabbits begin it, taking the trail with long, light leaps, one eye and ear

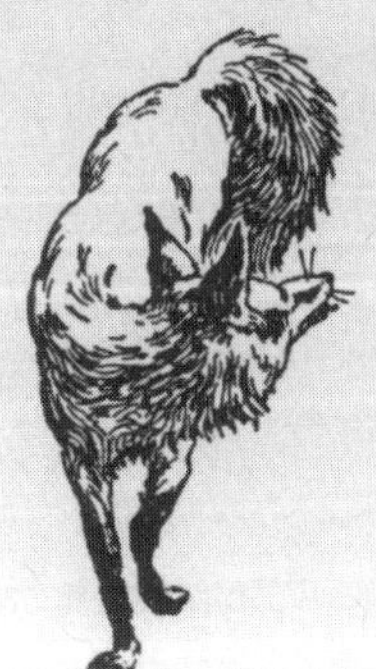

2.08 E. Boyd Smith, drawing of coyote looking at moon across "landscape" of text, from Mary Austin, *The Land of Little Rain* (p. 21)

and industrialization in California, *The Ford* (1917), and line drawings for *The Lands of the Sun* (1927). The frontispiece of *The Ford* need not concern us here. A wholly conventional, heavily romanticized halftone, it in no way complements the driving interests of the novel. For the other two books, however, both of them nonfiction and once again in the genre of the descriptive sketch, Smith did produce line drawings that are of some interest, although they never reach the level of artistry of those in *The Land of Little Rain.* Perhaps the most striking aspect of Smith's later work on texts by Austin is the keenness, in a letter to Houghton Mifflin, with which he remembered the earlier work.

The Flock, on sheepherding in California, is abundantly decorated with very nice head-pieces and tail-pieces, as well as interpolated small drawings, in addition to a frontispiece.[18] Unlike the line drawings in *Little Rain,* these are a mixture of clean pen-and-ink drawings (figure 2.09) and filled-in work reproduced in halftones (figure 2.10).

All of the pictures in *The Flock* except the small tail-pieces have framing lines drawn around them that in effect set them off from the text. Illustration and text are less integrated than in *The Land of Little Rain.* Less visually remarkable than *Little Rain,* even as it is usually regarded as a lesser achievement on Austin's part, *The Flock* is even so, in Smith's own understated words some years later, a "good looking book" (Smith to R. L. Scaife, November 16, 1926).

The 1926 letter in which Smith recalled *The Flock* with such evident satisfaction was written in the course of correspondence with Houghton Mifflin relating to plans for his illustration of *The Lands of the Sun,* a revised republication of Austin's 1914 *California: The Land of the Sun.* The earlier version was written on commission by the Los Angeles Chamber of Commerce to accompany a collection of watercolors of California scenes done by Sutton Palmer. Not readily available today, it is a strikingly handsome volume with thirty-two color reproductions tipped in on full pages of cream-colored stock, inside half-inch borders printed in a muted gold tone. The title page asserts that these are "described" in Austin's text. Such is not the case. Her descriptive prose is directed toward California itself, not toward the paintings. Because of their lush colors and handsome presentation, the pictures are indeed the dominant element, but in every case Austin's words are independent; they simple continue up to and beyond the inserted pic-

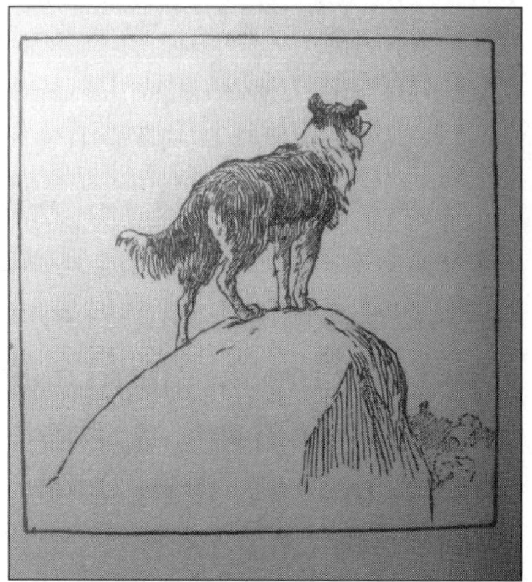

2.09 E. Boyd Smith, drawing of sheep dog, from Mary Austin, *The Flock* (p. 149)

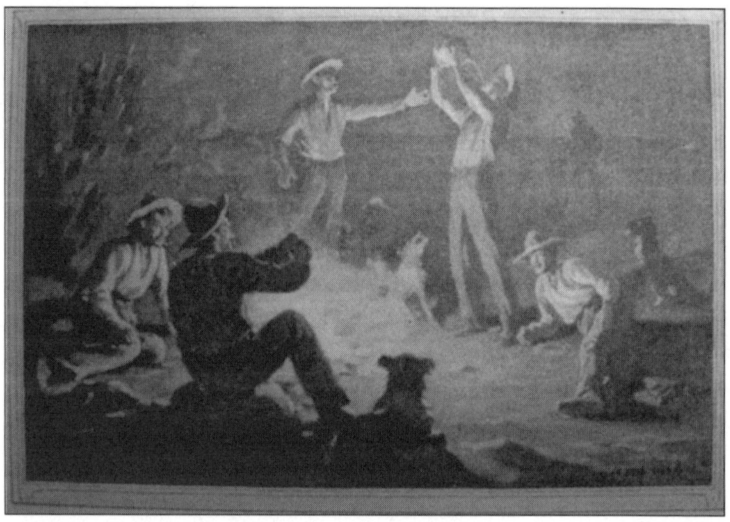

2.10 E. Boyd Smith, drawing of shepherds in fall camp, from Mary Austin, *The Flock* (p. 51)

tures, taking no notice of their presence. The independence of her text is demonstrated by its having been only scarcely revised for the Houghton Mifflin publication of *The Lands of the Sun* thirteen years later, where the reading field constructed by Smith's drawings is very different indeed.

The record of Smith's interactions with Houghton Mifflin's editorial staff about *The Lands of the Sun* shows that he was initially asked to provide only a frontispiece and a title-page decoration (R. L. Scaife to Boyd-Smith, October 28, 1926). The idea of making the book a companion volume to *The Land of Little Rain* emerged and gained specificity in the course of the correspondence. Once Smith was provided the manuscript for study—that is, once he was able to see the text itself so that he could begin to conceive pictures that would be complementary—he saw it as a "poetic" project and not at all an "obvious" one. It was his suggestion of drawings for the chapter half-title pages that crystallized the press's intentions on design. A fee of $300 was agreed on, both sides recalled that *Little Rain* and *The Flock* had been attractive books, and Smith committed himself to providing drawings that could be reproduced on rough paper, in a style similar to that of the *Little Rain* drawings. Whether he was also in correspondence with Austin is not clear; I have found no evidence that they communicated with each other. What *is* clear is that he had maneuvered himself into the position of being, in effect, the designer of the volume.

Following the agreed-on plan but having been given considerable latitude, Smith provided pen-and-ink drawings for the half-title pages of each of the nine chapters. These are, Smith asserted, of the "same character" as those of *Little Rain* (Smith to Scaife, November 16, 1926). That is more or less, but not precisely, true. A far higher proportion of the *Lands of the Sun* drawings include human figures (such as in figure 2.11). As a result, the volume gives a graphic impression of greater social density, with less focus on place in and of itself. Human presence in, and response to, landscape are stressed, more than the specificities of place and environment that were so lovingly yet unsparingly rendered in *The Land of Little Rain.* The low horizon line seen in many of the *Little Rain* drawings reappears, and the clouds are still recognizable as Smith clouds, as we see in the half-title decorations for "Sagebrush Country" (figure 2.12) and "The Twin Valleys" (figure 2.13).

In both of these half-title decorations, however, the image is placed so high on the page, so near the print, that it fails to convey a sense of a big sky.

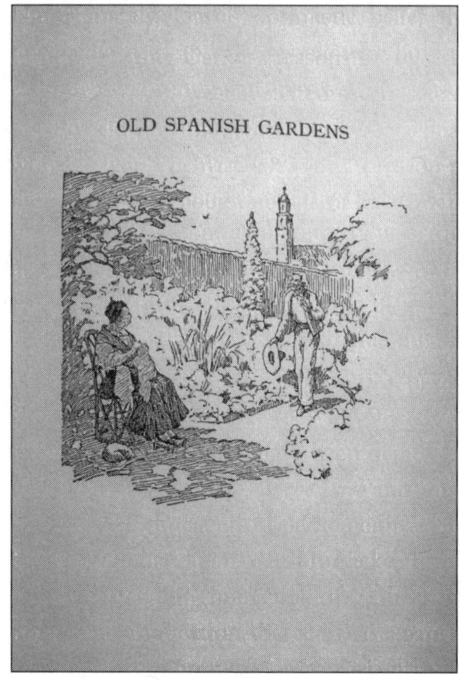

2.11 E. Boyd Smith, half-title page drawing for "Old Spanish Gardens," from Mary Austin, *The Lands of the Sun* (p. 99)

There is far less willingness, in Smith's work for *The Lands of the Sun,* to use white space for emphasis. We might note, too, that although "Twin Valleys" may recall the drawing of thirsty cattle in *Little Rain* (figure 2.02), the cattle here are rendered less convincingly and with less affective quality.

Smith's line drawings for *The Lands of the Sun* do, however, continue to convey a strong sense of desertness. The pictures in the 1914 *California: The Land of the Sun* most emphatically do not; there, we see lush scenes of flowers, streams, and eucalyptus groves. Where Smith provides a stark drawing of cattle on sparse, dry country for "The Twin Valleys" (figure 2.13), the same chapter in the 1914 *California* has seven watercolors, all but one showing water and with blue and purple mountains much in evidence.

Austin's own interest, in the text of the nine sketches in *The Lands of the Sun,* is more often in "compelling contours" (topography) and affective quality than in precision of observation (*Lands* v). We see this, for instance, in her attention to what she perceives as the nature of the appeal of the "Mother range," the Sierra Madre: "mass and line" (*Lands* 42). Besides its

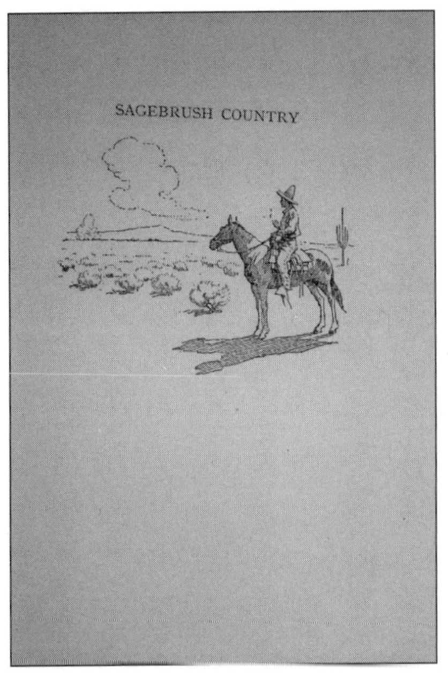

2.12 E. Boyd Smith, half-title page drawing for "Sagebrush Country," from Mary Austin, *The Lands of the Sun* (p. 169)

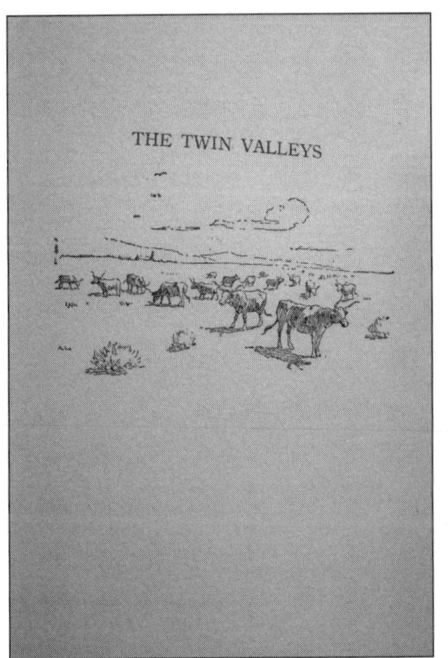

2.13 E. Boyd Smith, half-title page drawing for "The Twin Valleys," from Mary Austin, *The Lands of the Sun* (p. 145)

emphasis on large scale more than close observation, *The Lands of the Sun* differs from *The Land of Little Rain* in its more frequent focus on color, as in the following passage:

> The prevailing note of the San Joaquin is tawny russet. Gold it will be in the season resplendent as those idols which the Incas overlaid yearly with fresh-beaten leaf. In September the tall *barrancas* above Bakersfield and Visalia are yellow as brass, but all up and down the hill-rimmed hollow is every lion-colored tint contending still with the thin belts of planted orchard. (*Lands* 149)[19]

As observed in this excerpt, the later work also differs in its prose style, which unlike that of *Little Rain* has a quality of fullness or lushness. In "The Port of Monterey," for instance, we find catalog after catalog in which she names and describes tree after tree (*Lands* 84–86) or names various kinds of birds (*Lands* 79–81):

> Here the ancient murrelet fattens for the long flight to the Alaskan breeding grounds, and in the wildest gales the little nocturnal auklets may be heard calling to one another. . . . Long triangular flights of curlew drop down these beaches against the westering sun, with wings extended straight above their heads, furling like the little lateen sails come home from fishing. Sandpipers, sanderlings, all the ripple runners, the skimmers of the receding foam, all the scavengers of the tide, the gulls, Glaucous-winged, Herring, Ringbilled, and the species that take their name of the locality, may be found two or three miles inland, following the plough as robins do in the spring. When the herring school in the bay nothing could exceed the multitude and clamor of the Herring gulls. They stretch out in close order, wing beating against wing . . . (*Lands* 80)

The effect of such catalogs is of great plenitude—a marked contrast to the bareness of *The Land of Little Rain.* In this respect, it might seem to accord better with Palmer's watercolors, in the 1914 version, than with Smith's drawings in the 1927 republication. Even so, Austin's descriptions of place have, on the whole, a toughness and specificity better served by the style of the later volume, but able to stand up to either.

Repeatedly, in this book published almost a quarter-century after *The Land of Little Rain* but originally written in 1914, Austin animates the broad expanses of the landscape itself. In describing Carmel she notes "hills of softer contours, tawny, rippled like the coat of a great cat sleeping in the sun" (*Lands* 90). Her attention to small mammals remains precise:

> Any morning you may find about your bungalow innumerable prints, as of baby palms pressed downward in the dust, the tracks of the friendly little raccoon who may be heard babbling in the shallow cañons any moonlight night. Often I have left a cut melon under my window for the sake of seeing, an hour after moonrise, two or three of them scooping out the pink heart, spatting one another for helpings out of turn, keeping, in spite of the little gluttons you know them to be, a great affectation of daintiness. The night cry of these little creatures is difficult to distinguish from the love call of the horned owl. (*Lands* 94)

Even when given over to lush sweep or a kind of boosterism, her landscape description retains its photographic precision and its familiar directness. It retains, too, its commitment to a conception of the land as a place for living, rather than a pristine sanctuary for preservation. Here, she goes further, perhaps too far, insisting that "one must learn to think of the land in terms of human achievement" (*Lands* 155). The book ends with what I take to be (despite the plural "peoples") a celebration of the enterprising and entrepreneurial Anglos who have rushed to California for agricultural and commercial wealth: The High Sierra is "the source of that high confidence in their destiny and the purposeful friendliness of the Powers which characterizes the peoples of the West" (*Lands* 214). The idea runs directly counter to her earlier praise of the Native people and criticism of their Anglo oppressors.

In many ways *The Lands of the Sun* anticipates *The Land of Journeys' Ending,* Austin's major work about the Arizona–New Mexico Southwest. It is readable and at times, even now, interesting. But it does not give the sense of lived intimacy with a place that *Little Rain* does so well, nor does it make the whole of California into a microcosm as *Little Rain* succeeded in doing with a small portion of it, the dry Tejon. In *The Land of Little Rain,* a smaller geographic span and the life-forms that inhabit it command a closer look. The more precise visual nature of the text and the compelling visual presence of the book itself, with its remarkable complementarity between illustrations and text, explain why *The Land of Little Rain* continues to be regarded as Austin's most fully achieved book about the West, even as, for very different reasons, "The Walking Woman," from *Lost Borders* (to be discussed in Chapter Three) is customarily and rightly regarded as her most successful short story.

In 1924, slightly more than a decade before her death, Mary Austin moved to Santa Fe and built a home there. In these last years of her career, her rate of publication declined from the staggering (in some ways counterproductively so) output of her earlier career. Even so, she wrote four major books during her New Mexico years: *The Land of Journeys' Ending,* a nonfiction survey of the geography and history of New Mexico and Arizona; the novel *Starry Adventure;* her autobiography, *Earth Horizon,* with significant passages about southwestern culture and what she saw as Willa Cather's abuse of the Southwest; and the novella *Cactus Thorn,* unpublished until many years after her death, a work that links the southwestern landscape with assertive feminism and repays old grudges from Austin's personal life. In different ways in all of these books, visual experience is the key to understanding and the land itself is ultimately our reason for wanting and needing to understand human stories. "Study history," she admonishes us, "for the sake of the land" (*LJE* 195).

Both in its language and in its physical presence, *The Land of Journeys' Ending* is highly visual. It was published with an abundance of illustrations. Superficially, it might seem to be a companion book to *Little Rain* in that both are nonfiction, both are centered on place (the one California, the other Arizona and New Mexico), and both are concerned with the land and natural processes as the shaping determinants of patterns of human life. Even the titles are counterparts. Yet the differences between the two are more striking than the parallels. The language of *Journeys' End* is lush rather than epigrammatic, and its scope extensive rather than intensive. Moreover, *The Land of Journeys' Ending* is far more overtly concerned with history and with social commentary. Conceiving the Southwest, and more specifically its Native cultures, as an ideal, Austin repeatedly registers dismay at the history of assaults on Pueblo cultures by aggressive intruding forces—the Spanish and their missionaries and Americans and theirs. She had launched her portrayal of Native cultures as exemplary teachers of spirituality in *The Land of Little Rain* and continued it in *Lost Borders,* where she repeatedly vented her indignation at Anglos who mistreat Native Americans, especially Indian women. In *Outland,* a fantasy novel set in California (published in 1910 in England and 1919 in the United States), her idealized fantasy people seem modeled on Native Americans in many ways, including their sacred colors associated with the cardinal directions (*Outland* 46). By the time she wrote *Journeys' Ending,* she was widely regarded as an expert on American Indians.[20] At that juncture, she turned her attention to the powerful threats posed to Native life by Christianity and by Anglo political and economic forces.

Geographically, the visual and environmental scope of *The Land of Journeys' Ending* is vast and sweeping, rather than localized and intently viewed as it is in *The Land of Little Rain.* This difference of scope is both a strength and a weakness, and is probably the main reason *Journeys' Ending* is so difficult a book to evaluate, even as it is a richly rewarding one to read. Its impressive scope constitutes the achievement of an entirely different *kind* of vision, one more nearly resembling that of *The Lands of the Sun* and one Austin describes in her preface to that book as a sense of the country's "structural plan" and "compelling contours" (*Lands* v). It is in multiple senses an enlargement of the geological vision that in *Little Rain* is, for the most part, restricted to an interest in watercourses. Undeniably, *Journeys' Ending* suffers from the lack of the precision and focus of observation that characterize *Little Rain.* Even so, in its realization of color and form it is still a manifestation, although a more "synesthetic" one, of what Lanigan Stineman calls Austin's "photographic imagination" (180–83).[21] The loss of precision and focus is counterbalanced by the book's geographic and historical largeness, by the power of Austin's political and moral pronouncements, and by her shaping metaphor of converging journeys that irresistibly link time and space.

Although few readers would consider it Austin's best and most artistic book—an estimate usually reserved for *Little Rain*—it can nevertheless be considered an unjustly neglected work, and even a masterwork of the Southwest.

Taking just one of any number of good examples, we can see the largeness of scale that characterizes *The Land of Journeys' Ending:*

> This is a rim-rock mesa, red sandstone, topping the softer stuff and weathering in huge blocks like a ruined wall. Like the teocalli of the Aztecs, it rises from the mesa platform, a pyramidal, solitary mass of broken cones, from whose top, strea[m] cloud[s] like smoke of accepted sacrifice, following the high wind river. For a whole day's travel, east and west, it dominates the landscape to the north of the railway, a semicircular volcanic mass, having a secondary cone within, one clear creek, and a giant's tongue of black lava protruded down the shallow red sandstone cañon where the railway follows the old trail past Acoma to Zuñi. Tsotsil, it is called by the Navajo, in reference to the lava tongue, and, ceremonially, Blue Turquoise Mountain, sacred world altar of the South. But on the maps you will find it designated as Mt. Taylor. (*LJE* 376)[22]

In an assertion that notably implies rejection of the supposed standard desire of women to make domestic gardens in the West, Austin insists that "once you have accepted the scale it is as easy to be familiar with a grass-plot the size of Rhode Island or a plantation of yellow pines half as big as Belgium, as with the posy-plots of your garden" (*LJE* 35). But actually it isn't. The reader's mental vision cannot so successfully fasten onto a plantation of yellow pines or a semicircular volcanic mass as on a half-dozen marigolds or the uneasy movement of a single coyote on a night of full moon (so well realized in *Little Rain*) or the shape and color of spines on the cholla (seen elsewhere in *Journeys' Ending*). This matter of scale is a difficulty if we seek to compare Austin's relative achievements in the two books.

Even so, Austin's style remains, in this book of the large scale, richly visual and very much her own. We recognize the voice of *Little Rain* in her references to "small furred folk" and to the chollas having "a tree-like form and a social habit" (*LJE* 132,128). Plant life is especially well observed and put into words, and the emphasis on journeys, movement, and converging trails gives a quasi-visual sense of the large contours of the land. Such journeys are not only those of different human groups, serving her emphasis on multi-ethnicity, but of animals and plant life—pine trees "march" (*LJE* 34), plants in general make a "journey" of evolution (*LJE* 133–36). Even watercourses and air currents move along trails of sorts. Subtleties of color are dwelt on and lusciously realized, as when she makes a distinction between the hues of different trees, "the green of the junipers" being "slightly yellower" than that of the piñons (*LJE* 36). We see this dwelling on rich color here:

> In the snowy months there will be cumulus clouds topping the cañon walls, white as cotton bolls, burnt-orange tips of the willows repeating the note of the cliffs, and bright flecks of bluebirds' wings, interlacing earth and sky. When the snowdrifts in the shadows begin to take lilac tones, the drift of wild plums is feather white, the rabbit-brush white fluff over green, and the water shadows as green as the junipers. In September the wild plums are vermilion, with a bloom like the purple haze of the mountains, and after the plums the Virginia creeper tones with the frost-bitten red of the cliffs. Then the squashes piled in the fields, and the bright gold of the rabbit-brush bring out the yellow of the clays, and the adobe huts which otherwise tend to disappear into the earth from which they have been drawn, are blots of flaming scarlet and vermilion. In Española Valley where chile is raised for export, not only the house walls, but great racks of threaded pods make splashes of heartening color, clear and detached, color that gives you a full sense of its being eaten and absorbed. About this time the cottonwoods along the acequia madre begin to bear, in place of leaves, little heart-shaped fruits of light. . . . Along Tesuque River they come up burning like the bush in the midst of which was God. Toward the end of October the deep, self-contained blues, the delicate fawn, and the grape-black shadows of the winter landscape emerge. (*LJE* 177–78)

Such language can scarcely be captured in black-and-white illustrations. (And indeed, Austin told Alice Corbin Henderson in a letter written from New York that she dreamed about New Mexico's colors every night.[23]) In *The Land of Little Rain,* where the language also had color as well as, more notably, precision, Smith's clear, spacious drawings seemed entirely adequate. Here it would take an impressionist painting to hold its own with the language.

Perhaps it was because his task was so difficult, then, that John Edwin Jackson's illustrations for Journeys' Ending do not achieve a level of charm or absolute rightness of complementarity with the text equal to Smith's in Little Rain. Moreover, Jackson (1876–1950) usually did urban scenes, and these are outdoor scenes. They are very competent, to be sure, and they greatly add to the interest of the book as a total reading experience, but they fail to move beyond a certain inertness. The frontispiece, for example, captioned "Against the Evening Light the Sahuaros Have a Stately Look" (all the full-page illustrations are captioned with words from the text), is so dark with busy lines and shading that we get no impression of the intense light of southwest Arizona (figure 2.14). The drawing does strike the note of journeying that pervades and structures the text, and in that way it admirably serves the function of a frontispiece, but neither man nor horse nor donkey is particularized, and the disproportion between them and the outsized cacti is clumsy. The first of the chapter half-title page pieces particularizes the costumes and weapons of the Spanish conquistadors with whose incursion the book begins, but the men themselves are not individualized, the postures of the one on the left and on the right are stiff, and we get no sense of place (figure 2.15).

All of the chapter half-title pages in *Journeys' Ending* are adorned with similar illustrations about half a page in size. Like the one of the conquistadors, these are considerably more open and set off by more white space than the fourteen full-page pictures (including frontispiece) that are shown in the List of Illustrations, which with perhaps a single exception are closed in, darkly shaded, and cluttered with detail, their horizon lines so high that the sense of a big sky is lost. An example appears in figure 2.16. The chapter half-title page drawings, such as figure 2.17, give a sense of the region's spaciousness and big skies far more satisfactorily, and thus have greater complementarity to the text.

Unfortunately, several of the drawings for the chapter half-title pages are merely ornamental, lacking the narrative interest of the "Cactus Country"

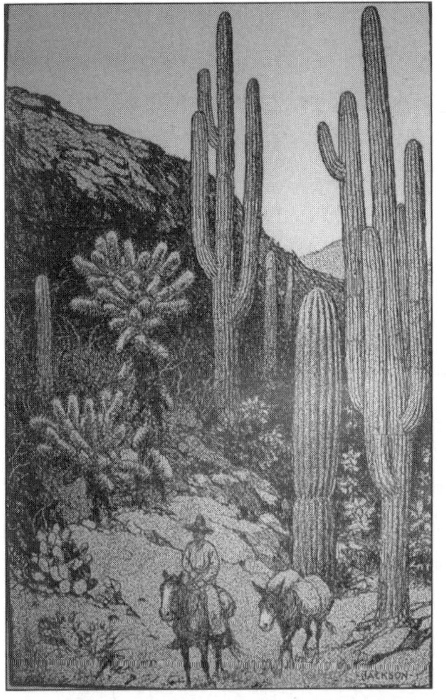

2.14 John Edwin Jackson, frontispiece to Mary Austin, *The Land of Journeys' Ending*

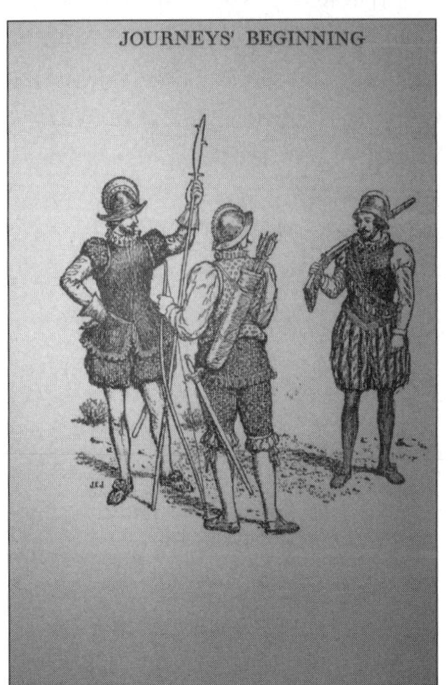

2.15 John Edwin Jackson, half-title page drawing for "Journeys' Beginning," from Mary Austin, *The Land of Journeys' Ending* (p. 1)

scene.[24] There are fifteen of these chapter half-title page drawings (I use so awkward a term because they seem to me to surpass what is implied by "head-pieces"), in addition to the fourteen full-page illustrations listed, plus one map, and an additional twenty-six small drawings inserted as tail-pieces or at the side edge of blocks of type. These mostly show heads of people, plants, or objects such as Native pots or baskets. Although the human portraits are more typecast than individualized, these small drawings are for the most part well done and interesting. Nowhere is there a picture showing violent conflict—the note that so often characterizes the masculine tradition in western art—but rather quiet mountain aspens, cliff dwellings "with a sense of cuddling safely against the mother rock" (*LJE* 79), and emblems of both Native and Anglo spirituality.

A total of fifty-five pictures, then, adorn Austin's text, making *The Land of Journeys' Ending* a lavishly produced book indeed. Only six years earlier, Houghton Mifflin had balked at paying more than $150 to W. T. Benda, a well-known illustrator, for line drawings for Willa Cather's *My Ántonia.* After Cather protested (in a letter to Ferris Greenslet, November 24, [1917]), the amount was raised to $200, but no more. As a result, the novel was published with eight line drawings distributed mostly in the earlier half of the book, rather than the twelve that Cather, who was very much in control of the art for *Ántonia,* had intended. Compare these eight drawings with the fifty-five in *The Land of Journeys' Ending.* The willingness of Austin's publisher, Century, to provide so much more lavishly for the book testifies to her status at the time. Clearly, the Century editors felt that she was an authorial commodity worth investing in and her subject one that would have a market. The author, by 1924, of many books, Austin was well established, whereas Cather was only beginning her period of greatness and recognition when she was getting *My Ántonia* ready for publication.

Time has not dealt gently with Austin, however. Few people now recognize her name, whereas Cather's is one of the standard names of the American literary heritage. This is true despite a significant Austin revival in the 1980s. In part, the erosion of her reputation may lie in the sheer number of her books; we may well think she published too much. With no source of income but her own writing and occasional lecturing, she sometimes pushed into print material that lacked the polish of her best work. In part, too, it may be because she was so willing to scold and lecture, and as a result developed

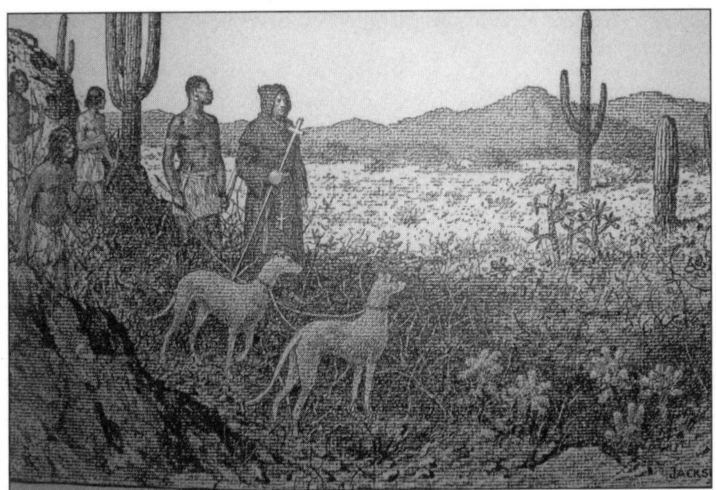

2.16 John Edwin Jackson, "Fray Marcos and Estevánico . . . Going North by Trails the Indians Showed Him . . . His Greyhounds Well in Leash," from Mary Austin, *The Land of Journeys' Ending* (p. 13)

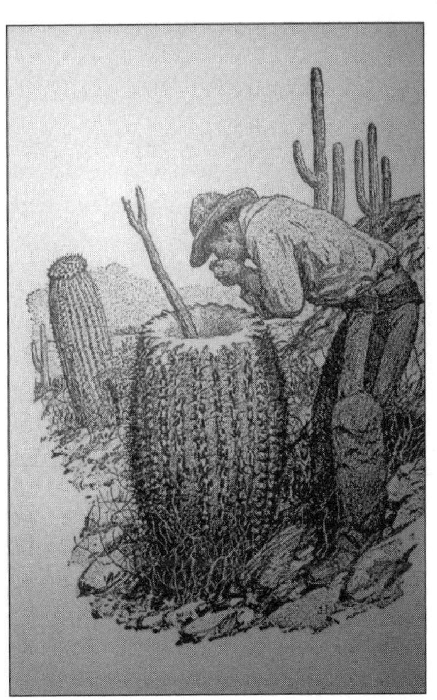

2.17 John Edwin Jackson, half-title page drawing for "Cactus Country," from Mary Austin, *The Land of Journeys' Ending* (p. 117)

a negative personal reputation. Largely, however, Austin's eclipse must be attributed to the fact that she was not at her best in the novel, the genre of choice of twentieth-century readers, but rather in the less favored genres of the sketch and the descriptive essay. In an increasingly fast-paced culture, fewer and fewer people have had the patience to read quiet descriptions of natural phenomena and scenes. To be sure, Austin should rightly be thought of as an ecological writer rather than a descriptive nature writer. Her primary interest is in systems of life existing within environments. Mark Schlenz defines this interest as a Boasian concern with "human societies in ecological contexts" (66). One might expect, then, that her insistent ecological emphasis would have enhanced her reputation over the years. But it is often easiest to perceive her writing as appreciative landscape description—a mode scarcely admired by most readers in the past half-century or more. And it has not helped her reputation that as her major book of ecological writing, combining geography, geology, and history, *The Land of Journeys' Ending* is less keenly visualized and distinctive in style than her first book.

Journeys' Ending has never had as many readers or as much critical attention as *Little Rain.* It is denser and less often enlivened by the distinctive wittiness that *Little Rain* possesses in such abundance. At the same time, it is less intensively, if more extensively, informed. At the time of its publication, Austin was only in transition to being a resident of the area she writes about.[25] Rather than the close observations afforded by many years of residence, hiking, and camping that pervaded *Little Rain, Journeys' Ending* was based on the gleanings of periodic visits during which Austin traveled mainly by car. Goodman probably shortchanges the extent of the familiarity Austin was able to build up in that way by saying that her "impressions" were gained in a single year's "sketching trip" through the Rio Grande Valley and southern Arizona with Santa Fe artist Gerald Cassidy and his wife (Goodman 117). According to her biographer, she had been making "frequent sojourns" with her friend and possibly romantic interest Daniel MacDougal of the University of Arizona, including visits to the Desert Laboratory near Tucson in 1919, 1922, and 1923.[26] Still, one concludes that Austin's own statement about her lack of detailed acquaintance with California as a whole in *The Lands of the Sun*—that she did not know it with the "close-studied intimacy" of her knowledge of the Owens Valley (*Lands* v)—seems to apply to her knowledge of New Mexico and Arizona as well.

Through historical sweep and her ability to visualize landscape in powerful overarching terms, she was able to go far toward overcoming this lack of close intimacy in writing *The Land of Journeys' Ending,* but it never achieves the closeness of vision and personal involvement that we find in *The Land of Little Rain.*

To be sure, the breadth of historical vision Austin displays in *Journeys' Ending* is impressive, probably as impressive as her visual grasp of large geographical masses and her ability to put them into words. New Mexico and Arizona are huge expanses of territory with complex histories and rich human diversity. There could scarcely be a writer better suited to address this large and beautifully complex human geography than Austin, whose interest in and devotion to the cultural diversity represented by Native Americans and long-time Hispanos, as well as by women, are abundantly demonstrated in the much earlier *Lost Borders* and *The Flock* as well as *The Land of Little Rain.* Introducing *The Land of Journeys' Ending* by way of historical figures Cabeza de Vaca, Fray Marcos, and Estevánico, she approximates these early Spanish intruders' experiences to those of contemporary first-time visitors by considering the nature of anyone's first impressions of the region. One's first sense of the land, she says, is of strength; it is "like the middle life of a strong man, splendidly ordered" (*LJE* 3). One's second sense is of geologic process. She returns to these twin emphases—geologic process and the linkage of human life to the land—throughout the book.

Two ideas that are emphatically established are that the Southwest is not actually a desert and that the nature of the place determines the nature of human activity within it. The Southwest's "undeserved reputation for desertness" she attributes to a "prevalence of a single type of growth over enormous areas, combined with the lack of surface cover for the raked, fire-colored sands" (*LJE* 37). In fact, as Austin correctly points out, much of the area receives snows in winter and a rainy season in summer (now popularly called the monsoon season). She concedes that at mid-August, when the rainy season is finished and heat has dried everything up, the land does take on "that aspect of life defeated which is the accepted note of desertness." Since most visitors come in the early fall, because temperatures are moderate then, what they see is this "defeated" appearance. But the "initiate"—among whom Austin certainly counts herself—know that "the secret charm of the desert is the secret of life triumphant," not defeated at all (*LJE* 56). Unlike those who have seen these arid reaches in terms of deadness, she finds it a place of vitality, although not of an obvious or easy kind.

The contrasts Austin observes in this passage on climate, and in passages on mountainous terrain alongside flat expanses, make for an "intensely dramatic landscape." This fact, she says, and the "introverting effect of isolation" have together shaped social patterns in the Southwest. They have contributed, for example, to the starkness of the passion play observances of Los Hermanos Penitentes, the lay religious orders of the Penitential Brotherhoods (*LJE* 355).

Austin's interest in the harsh practices of the Penitentes (which would soon engage Cather and O'Keeffe as well) had been exhibited many years earlier by her sometime mentor Charles Lummis in, for example, a chapter called "The Self-Crucifiers" in his book *Some Strange Corners of Our Country* (1892). Considering the closeness of Austin's acquaintance with Lummis around the time *Strange Corners* was published, it seems likely that she knew of this essay. The word "strange" in his book title exemplifies his habitual exoticizing of the Southwest, and the term "self-crucifiers" indicates the perversity he saw in these religious devotees. He writes of their penitential practices, which reach an annual culmination on Good Friday, as a disease that afflicts the most "ignorant and fanatic" of Mexicans (90–91). Lummis's account, then, is tinged with a judgmental racism directed toward readers' responses of horrified fascination. His "intent[ness] on writing about the most folkloric and romantic elements of Native American and *mestizo* culture" has led Héctor Calderón and José David Saldívar to label him "patronizing" (quoted in Anderson 88).

Like Lummis, Austin liked to boast of her familiarity with rites forbidden to outsiders. She was indeed equally willing to capitalize on her "insider" status by contributing to a Santa Fe Railway brochure entitled *They Know New Mexico* (Weigle, "From Desert" 129–30, 136). Unlike Lummis's, however, her account of the Penitentes in *The Land of Journeys' Ending* is given in a tone of serious and even respectful interest. She ponders the "ultimate gain in peace and spiritual insight" derived by society as a whole from those who "have taken the Trail of the Blood" (*LJE* 363). Willa Cather's treatment of the Penitentes in *Death Comes for the Archbishop,* three years later, would be judgmental, like Lummis's, but like Austin's would stop short of sensationalism.

Comparison of Cather's *Archbishop* (1927) and Austin's *Land of Journeys' Ending* (1924) is instructive. Austin was far more willing to make blunt criticism of both the Spanish and the American imperialists, including missionaries, who came into the Southwest and disrupted its traditional ways of life. In contrast to the tone of sad regret that Cather would take in *Archbishop,* Austin speaks of the displacement of the Navajo to the Bosque Redondo as a "disgrace to America,—supposing Americans capable of feeling disgraced by their own conduct" (*LJE* 221). In sharply barbed language, she speaks of the Spanish as "gaudy, gold-greedy young Dons" who "came swaggering out of Culiacan" and of the United States, with its takeover of all of northern Mexico, as "this most Christian but un-Christlike civilization of ours" (*LJE* 235–36). The true Americans, she implies, were the people of the pueblos, because they steadfastly tried to maintain that principle "everywhere spoken of as American," freedom of religion (*LJE* 237). Instead of seeing the U.S. seizure of the territories that we call Arizona and New Mexico as a benefit to the Native populace, then, as Cather does, she sees the pueblos as having fallen "into the clutch" of a society "knowing neither the land nor its inhabitants" and "caring only for what they could get out of them" (*LJE* 235, 238). In a rhetorical turn that would have been, and would now be, shocking to most Americans, she equates the "gringo" with the then generally reviled Spanish, Navajo, Apache, and Comanche as making up the "five fingers of the Left Hand" of God that closed crushingly on the pueblos (*LJE* 238).

Austin views the Southwest, in *The Land of Journeys' Ending,* in both the sweeping terms of geology and the minute ones of botany; in the colorfully aesthetic terms of the painter; under the long perspective of the historian; and with the immediacy of the social critic. Here, as in her earliest writings, she draws on her intensely visual way of experiencing and imagining place to picture a Southwest far removed from the inviting arena for adventure and conquest seen by the most influential of her male predecessors.

3

GENDER AND EQUALITY IN AUSTIN'S SOUTHWEST

She had walked off all sense of society-made values, and, knowing the best when the best came to her, was able to take it.

Mary Austin
"The Walking Woman," Lost Borders

It's all about rounding that next bend in the river.
What will engage or assault your eye?

Margaret Randall
"Around the Bend," Into Another Time

In a passage in her New Mexico novel *Starry Adventure* (1931), Austin makes an argument that visual apprehension—seeing—constitutes a kind of direct knowledge distinct from either intellect or feeling. Her hero, Gard, and his friend Jane have just observed "a vast twilight canopy of moving stars, cut about the bottom in pointed scallops of blackness that were the circling ranges" of New Mexico's mountains (*SA* 129). At once, as if the conversation arises directly from what they have seen, Jane asks Gard whether he still experiences, as he did as a child, a conviction of there being a "starry adventure" in store for him. Yes, he says, it still comes, in moments of intense visual experience of the land and the sky—for example, if it's "early in the morning, if I wake and it's white, but the stars are shining" (*SA* 129). Jane is the only person to whom he has ever confided this conviction, and now she tells him that she, too, has such a feeling, but only in New Mexico, never in New York, where she now lives. Gard complains that people "keep bothering" him—they can't seem to "*see!*" The two explore these insights, Jane's voice coming first:

> "I guess David [Gard's best friend] is one of those who don't see, either. He knows a lot; more than any boy I ever met. But he doesn't see anything. And Laura [Gard's sister], she sort of sees; but only a few kinds of things." Gard was much struck. It never occurred to him to analyze the people that he loved. But Laura and David; she had hit them off exactly. They knew a lot and they worried because you didn't know it; but as for *seeing* . . .
>
> "I guess David sees engineering things all right." His friend wasn't to be belittled.
>
> "Like my father sees business. But there's such a lot of other things." (SA 130)

Among the many new understandings that come to Gard in this conversation is the realization that Jane thinks she may be "in" his adventure and that, yes, "'girls *are* in things now.'" He continues to ponder it: "Yes, girls were in things. Had a right to be, votes and everything. All that stuff about women being off by themselves was over, canned" (*SA* 130).

This remarkable two-page passage in what has been a much-neglec ted novel provides us the crux of Austin's writing about the Southwest: a fusion of place, vision, and gender equality.[1] Only a direct indication of her sense of the complex sweep of regional history—an element that appears primarily in *The Land of Journeys' Ending*—is missing. The principle she stated in her essay "Regionalism in American Fiction," that in a true regional literature place itself should be "the instigator of plot" (138), is evident in the way Gard and Jane's conversation develops out of what they are experiencing and their shared sense that a vision for their lives comes to them only *in* place, this place. Austin's sense of the primacy of visual experience appears in their discussion of people who know things but do not *see.* Indeed, it appears even in the movement of the sentence in which Gard and Jane *first* perceive "pointed scallops of blackness," and *then* identify them as mountains. Austin's belief that there are things more important than money-making is evident in the barb at Jane's father. Her conviction that women were indeed "*in* things" and were entitled to equality with men—a conviction shared by some men, such as Gard and David—is obvious. Perhaps less so is her belief, clearly evident in other writings, that the West provides an opportunity for women to take such a place in society. Implicit in the scene, too, is the idea that the Southwest provides, on a grand scale, the space needed for people to pursue "starry adventures."

It is unfortunate that *Starry Adventure* has not attracted many readers, even among those who have participated in the Austin revival of the 1980s and after. Perhaps its quirky title is a deterrent. Even so, it is a work that stands up to multiple readings, and one arguably of major social significance in its reconceptualizing of what the Southwest may mean for America. If its emphasis on physical and spiritual vision links the novel to much of Austin's earlier writing of place, its insistent reconceptualizing of both male and female gender roles links it to others of her western writings not yet discussed here. To read this major late work and to assess its vision of the Southwest as a place of equality and a place for living, we need to turn back to some of her earlier books, especially *Lost Borders* (1909), and also reach forward to the novella *Cactus Thorn,* written during her New Mexico years but not published until 1988, more than half a century after her death.

The central unifying element in all of Austin's voluminous works, running through and beyond her interest in the West and Southwest, is a vision of equality between the sexes.[2] Her insistence on gender equality was indeed a major cause of the breaking off of her mentoring by Charles Lummis.[3] A particularly clear statement of her concern for the need for change in women's lives—"feminism is the inherent hope of women to be esteemed for something over and above their femininity"—appeared in Lummis's magazine *Out West,* but in 1914, when he was no longer editor. It is a concern evident in all of her novels, beginning with the little-read *Isidro,* in which the heroine appears in disguise as a male during much of the book and teaches her prospective husband some new ideas before settling into their marriage. It is equally evident in her second California novel, *Santa Lucia* (1908), with its critique of marriage and restrictive assumptions about the scope of women's lives, and in *Outland* (1910), a fantasy of escape to a better, more peaceful society. In *Outland,* California's coastal range and redwood forests serve as a place permeable to humans but chiefly inhabited by quasi-human "outliers" in whose society women are strong and fast, like men, and men are nurturing, like women. Only after learning from such a society can the male of the Anglo pair who are the central characters gain sufficient emotional honesty for the romantic plot to reach consummation—a consummation rendered in terms of Austin's favorite image, the trail.

Outland's fantasy of a better life in California's forested coastland, in a newly developing multiethnic society, continues Austin's attempt to merge her response to physical environment and concern for its wise use with a respect for Native peoples and an insistence on gender equality. Her fusion of feminism with interest in place and environment in her writings about the West is one of her greatest distinctions.

More successful artistically than any of these novels, however, and certainly better known, are the linked short stories of *Lost Borders* (1909). And here we return to the role of illustration.

In correspondence with Houghton Mifflin about the publication of *Lost Borders,* Austin wrote to her production editor, W. I. Booth, "I sincerely hope you will not insist upon illustrating it. I am strongly prejudiced against illustrated fiction except for children" (letter of April 27, 1907). It is a surprising statement, given her success with *The Land of Little Rain* and the fact that she had considered illustrations to be so important a part of *The Flock,* published only a year before this letter, that she made provisional drawings herself. Perhaps her momentary virulence against pictures sprang from her previous experience with publishing a book of fiction. The illustrations of *Isidro,* done by an artist named Eric Pape, had none of the distinctiveness of E. Boyd Smith's work for the two books of sketches. They consisted of four conventionally romanticized, heavily shaded pictures, two emphasizing the love story and two the adventure story aspects of the book. The energetic heroine, Jacinta (sometimes, when in disguise, referred to as El Zarzo, The Thorn), who draws "deep breaths of freedom and relief" when she goes out alone on horseback in boy's clothing (*Isidro* 353), is shown languishing on the arm of her man. It is easy to understand that Austin would not want illustrations if she thought they would again misrepresent her work.

Contrary to her stated wishes, however, *Lost Borders* was indeed published with illustrations. Curiously, the name of the artist does not appear on the title page, but it is discernible on the plates themselves: Denman Fink (1880–1956). Fink's seven drawings, all in halftone reproduction with full modeling (shading for an appearance of roundness), are a striking contrast to Smith's open line drawings in *Land of Little Rain.* Nor for the most part do they convey a strong sense of place, the quality Smith's drawings most emphasized. The two most notable exceptions, in that they *do* give a compelling sense of place, are the drawing of a man and woman riding across grassy plains in "The Woman at the Eighteen-Mile" (figure 3.01) and the one of Catameneda, a Paiute woman, assisting an Anglo man through a storm in "Agua Dulce" (figure 3.02).

Primarily through Catameneda's protective and determined posture, the picture in figure 3.02 achieves a truly remarkable sense of character without even showing the faces of the two figures. Likewise, it gives a sense of place without showing place at all, merely by indicating the swirling of the fierce wind while the wider scene remains blank. White space is used here to expressive advantage. If Fink's illustrations for *Lost Borders* generally fall short of conveying the strong sense of place that we might expect, given Austin's title, they succeed admirably in focusing on relationships between male and female—which are finally, after all, the main thematic emphasis of the volume in all its stories. Human figures are shown in arrangements conveying strong emotional interactions.

Austin uses the West, in *Lost Borders,* as a setting in which the injustices of male–female relations become starkly evident. Although Cynthia Taylor errs in calling it Austin's second book (it was her fifth), she is correct in stating that both *The Land of Little Rain* and *Lost Borders* are "in some ways about the possibility for responsible civilized life in the West and the role that women and native peoples must play in that life" (120). Again and again the female characters are treated unfairly and are not accorded equality. That is particularly true for Native American women subjected to such shameful practices as "mahala chasing" or having their children dismissed as "a handful of little half-breeds" (*LB* 30). Having demonstrated in *Little Rain* her respect for Native spirituality and ways of living in harmony with the environment, Austin becomes in *Lost Borders* explicitly and incisively resistant to Anglo prejudice toward Native Americans, as well as conventional denials of equality between the sexes. Margaret Jacobs seems to me to misread when she finds Austin's point about sexual relations to be that "'lost borders' could make a woman both emancipated and vulnerable" (80). Rather, I believe her point was that even here, where one might suppose oneself to be free of the corruptions of eastern white society, exploitation of women by men not only continued but was exacerbated by racial inequality.[4]

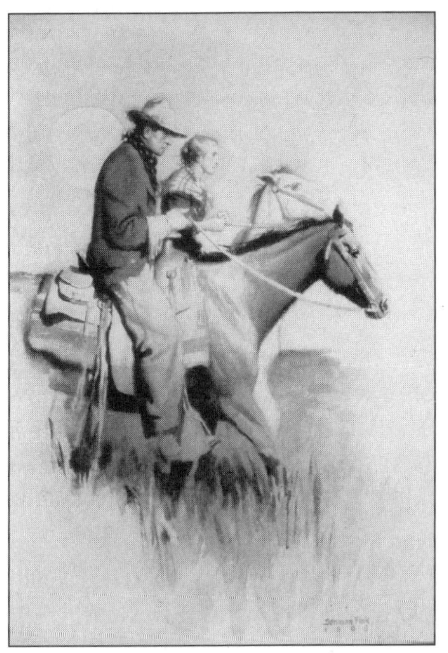

3.01 Denman Fink, illustration for "The Woman at the Eighteen-Mile," captioned "The moon was half high when the sun went down," from Mary Austin, *Lost Borders* (facing page 104)

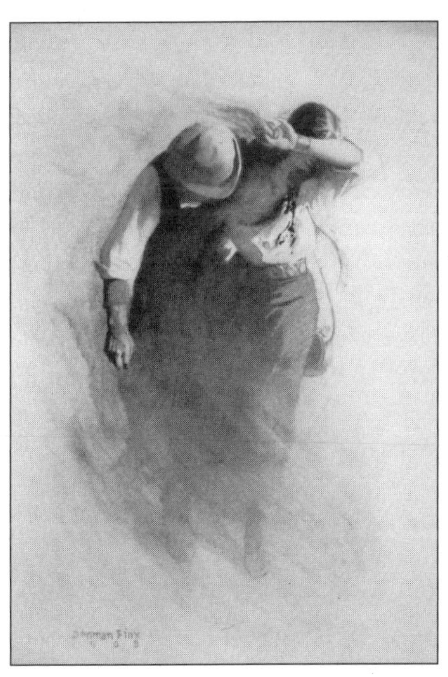

3.02 Denman Fink, illustration for "Agua Dulce," captioned "Catameneda laughed as she braced him with her firm young body," from Mary Austin, *Lost Borders* (facing page 90)

Austin's protests against a racialized exploitation of women in the California setting echoed, in some ways, those of Helen Hunt Jackson, whose wildly popular *Ramona,* some twenty years before, featured a mixed-race (Scottish and Native) heroine of elite Spanish upbringing who falls tragically in love with an Indian. The murder of Ramona's Indian husband by a white settler, who thereby "destroys the interracial relationship," was a fictionalization of an actual event (Padget, *Indian Country* 94–95). Austin's dismissal of *Ramona,* in her autobiography, as "a second-rate romance" (*EH* 186) may have been prompted not so much by the book itself as by the use to which it was put by promoters intent on attracting tourists to California and its missions. More directly, her judgment would have been impelled by Jackson's "idyllic" account of the lives of "elite Californios" before the U.S.–Mexican War (Padget 79–80). Jackson had in fact quite knowingly cast a "romantic aura" over her tale as a "sugar pill" to induce readers to swallow her message of justice for Native Americans (May 109). Austin, intent on writing in a more plainspoken way about societal shortcomings as well as the harsh natural environment in the area, recoiled against such romanticizing. (We may well think she perpetuated it in her own novel of pre-1848 Spanish and Native culture, *Isidro.*) In *Lost Borders,* however, she both criticized abuses that had preoccupied Jackson and featured assorted versions of the female healer and source of wisdom, a character type represented in *Ramona* by Aunt Ri and already well developed by Austin herself in Seyavi, the basket maker.

In the opening sketch of *Lost Borders,* "The Land," Austin states flatly that women (clearly, she means white women) find it difficult to "cast off old usages" and surrender to a love for the desert. Women dragged west as pioneers, she says, into arid regions where the skeletons of dead cattle are "almost invariably" found with their heads "turned toward the places where water-holes should be," hate equally the land and the life they are forced to lead there. Yet she immediately defines herself as an exception by insisting, in the same sentence, that the land they hate is strangely beautiful, "stretching interminably whity-brown, dim and shadowy blue hills that hem in, glimmering pale waters of mirage that creep and crawl about its edges" (*LB* 9–10). Austin's description, with its subdued colors, its spaciousness, and at the same time its harshness, epitomizes her at once enamored and unvarnished view of the West.

After this opening, the genre of the *Lost Borders* pieces becomes more story-like—although, to be sure, a significant aspect of Austin's achievement was her evasion of generic borders as well as geographic ones. Story after story presses on Austin's readers an awareness of how different the relations between the sexes ought to be. "Out there where the borders of conscience break down, where there is no convention," she begins "The Land" (*LB* 3). But as she goes on to show, the same things happen "out there," as regularly as if there were conventions but without their measure of protection in the absence of conscience. She establishes at once, in this first piece in the volume, her insistence that natural beauty and natural harshness are equally real. "Pure desertness clings along the pits of the long valleys and the formless beds of vanished lakes. Every hill that lifts as high as the cloud-line has some trees upon it, and deer and bighorn to feed on the tall, tufted, bunch grass between the boulders" (*LB* 9). But the masculine mind, she believes, rejects the coexistence of opposites; it assumes that one or the other must be false—"there is something incomprehensible to the man-mind in the concurrence of death and beauty" (*LB* 9–10). A woman of the desert, though, is not only "tawny" like it, but possessed of a corresponding "largeness to her mind" that accommodates contradictions. Apparently such women need to do so, having experienced both the beauty and the harshness. This is especially true of Native women, since the "convention" of racial prejudice survives in the desert along with conventions of sexual inequality.

Turwhasé, the Shoshone woman of "A Case of Conscience," is a good example. She delights in the attentions of a white man, a "lunger" who needs her nursing as long as he is sick. But as he gets well he determines to go back to white society and decides she is "hopeless," meaning socially unpresentable (*LB* 32). They have had a baby, which he has treated as a "plaything of which he was very fond." Now he demands possession of the baby girl, thinking to take her away and educate her as a white child. Soon discovering that the care of a baby is not so easy as he supposed, and realizing that whites notice her mixed race, he decides she is "a nuisance" and it might be "the best thing" if she died (*LB* 36). But Turwhasé has followed him. Appearing outside his hotel door, she takes the baby back, insisting "Mine! Mine, not yours!" Spurning his money, she returns to the desert and a life that will be more difficult than any he has ever imagined. Except for its setting and the woman's assertiveness in claiming her own, it is an old, tired story. And that is Austin's point.

"The Ploughed Lands," immediately following, tells a similar story of a Shoshone woman, Tiawa, who nurses a white man back to health after he nearly died of thirst because he failed to carry enough water in the spring when the earth looked beautiful and flowery. Curly Gavin's carelessness came, as Austin has already insisted, from the male inability to entertain what seem to be contradictions. She makes the point again: "It is as easy, I say, to believe that such a land could neglect men to their death, as for men to believe that a lovely woman can be unkind" (*LB* 43). Tiawa herself was as "young and comely" as the spring (42) and fulfilled his expectations of pretty things by being "kind," but he did not fulfill her expectations of fair dealing. As she says later, she "did not know then that a white man could take service from such as we and not requite it" (*LB* 46). She helps him as far as the plowed lands—the borders of white society—and there he makes it clear that he has no further use for her. Clearly, these white men's expectations that pretty women also be kind are not expectations they apply equally to themselves, and if they think mildness necessarily goes along with beauty in the natural world they are fools.

Men's tendency to associate beauty with love is especially galling to Austin, who did not possess physical beauty. She seems to have believed that it was her appearance that deprived her of the satisfactions of a loving relationship. *Lost Borders* was at least in part an effort to work out this personal problem. In *Outland* as well she seems to have been writing through the pain of her own awareness of a lack of physical attractiveness, using setting and the fantasy of a more natural society as ways to imagine erotic satisfaction. The narrator of *Outland,* Mona, has wanted her emotionally stilted suitor, Herman, to wake up to love, but instead sees him becoming infatuated with a young girl among the Outliers who is strikingly beautiful. "To see him excusing treachery for the sake of a tinted cheek or the way a wrist was turned, set me white hot and throbbing," she says (*Outland* 230).

Perhaps the worst of the swaggering males in *Lost Borders* who value women for only the shallowest of reasons is the flirtatious shepherd Louis Chabot, in "A Bitterness of Women." Chabot is a great success among young and pretty girls until he is mauled by a bear and left hideously disfigured. Then the only woman who still cares for him is Marguerita, the half-French, half-Mexican woman he had earlier toyed with and jilted because, as he bluntly told her, she wasn't pretty enough. "Swarthy and heavy of face," with thick ankles and a hint of a mustache on her upper lip, Marguerita "had no figure, which means she had a great deal too much of it" (*LB* 170).[5] Despite having been rejected by the proudly French Chabot when he was good-looking, she takes him back in his disfigured state and proves utterly faithful and loving. On his part, however, he still sometimes shows dissatisfaction at her not having "grow[n] any prettier after she was married" (*LB* 178). The hint of unironized racial antipathy in Austin's accounting for Chabot's failure of affection (clearly, Marguerita's objectionable appearance is attributed to her Mexican blood, even if his inability to see beyond it is condemned) is an unfortunate demonstration that even a woman writer who resisted stereotypes of gender might participate in Anglo racism—and this despite the fact that she often sharpened the point of her criticism of men's behavior toward women by linking it to racism when Native Americans were involved.

Austin makes it clear that gender inequality is equally venomous when race is not at issue. The wife deserted after seventeen miserable years in "The Return of Mr. Wills" finds that she can struggle along better without her husband than with him. When he comes back and "settle[s] on his family like a blight" (*LB* 62), she can only hope that the "insatiable spirit" of the desert will "reach out and take Mr. Wills again" and this time he won't come back (*LB* 64). The stories in *Lost Borders* are all stories of "betrayed and deprived women" (Pryse xxix), and all make essentially the same point, that men expect to receive loving care from women while exploiting them in return. Men's failure to perceive the moral obligation that goes with their toying with women is the equivalent of going west and doing nothing better with the experience than tell "mostly untrue" stories, the kind that regularly involve adventures and beautiful maidens (*LB* 79). In a pointed coda to "The Last Antelope," Austin poses a parallel between foolish males who are unable to appreciate women's qualities if they aren't beautiful and foolish newcomers to the West who tell tall tales (or perhaps write Westerns?) and don't respect the land.

One wonders if Austin had Owen Wister in mind in her reference to "mostly untrue" stories. *The Virginian* was published only a year before *The Land of Little Rain* and seven years before *Lost Borders*. My conjecture that this reference and indeed Austin's western writings in general were to some extent reactions against Wister's phenomenally popular and trend-setting novel has been stimulated in part by Susan Rosowski's similar conjecture relating to Willa Cather. Unfortunately, Rosowski was a decade off in identifying 1902 as the year of not one but two publishing events that "signaled the twentieth-century's gendered responses" to the West—*The Virginian* and Cather's first story, "Peter" (*Birthing* 11). "Peter," in which (as Rosowski continues) Cather "announced her commitment to freeing women from the alterity of the Western's script," was published in 1892, not 1902. Even so, her point is well taken. Cather's as well as Austin's project was a reaction against established conventions. Although Wister produced *The Virginian* slightly after, not before, both of them began to write, the "script" had been established in dime novels,[6] romantic histories, the political discourse of Manifest Destiny, and, as we have seen, the visual art of the West.

Lost Borders culminates with "The Walking Woman," the memorable story of an almost mythical but very real woman who freely "came and went about our western world on no discoverable errand," often in a "kind of muse of travel" (*LB* 196). An errand is a task imposed by others. Instead, she goes where she chooses. Fearlessly frequenting the haunts of rough men living without women, she is adequate to whatever demands her environment places on her, such as a sandstorm that threatens to scatter the flock of a shepherd named Filon Geraud she meets and falls in with. Spontaneously dropping into the role of partner, she helps Filon keep his flock together, takes satisfaction in her good work (as Austin says, in doing rather than "seeming"), and stays with him for the rest of the season, becoming his woman as well as his partner in work. When advancing pregnancy makes her unable to keep up on the trail, he has to go on without her, continuing the annual migration with the sheep that are his life. The baby dies, and the Walking Woman resumes her solitary rambling. "She was the Walking Woman. That was it. She had walked off all sense of society-made values, and, knowing the best when the best came to her, was able to take it" (*LB* 208). The best, according to Austin, or the narrator, includes having a child. The narrator's "the mouth at the breast," and Walking Woman's brief reply of "the lips and the hands . . . the little pushing hands and the small cry," make it clear that she subscribes to that belief, but without giving up her independence. Through her combination of freedom, competent work, and motherhood, she demonstrates the escape from limitation by conventional gender roles that Austin envisions and seeks to promote for other women. Like Seyavi, the Paiute basket maker who appears in both *The Land of Little Rain* and *Lost Borders,* who successfully "set her wit to fend for herself and

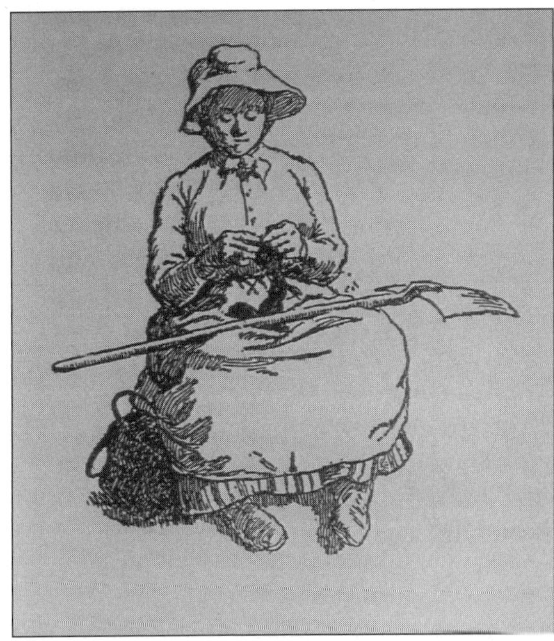

3.03 E. Boyd Smith, drawing of woman defending family water rights, from Mary Austin, *The Land of Little Rain* (p. 141)

her young son" alone (*LLR* 103), she embodies qualities of independence and adequacy in what would seem to be an impossibly adverse environment.

For Austin, both the rigors and the satisfactions of life in the spacious, harsh, and beautiful West are personified in these two strong women, one Anglo and one Native. We could add to the list the woman in "Other Water Borders," in *The Land of Little Rain,* who knits and watches her children while guarding with a long-handled shovel her family's rights to an equal share in the irrigation ditch. Smith's drawing of this woman (figure 3.03) has a humorous tinge, but she is to be taken seriously. Such women are examples of a new female freedom and a new quality of female strength, but at the same time examples of persistent nurturance, making the West and the Southwest a place for living as well as for adventure.

Both Austin's emphasis on the ways in which geography shapes human life and her insistence that assumptions about gender be revised are brought to fulfillment in *Starry Adventure.*[7] This final novel, with its abundant word-pictures (published without illustrations, as almost all novels were by the

1930s), and the belatedly published *Cactus Thorn* are the culminating works in Austin's sequence of feminist stories and novels set in the West.

To the Sitwell children, Gard and Laura, who are the main characters in the opening chapters of *Starry Adventure,* the land is "held down . . . named and identified through the people who lived there and the things that had happened" (*SA* 51). By establishing this "continuity of lived experience in a particular place," Austin constructs what Mark Schlenz calls "an inhabitory ethic" (76), showing that region and those who inhabit it form a single whole. The centrality of home and domestic life in such an ethic is evident throughout, but most notably in the culminating scene when Gard makes a circuit of his and Jane's house preparatory to going to bed, the night preceding their departure on a trip around the state to gather material for a book about—suitably enough—domestic architecture. Homes within homes, circles within circles. It is this central idea of the West as a place for living that makes so thematically appropriate Gard's occupation as builder specializing in the restoration of Spanish Colonial houses, in partnership with an architect who encourages him to develop his historical knowledge of regional housing. The same central idea also serves Austin's construction of a new gendering of domestic and social relations and ultimately a new gendering of region. Her aims in her only novel set in New Mexico are high indeed.

Starry Adventure is a case study in how place can be virtually "another character" in the story, as Austin argued in "Regionalism in American Literature." We have seen its function as "instigator of plot" in Gard and Jane's conversation about women's new roles, but the New Mexico landscape instigates plot even at the very outset of the novel. A five-year-old Gard (clearly a male stand-in for Austin herself, as Jim Burden is for Cather in *My Ántonia*) lingers outside his home on the family ranch, watching the sunset over the mountains. "Suddenly," as he watches the banks of "sunlit and towering" thunder clouds, the "wonder was all about him. The edges of the banked clouds were brightly gilt, the torn films flushed crimson, the gleaming cumuli behind them came hurrying; heaping and wheeling. Great sword-like beams of light slashed between them . . . the sword of the Lord" (*SA* 1, 4). Gard is convinced he has seen God in nature, or as he later thinks, the God of New Mexico. From this point on until the novel leaves him as an adult and a prospective father, he feels destined to a grand and sacred mission, his "starry adventure."

Like so much of Austin's writing, the language of this novel is highly visual. Even Gard's feelings toward others tend to be defined visually. He thinks of Eudora Ballintin, with whom he has an affair, as a "flaming blondness" or as a "goldfish . . . gold in a cool green pool . . . pure gold" (*SA* 263, 298).[8] Equally lush, richly colored landscape descriptions pervading the text might seem overwritten if they were not so intrinsically enmeshed with both plot and theme—and if, moreover, they did not gain acceptance by being located in the point of view of a child. In this, Austin makes a distinctive adaptation of the long-established and at times (in other hands) unthinking practice of writing about the Southwest from the perspective of the Anglo newcomer from the East. In *Starry Adventure,* the newcomer is the child Gard Sitwell, whose family has come to New Mexico because his father is a "lunger," the common New Mexico expression for a sufferer from tuberculosis. Both unfamiliarity and the naiveté of his age qualify Gard to see things freshly. By adopting his naive perspective, Austin is able to impart a special quality of wonder to her descriptions of landscape, making his perceptions of the stunning scale and beauty of his surroundings available to the reader's sympathy. Gard's world is one in which mountains unaccountably loom up over him, almost like live beings, evoking both the wonder and the fear that comprise awe in the aesthetic of the sublime. Feeling very small in this looming, majestic landscape, and lacking the hardened sophistication of an adult, he is fully open to intense experiences of color and wonder.

The association of majestic landscape with spiritual exaltation established in the opening scene when he watches the sunset continues throughout the novel. Austin's descriptions, florid as they may sometimes seem, reflect knowledge of the area. Place names are a combination of the fictitious with the actual. "From here you could see all across the valley toward the Rio Grande south and west to the blue keep of Jémez and the square-topped tail of Pedernál. North on a clear day, two or three white domes of the Rockies swam into view beyond the Colorado line, suspended in opalescent air" (*SA* 67). All these are real places. Spirituality seems to spring directly out of the earth itself; it is not an abstraction imposed on it. The ineffable is a "strange, surging warmth which came out of stars and trees and mountains and made itself felt inside you." When this "Something" comes on a particularly beautiful day, it is "in" Gard and "in" the "faintly lilac-blue" broken glass and the blue pentstemon flower he has been looking at. "It was in the bee that bent the blue-and-lilac cup; it was the bee and it was Gard; and it was the young piñon. It had speech with him. The boy looked up and noted how the ember red of the mountain warmed toward him friendlily" (*SA* 70).

The New Mexico of *Starry Adventure* is not only a landscape of glamour, then, but of meaning. The clear air affords clarity of both physical vision and spiritual vision. At times when the adult Gard is troubled and distracted by his affair with Eudora, he neither sees what is around him nor feels its spirituality, but when he begins to come out from the cloud of that distraction he again notices things. A "clear and high-keyed" morning is "one of those mornings of New Mexico that more than any other give the sense of altitude, the earth rolling eastward, the mountains rearing purposively," while the very weeds take on a kind of splendor, with "hints and glints of gold as though what had left the air so thin and fluent was the drawing down of the gold, crisp, delicate curds of gold, thickening to a crust" (*SA* 357). Vastness of landscape affords vastness of aspiration and moral purpose. As Gard thinks to himself, simply, "There was room" (390). Returning to himself after a period of distraction and moral confusion, he literally returns to his own place. He drives to the family ranch, "the Land" that "never betrayed you," turns off the motor of his car, and sits behind the wheel to watch the sunrise. Doing so, he experiences a return of the glory that has spoken to him out of the landscape since early childhood:

> [L]ong blades of light began to slash the shadows of the mountains, gilt on the green of the Prado. The adobe walls of the houses brightened answeringly. The tall potreros remembered the fires from which they came. Splendor of the morning! Gard rested, leaning on the steering wheel. It was good to be able to feel again the roll of the earth eastward. (*SA* 393)

In writing *Starry Adventure*, Austin was purposely responding to Cather's *Death Comes for the Archbishop*, published four years earlier. Both phrasing and punctuation in this passage about Gard's return to himself echo, in the parallel phrase "Splendor of the morning!," the archbishop's spiritually elated and perhaps somewhat overwritten "Into the morning! into the morning!" Unlike Cather's archbishop, though, the central consciousness here is not yet afflicted with imperial nostalgia. Were it not for the merest glimpses of white guilt (in one corner of his mind he ponders selling off the old pastures for a housing development), we might believe Gard's awareness of the southwestern landscape to be entirely innocent.

Even as Austin's use of Gard's childhood perspective in the early chapters of the novel allows us to accept his perceptions of landscape at face value, it also facilitates her social criticism. As a child witness, his impressions of human society are rooted in a naiveté much like Huckleberry Finn's in Mark Twain's classic tour de force of narrative point of view. Largely, it is distinctions of religious labeling that cause Gard puzzlement—Presbyterian? Methodist? Cath'lic? Christian? Heathen? Natheist? (His friend David's father is "a Natheist.") His own ambition to be a Heathen when he grows up is at once amusing (his sister tells him he won't be allowed to be one) and an expression of a religious dimension to the mental freedom Austin associates with the Southwest's spaciousness. But Gard's naive point of view is also useful for observing the prejudices that New Mexico's Anglo newcomers bring with them. When he goes to a mission school, he observes that the children the Anglo teachers call "inmates" are the same ones also commonly called "natives," a term he understands to mean that they "spoke Spanish among themselves and looked like Pablo and Aloysia Liberadita," employees on the family ranch whom he regards with respect (*SA* 52). He notices, too, that the American ranchers who attend Bible study "behaved exactly as if the inmates were invisible" (*SA* 53). The reader, possessing a frame of reference that Gard does not yet have, is able to label the system he is witnessing by its accurate name: racial prejudice.

The racial attitudes of the novel as a whole are not, however, so simple and clear-cut as those implied by Gard's childhood perceptions. We know that one reason Austin herself regarded the Southwest through a shimmer of idealism was its long-established multiethnicity. She can only have seen attitudes such as those of the Anglo teachers and missionaries as a blight on what she wanted to maintain was "the seat of the world's next great culture" precisely because it was a long-established multiethnic society (Wynn 252). Even so, we wait in vain for authorial correctives as racial prejudice slips into Gard's mind as well. At various points his thoughts incorporate phrases like "dirty Native" and "uncontaminated Spanish blood," and when he sees his flirtatious step-grandmother "talk[ing] to Alfredo as if he were a white man," he feels a need to explain to her how one was supposed to speak to natives (*SA* 61, 99–100, 153). "Native" is obviously an appropriate term when used in reference to the various peoples more commonly called Indians; it recognizes their primacy in place. But in *Starry Adventure* Austin uses the word to refer, with only rare distinctions, to Hispanics and Native Americans alike. Was she, perhaps, merely indicating the longer claim of Hispanics (or to use the more precise regional term for families whose New Mexico roots go back to Spanish Colonial times, Hispanos) as compared to Anglo latecomers? That does not seem to be the case. She seems to use "native" in a labeling or othering way referring to such characters' darker skins and Spanish language. Indeed, it seems to refer to these qualities as if they were stigmas.

In short, Austin falls into all-too-common patterns of Anglo perception even while showing, in the interactions of the novel, that she values New Mexico's multiethnicity. She never sufficiently distances her attitudes from those of a prejudicial color consciousness on the part of various characters or from those (common in the Southwest) that accord higher status to Hispanos than to the typically darker-skinned families of mixed ancestry who came to the area from Mexico during the major flow of immigration resulting from political upheavals in the late nineteenth and early twentieth centuries. Gard's erring step-grandmother's lover, with whom she runs away to Mexico, is referred to disparagingly, with no authorial demurral whatever, as a "Mex." The condescending tone attached to the word "native" is most blatant at a moment late in the novel when Gard, now as enlightened as he is ever going to be, comes in his car to rescue Jane, who has gone out on horseback and been caught in a hail storm. When he finds her, he "*whistled* up a *native* boy who had come out of a house to see what the extraordinary Americanos were about this time, and *told* him to ride the horse back to Rancho Antígua" (*SA* 411, emphases mine). It is a disappointing turn in a novel that in so many ways is admirably open-minded and illuminating.

With respect to gender, *Starry Adventure* works hard to show that freer lives for women mean freer lives for men as well and to associate the female with landscape in elevating, not demeaning, ways. Both Laura, Gard's sister, and Jane, the childhood friend he eventually marries, are afforded opportunities for meaningful work in the world (although Laura recognizes that even with suffrage and the right to pursue careers, women are still treated in second-class ways). Both are able to dress sensibly and engage in vigorous activities such as riding and climbing that seem suited to life in the West but were thought, not so very long before Austin wrote, to be appropriate only to men (or lower-class women). For all its narrative disapproval of Eudora Ballintin, the novel never implies that she should not have an active and eager sex life, only that if she expects to assume the role of *patrona* she can't brandish her sexual freedom before the eyes of a traditional rural society with impunity. Gard himself, as he gains confidence, maturity, and sexual presence, pursues interests and roles conventionally associated with women rather than men. The final definition of his vaguely conceived and long-awaited "starry adventure" comes from Jane by way of an analogy with pregnancy. Male questing, in this novel, is an inner state akin to the gestation of a baby.

The spirituality associated with landscape is also associated with the female. Gard's and Laura's mother's voice, when she reads to them when they are children, goes on and on in their sleepy awareness "like the gurgle of the acéquia when the creek is full from rains on the mountains" (*SA* 87), and his sense of the "surging warmth" of the divine, the God of New Mexico, is "most like what you felt for your mother" (*SA* 70). The pretentious Eudora may describe the New Mexico landscape as "phallic"—a term that plausibly recalls the jutting ruggedness of such views of the West as Bierstadt's and Russell's—but to the still groping but nevertheless intellectually honest Gard it has "the noble curves, the brooding quiet of maternity" (*SA* 277).

I have referred to *Starry Adventure*'s having been in part a response to *Death Comes for the Archbishop.* Both in her autobiography and in her article on regionalism in literature, Austin castigated Cather for having used the New Mexico setting only as a background and for having betrayed a lack of concern for the local culture. Certainly *Starry Adventure* seems designed to counteract such a misuse. It is surprising, then, to learn that Austin had written at least part of it as early as mid-1916, eight years before she moved to New Mexico; that she was far enough along to expect it to go to press by mid-1917; and that its setting was to have been Los Angeles (Austin to Ferris Greenslet, Houghton Mifflin, June 8, 1916, and July 12, 1916). Yet the novel as finally published in 1931 is so firmly and convincingly rooted in the soil of New Mexico that one can scarcely imagine its having been begun in any other way. How Austin managed to reconceive and rewrite it so drastically, with a southwestern setting so intrinsic to the book as a whole, is a mystery. Perhaps she only reused the title of a discarded work.

* * *

The short novel *Cactus Thorn,* written between *Land of Journeys' Ending* and *Starry Adventure,* returns to the desert country of California. Geographically, its affinities are more with Austin's earlier works, especially *Lost Borders,* than with the others she produced during her years in New Mexico. It emphasizes desertness more than her writings about New Mexico do.[9] Even so, it shows strong continuities with *Starry Adventure.*

As we have seen, Austin's view of the landscapes of New Mexico and Arizona was characterized by grandeur and majesty. Only the "Papagueria" chapter of *The Land of Journeys' Ending* explores a territory as harsh, arid, and, for large expanses, as flat as that of *Cactus Thorn:* the dry, sandy country south of Tucson, where the mission of San Xavier del Bac still attracts tourists as well as the devout. Yet as *Journeys' Ending* well establishes, there is great geographic variety in this vast region. Despite its return to California, then, the setting of *Cactus Thorn* bears commonalities with the books about mountainous New Mexico. Primarily these are commonalities of palette, with shades of orchid, rose, and gold predominating, along with clarity of air and light.[10] The result is that in brief passages of description Austin's desert in *Cactus Thorn* has a gorgeousness comparable to that of the mountain scenes in *Starry Adventure* and *The Land of Journeys' Ending.* Here is an example:

> It was very still where they stood on the very crest of the range; even the wind had ceased to stir. Sweetwater lay hidden under a lilac haze, and over the vast assemblage of ranges rose far to the west a single snowy crest that seemed to float on opalescent air. (*CT* 48)

And yet another:

> It was well on into the long twilight when he caught sight of her, one of those hours that come only at the end of spring, when the sunlight, caught in an invisible web of atmosphere, makes itself molten, and spreads itself along the ground like gold. Overhead, the earth's penumbra was filled with pellucid dusk, shattered from point to point by the shrill cry of the nightjar. (*CT* 42)

Still, for the most part the visual natural world of *Cactus Thorn* is one of bare sand, cactus, and rattlesnakes—a bare world that serves its central character, Dulcie Adelaid, as a bedrock of truth. Accordingly, in speech and in appearance, she herself is simply what she seems; she wears no decorative foliage of disguise. And reflecting her clear-eyed knowledge of her surroundings, the book does not mitigate the desert's harshness. Especially when Dulcie Adelaid's estranged husband wanders drunkenly off into spring-less country as a sandstorm is gathering, we are reminded of Austin's plainspoken line in *The Land of Little Rain,* "To underestimate one's thirst, to pass a given landmark to the right or left, to find a dry spring where one looked for running water—there is no help for any of these things" (*LLR* 6).

Why does she write passages of such decorative lushness in a work of such thematically significant bareness? Aside from its inherent delight (if one has a taste for such picture-prose), the language of splendor seems as emblematically important to her here as the language of harshness. Indeed, the word "setting" is scarcely adequate for how place functions in *Cactus Thorn.* As Austin demanded of a true regional literature, place becomes an actor in the story as well as an emblem of a quality of life that the novella is designed to espouse. Less specific as to location than she is in *The Land of Little Rain,* Austin is also less occupied with observation of details. Instead, she is concerned to show how the occasional visual splendor of the desert setting lifts the aspirations of her characters—especially the high-aspiring politician Grant Arliss, modeled on journalist Lincoln Steffens—and how its harshness anneals their strength, especially that of the unwavering Dulcie Adelaid. Place shapes character.

We see this especially in Dulcie Adelaid. Unlike Grant Arliss, whom she meets at a desert train station and who then becomes her lover, she is adequate to the rigors of the desert, even to the point of merciless use of her "thorn," that is, her dagger; and she, unlike her drunken estranged husband, can stay on the trail. Literally, she knows essential trails well enough to see them in her mind even when blowing dust obscures them. Figuratively, she stays on the trail by persisting in her determined course, even to the point of wielding her dagger, with lethal results, when Grant does not prove equally honest. The fact that *Cactus Thorn* lay unpublished until many years after Austin's death may relate to the starkness of Dulcie Adelaid's murder of Arliss and more generally to the assertiveness with which it links the southwestern landscape to a feminist vision. Melody Graulich writes that it was "apparently . . . rejected by Houghton Mifflin" (Foreword viii). We can conjecture that the publisher considered its starkness of vision a commercial impediment.

We have seen that in *Starry Adventure* gender roles are not assigned by rigid convention. Women are free to take jobs and to engage in vigorous outdoor exercise, and men are free to find fulfillment in domestic architecture and household routine. Both male and female are free to pursue sexual fulfillment, and both are equally responsible for dealing honestly with their sexual partners by regarding the sexual bond as a mutual commitment that cannot be broken by either without the consent of the other. And it is the woman, Jane, who leads her bewildered lover to something approaching clearness of vision in thinking about his life's goals. All of these motifs—the equality of male and female, the seriousness of the sexual bond, and the role of a woman as guide to understanding—were developed in *Cactus Thorn* before their extension in the longer work, where similar ideas were shaped toward a happy ending of equality between a strong woman and a feminized man.

Pat Mora writes in her poem "Unrefined," "The desert is no lady."[11] Austin would seem to agree. In Dulcie Adelaid she creates a woman who is all natural grace and strength, with no ladylike posturing or coyness. Nor did Austin regard herself as a lady, with all the baggage of social convention that term evokes, but rather as a woman—a wayfaring, freethinking woman who came to the awakening that allowed her to see her trail in life when she went into the desert on her own and found wild grapes that alleviated her malnutrition. What she learned from that experience was "revolutionary," given the gender constraints of the 1880s: that women, as fully as men, have to make their own way in life. Or as she puts it in *Earth Horizon,* she learned that "there was something you could do about unsatisfactory conditions besides being heroic or a martyr to them, something more satisfactory than enduring or complaining, and that was getting out to hunt for the remedy" (*EH* 195). Such an approach was decidedly unladylike, but never unwomanly. And Austin defined the desert itself in much the same way:

> If the desert were a woman, I know well what like she would be: deep-breasted, broad in the hips, tawny, with tawny hair, great masses of it

> lying smooth along her perfect curves, full lipped like a sphinx, but not heavy-lidded like one, eyes sane and steady as the polished jewel of her skies, such a countenance as should make men serve without desiring her, such a largeness to her mind as should make their sins of no account, passionate, but not necessitous, patient—and you could not move her, no, not if you had all the earth to give, so much as one tawny hair's-breadth beyond her own desires. If you cut very deeply into any soul that has the mark of the land upon it, you find such qualities as these. (LB 10–11)

The passage labels itself as being about the desert and also about those (implicitly female) persons who live in the desert in a sympathetic rather than resentful way. It serves equally well as Austin's statement of what the West is "like": like a woman, but a woman of a certain kind—strong, adequate, and free. The desert, or more expansively the West, is like the Walking Woman, the sturdy wayfarer who serves as a spirit of place, who has "walked off all sense of society-made values" (LB 208). Desert values must come from nature, from bare reality. The interpersonal values of honesty and fair treatment, then, which Austin endorses in her stories of the desert, are to be taken as absolutes of reality, not as mere social conventions.

"Tawny," the color-adjective that appears twice in the passage beginning "If the desert were like a woman . . . ," is one of Austin's favorites. It also turns up in *Earth Horizon, The Lands of the Sun,* and elsewhere. It is a word that evokes the sunlit bleached-brown of sand and, equally well, the pale yellowish-brown coat of a puma, which in "One Hundred Miles on Horseback" served as another key image for her discovery of both self and place when she was newly arrived in California. In *Earth Horizon,* "tawny" colors are associated with solitary encounters with reality. Austin recalls that her first sight of the Tejon when she rode in on a buckskin horse was of a place treeless and bare of grass but covered with "sparse knee-high sagebrush; all tawny pale with summer heat" (*EH* 190). Her mother and brothers, who made that entry with her, seem to have been erased from this passage; it is as if she alone confronted that "tawny pale" expanse. And just as she found solitary walking to be the cure for a "torpor" induced by malnourishment and a deep sense of lostness, so, she recalls, she found a spiritual cure in the same way. In the spring of her first full year in California she was "walking" alone when she spied "poppies coming up singly through the *tawny,* crystal-sanded soil" (*EH* 198, emphasis mine). The passage demonstrates once again the visual nature of Austin's meaning-making, but its significance goes further. The unexpected sighting of the poppies, an emblem of the beatitude of returning life and beauty even in a seemingly hostile environment, restores her to her sense of essential self, the "I-Mary" she had realized in early childhood when, outdoors and alone, she met God. Her sense of the "sweetness of ultimate reality" would thereafter "never . . . go away again; never . . . be completely out of call" (*EH* 198). The word "tawny" carries us from earth to metaphoric woman to sense of place to spiritual authenticity, all linked through images of trails and free walking (Graulich, Afterword 376).

Austin's vision of the female presence in the arid West is by no means ungendered, but still it is one we must label androgynous, rather than feminine. Like the Walking Woman, it is a distinctively strong, sturdy, free-spirited presence. The West offers freedom from artificial conventions. Its spaciousness becomes a metaphor for open possibility. The nature of that space is not idyllic; Austin repeatedly shows us the harshness of a life lived there. But the facing of harsh conditions is part and parcel of the liberation she desires for herself and holds up as a model for others. Such qualities are embodied in Seyavi, the strong but at the same time maternal Native woman who appears in both *Little Rain* and *Lost Borders,* and in the Walking Woman—both strong women who embody the rigors and the satisfactions of life in the spacious, harsh, and beautiful West. Both are powerfully maternal figures.

In *The Lands of the Sun,* motherhood is ascribed to the very mountains themselves: "Looking up suddenly at the Mother Mountain [in the "Mother range," the Sierra Madre] brooding above the plain, it is easy to understand how the symbol of aloof but solicitous care came home to the primitive mind, always peculiarly open to suggestions of humanness in nature" (*Lands* 42). There Austin celebrates, primarily by simply naming them, the "mighty rivers" and the "lesser singing streams" that feed them: the Kern, the Kings, the Kaweah, the Tule, the Merced, the Tuolumne, the San Joaquin, and the Sacramento. She speaks of mountain streams in terms that elevate the land itself to heroic status, as opposed to constituting it as a setting for heroic deeds. The sight of these streams "is as beautiful and as terrifying as the sight of youth to timorous age. They go leaping with their shining shields and their shouting shakes the rocks" (*Lands* 209).

As we would expect of a devoted naturalist who admired John Muir (Goodman 108), Austin recognizes and deplores the pollution and trashing of the land and streams that come in the wake of Anglo settlements. She writes of the contrast between the "outraged loveliness of the coastal slopes" and the "evidences of planlessness, the unimaginative economic greed, the idiot excitation of mere bigness, the strange shapeless ugliness" brought by development (*EH* 186). Because of her family's impatience to reach their land in the San Joaquin Valley, she was prevented from "giving herself up wholly to the mystery of the arroyos" when she first arrived, and she was later unable to return and do so because "the place of the mystery was eaten up, it was made into building lots, cannery sites; it receded before the preëmptions of rock crushers and city dumps" (*EH* 187–88).

This sensitivity to the ruin of the natural environment creates a rhetorical problem, since Austin wants to foster an idealized southern California as a place for agrarian living while at the same time recognizing and valuing its inherent harshness. In Barney Nelson's words, she "questions and reinvisions the dichotomy between the wild and domestic"; she envisions the West as "a home, not a playground" (*Wild* 22, 136). A shifting and sometimes uneasy balance develops between criticizing the depredations of Anglos on the land and celebrating settlement and irrigation for agriculture. "Always," Austin recognizes, "there is a war on between horse and cattle men and the wolves" (*Lands* 181). That same war is waged by timber and mining interests: "The glutting of the lumber region [around Mendocino] has been accomplished as wastefully, as violently as the search for gold. All up the valley, tall prophets of the rain have been butchered to make a lumberman's fat purse" (*Lands* 163). It is waged, too, by the sheepherders Austin nevertheless admires and whose company she enjoys. Although Nelson argues convincingly that Austin's purpose in *The Flock* was to issue "a series of direct challenges to Muir's published denigration of sheep and sheepherders" and that Muir's *My First Summer in the Sierra* (1911) "may well have been written in reaction to *The Flock*" (*Wild* 75, 77), we also find praise of Muir in Austin's writing. It seems to me, finally, that Austin was considerably more conflicted in her thinking about the use of California's land and Muir's preservationism than Nelson allows.[12]

This tension between environmentalism and the promotion of land use for community-building and practical work is inherently tied in with Austin's insistence on a female and maternal presence in the West. We need to bear this connection in mind if we are to understand the place of *Cactus Thorn.* Any estimate of *Cactus Thorn* and how it gathers up and defines Austin's earlier works into a merger of place-writing and gender-writing must take into account the portrayal of Dulcie Adelaid in terms that are continuous with her desert home and the story's emphatic rejection of her exploitation by a representative of the eastern power structure. Austin's females were never sirens or satin dolls. If in *Starry Adventure* she insisted on a man's right to center his life on house and home, in *Cactus Thorn* she praised a woman's power to assert both her equality with the male and her adequacy to the stringencies of her environment. Constructing a desert aesthetic of both grandness and austerity, Austin saw the West as an emblem of honesty and discipline—a landscape lesson her female "Cactus Thorn" has imbibed all her life but which the self-indulgent male easterner, Grant Arliss, never learns.

4

WILLA CATHER: PICTURES AND WORD-PICTURES ON THE GREAT PLAINS

Every one knows how much more interesting is an illustrated book than one without pictures.

Willa Cather
"Editor's Talk," National Stockman and Farmer

Evening and the flat land,
Rich and somber and always silent;
The miles of fresh-plowed soil,
Heavy and black, full of strength and harshness;
The growing wheat, the growing weeds,
The toiling horses, the tired men;
The long, empty roads . . .

Willa Cather
"Prairie Spring"

Willa Cather's sense of the world was strongly visual. She was acutely observant of details as well as visual composition and scenic vistas. We know, too, from the marginal notations she made in the field guide to wildflowers that she carried for more than twenty years, F. Schuyler Mathews's *Field Book of American Wild Flowers* (1902), that she shared Mary Austin's capacity for botanical observation in particular.[1] The margins are heavily marked with checks or lines beside individual entries, indicating that she had identified some one hundred and fifty-six distinct varieties during her walks in Nebraska, at Jaffrey, New Hampshire (where she liked to go in the fall), on Grand Manan Island (where she and Edith Lewis had a summer home), and in one instance in Virginia, the state where she was born. Frequently she indicated the date on which she saw a particular plant as well as the place, and occasionally she even added details to Mathews's already detailed descriptions. Her notes of this kind are astonishingly precise. Into the description of the "small dense clusters" of flowers on the arrow-leaved tearthumb, for example (108), she inserted the observation that the clusters are club-shaped. When Mathews described the leaves of the white woodland aster as "smooth" (484), she corrected him by noting that on the underside they are bristly along the veins. We see in these annotations in Cather's cherished field guide an effort to observe the natural world as closely as possible and to describe it as minutely as possible, in the most accurate language she could muster.[2]

The practice of close observation that Cather brought to bear during her customary walks, hikes, and climbs translates itself, through the medium of her lucid prose, into precision of rendered details. Her descriptions evince a kind of eye–hand coordination—a linkage of visual keenness to writerly virtuosity. To note just three examples: from *My Ántonia,* the "tracings like ripple-marks" or "curly waves" at the edges of thin terraced snow (62); again from *Ántonia,* the "thread of green liquid" oozing from the "crushed head" of the rattlesnake Jim kills (45); and from *One of Ours,* the ring of "dark sediment" in the washbowl that greets the early-rising Claude (3). Her fiction is replete with such small visual details.

Cather does not so much amass details, however, as focus on specific details one at a time. It is largely this isolation of details against an uncluttered background—perhaps like the microscopic views she would have experienced as an aspiring scientist in her adolescent years—that accounts for the visual acuity of her writing. Like the line drawings she chose to illustrate *My Ántonia,* her details are characteristically surrounded by empty space. Throwing the bulk of the furniture out the window, as she proclaimed a desire to do in "The Novel Démeublé" (*On Writing* 42), she allows the reader's eye, along with her own, to focus on the selected pieces that are kept. In *My Ántonia,* out of what must have been a prairieful of grasshoppers, she chooses one and lets us view it up close as Ántonia cups it in her hand, and then slips it into her hair for safekeeping. We even hear its faint chirping. In *A Lost Lady,* she shows us the "pointed tip" of only the last in a row of poplars, with the "hollow, silver winter moon" above it (40). In *Lucy Gayheart,* the "point of silver light" of the evening's single first star, rather than a skyful (9). From being set alone against blankness, these isolated presences not only gain a luminous significance, as critics have often noted, but gain, as well, clarity of visual presence. Examples are scattered throughout her publications, both fiction and nonfiction, as well as her letters. When she insisted that Claude, the naive but affectionately regarded central character of *One of Ours,* "does not see pictures," she was explicitly distinguishing between his fictive view of the world and her own.[3] She herself did see pictures—visual compositions—as well as the details of those pictures.

It seems entirely in character, then, when we learn in a 1919 letter that her choice of a Christmas gift for an old friend was a print of Albrecht Dürer's familiar watercolor of a hare.[4] Showing a single animal on an empty white ground, the painting is rendered with such clarity that one can distinguish individual hairs in the fur. Cather's choice of this particular print was perfectly in keeping with her way of seeing the world, which was also her way of rendering the world in her fiction. Like the painting, her writing was focused, finely but selectively detailed, and freed of background clutter. As Eudora Welty once discerningly pointed out, her fiction tends to occupy either far panoramas or clear foregrounds, with vacancy in the middle distance. Her selected details are typically surrounded by a blankness of the unsaid or the disregarded, just as Dürer's hare is set against blankness. In a familiar passage in Elizabeth Shepley Sergeant's memoir, when Cather wished to convey the sense of her new heroine as she was beginning *My Ántonia,* she reached for a single glazed jar and placed it by itself on the clear space of Elsie's desk (149). The anecdote illustrates very well the visual nature of her thought processes. The concrete image of the jar, so vividly established in the reader's mind, becomes emblematic of the abstract idea of the heroine's centrality in the novel. It makes the idea real. (Even so, what Cather wrote to Sergeant about *O Pioneers!* is true of *Ántonia* as well: that the land itself is the center of the novel.[5])

Cather's letters make it clear that she was also keenly aware of the illustrations of her works and had strong feelings about them. She is known to have disliked the illustrations of her first novel, *Alexander's Bridge,* and of "Two Friends," published in July 1932 in *Woman's Home Companion.* The month that "Two Friends" appeared, she wrote to her friend Carrie Miner Sherwood, whose father was the prototype for one of the two main characters, to apologize, saying that the magazine had assigned the story to an artist who knew nothing about the West and thought everyone looked like a galoot.[6] I confess that the two figures as drawn by Walter Everett do not look like galoots to me. Perhaps she felt that Carrie would be offended by seeing the representation of her father portrayed without a suit jacket, in the full glory of his suspenders. For the W. T. Benda illustrations of *My Ántonia,* however, Cather was fully involved, and was so pleased with the results that in July 1918, near the end of a series of contentious letters she exchanged with Houghton Mifflin, she insisted to her editor, Ferris Greenslet, that the illustrations should be regarded as an integral part of the text (*Calendar* #424).[7]

Cather took an interest in every aspect of the physical appearance of her books, from paper and type font to the color of the binding and the design of the cover. It is scarcely surprising that her sense of craft should extend to such matters, since she had spent six years, from 1906 through 1911, as editor or managing editor of *McClure's Magazine,* one of the most successful and also one of the most lavishly illustrated magazines in the United States. Art and layout were never her primary responsibilities, but we know that she was at least somewhat involved in decisions about illustrators and illustrations, as well as the selection of articles and stories for publication. In November 1917, she told Greenslet that she had arranged for illustrations except during rare intervals when the magazine employed an art editor (*Calendar* #399). Her letters bear this out. She tells S. S. McClure that she is holding up the next issue because of needing illustrations for the first article (perhaps the first of her articles on Mary Baker Eddy); she offers a contributor a thousand dollars for three articles including illustrations and writes again to arrange a working session to plan them; she writes to an illustrator who was miffed with the magazine, to woo him back into the fold; she asks a contributor to collect photographs to illustrate his upcoming article; she tries to coax what she wants out of an artist whose first try did not please her; and in 1913, after leaving her full-time editorial role, she praises McClure on the illustrations of the "autobiography" she ghostwrote for him.[8] A sensitivity to illustrations and their stylistic compatibility with text is demonstrated by a letter to her sister in December 1908 saying that she is sending some children's books for Christmas presents. She goes on to comment on what she saw as the tiresomely splashy quality of children's book illustrations by Maxfield Parrish and Jessie Willcox Smith.[9]

The actual pictorial work published in *McClure's* during the years of

Cather's close involvement is equally important as a context for considering her preferences in illustration and the illustrations of her own western works. She left a teaching job at Allegheny High School in Pittsburgh in early June 1906 and was at work at *McClure's* before the end of the month (Bohlke 173; see *Calendar* #112 and #113). Beginning with the May issue, by which time she must have been reading it very closely (although indeed she was quite aware of S. S. McClure and his magazine well before then), and continuing through March 1912, when she left for Pittsburgh before going on to Arizona to visit her brother, I find some twenty-three stories and three poems that can readily be labeled Westerns. All of these except the poems (two by Charles Lummis, a prime member of the "quaint and picturesque school" of writing about the Southwest, and one, "Prairie Dawn," by Cather herself) are illustrated.[10]

The illustrations of western material published in *McClure's* during Cather's years included the work of some of the best-known illustrators of the time, some of them artists still celebrated, such as C. M. Russell, then at the height of his powers, and E. L. Blumenschein. N. C. Wyeth, only beginning his career, provided illustrations for western material in the May 1906, August 1906, and May 1908 issues. Wyeth had studied with master illustrator Howard Pyle and imbibed Pyle's colorful but realistic style. Indeed, most of the illustrations of western material in *McClure's* in those years were in a style of romantic realism. The years 1906 through 1908 represent a brief period in Wyeth's long career when his work reflected a trip west during which he traveled and worked in Colorado, Arizona, and New Mexico. His interest would soon shift. As we would expect, his work on western materials for *McClure's* was highly competent, but at the same time it was deeply conventional in its emphasis on masculinity and violent action. A picture for "Arizona Nights," published in May 1906 in halftone reproduction, showed a man holding a gun on some toughs at a bar. For the nonfiction "Story of Montana" in the August 1906 issue, his painting, reproduced in full color, was of a holdup.

Not surprisingly, since that is what readers would have expected, similar conventions characterize the illustrations of most of the other western material in *McClure's* during Cather's years. Blumenschein's pictures for "The Unexpected," by Jack London, published in August 1906, depict male violence and female reformism. In the same issue his drawings for "Archie's

Baby," by *McClure's* staffer Viola Roseboro', show rough miners and a child, in what might be called the Bret Harte manner. Charcoals by Blumenschein accompanying "Two Men and the Desert," by Frederic L. Wheeler, in the February 1907 issue, show horses and a saloon. In the January 1907 and March 1907 issues, charcoal drawings by Martin Justice portray rustics, cowboys, barrooms, and fighting in a comically exaggerated manner. In June 1907, "The Tale of a Cayuse" was illustrated in charcoals in a heavily romanticized style, with the largest of the pictures showing a fight. Charcoals in an equally romantic mode in the March 1912 issue show a harsh and forbidding western landscape. From her own professional experience, then, Cather had abundant opportunity to be well acquainted with conventions of western art and the equally conventional, heavily shaded style that had become dominant with the introduction of halftone processing. Her own "Bohemian Girl," published in the August 1912 *McClure's,* was illustrated by Sigismund de Ivanowski in heavy charcoals emphasizing interior scenes and sexual romance (figure 4.01), with minimal attention to the geographic spaciousness and freedom of movement that are so compelling in the story.

These same years afforded Cather a familiarity with the work of W. T. Benda (1873–1948), whom she would choose as illustrator for *My Ántonia,* and—just as importantly—the opportunity to become familiar with drawings done in a less conventionalized, less cluttered, more open style. Among the illustrations that *McClure's* published in this more open style were some drawings by Charlie Russell in July 1910 for a story called "Corazón," by George Pattullo. These are conventional enough in subject matter, with horses, a covered wagon, and lively cowboy action, but are surprisingly (for Russell) minimal in style, with backgrounds of open or empty skies (see figure 4.02).

Empty backgrounds were not unusual in magazine art, but neither were they typical. Line drawings in the July 1906 and March 1908 issues also made considerable use of white space, one of them wrapping around the print on the page in a way reminiscent of E. Boyd Smith's drawing of the coyote and the bright moon in *The Land of Little Rain.* (This was called vignette-style illustrating; the artist prepared "images isolated in fields of white so that copy could be laid around the art work."[11]) We can be especially confident that Cather was aware of these pictures since one of them was on the page facing the beginning of the eleventh number of her own mate-

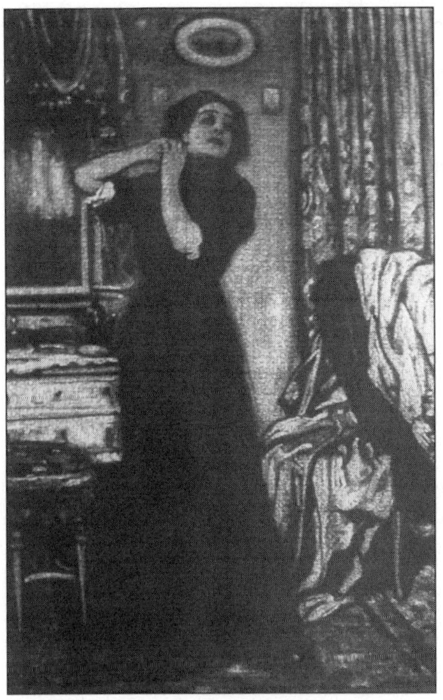

4.01 Sigismund de Ivanowski, illustration for Willa Cather's "The Bohemian Girl," captioned "Clara Vavrika was tying a wine-colored ribbon about her throat . . . ," *McClure's Magazine,* August 1912

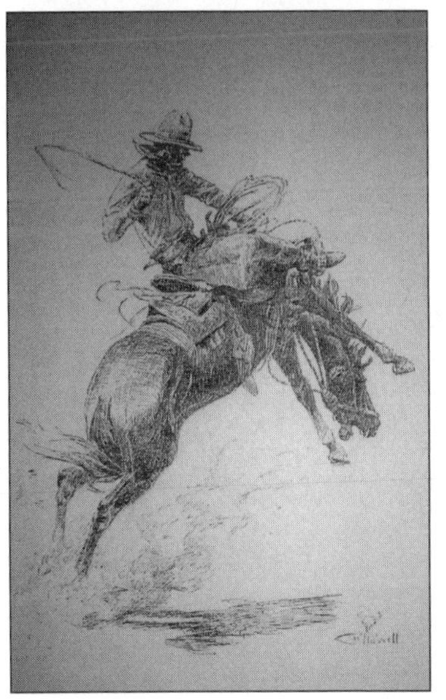

4.02 C. M. Russell, illustration for George Pattullo, "Corazón," *McClure's Magazine,* July 1910

rial on Mary Baker Eddy. A group of rather bare line drawings in the December 1908 issue included one with a big sky and no horizon line. These are the kinds of techniques she would later want for *Ántonia.*

Illustrations by Benda appeared in ten separate stories while Cather was editor. Few, however, were characterized by the minimalism of his later work for *My Ántonia.* For the most part they were in a heavily shaded, romantic style that could often be described as cluttered—most conspicuously so, perhaps, in his gloomy picture of a wrecked ship for Sarah Orne Jewett's poem "The Gloucester Mother" in October 1908. Certainly Cather would have been aware of this example of Benda's work, since she was personally devoted to Jewett and would have paid close attention to any publication of hers. Benda's work for Jack London's "The House of Mapuhi" in the January 1909 issue was equally heavy and cluttered. Still, a few of his illustrations for *McClure's* allowed Cather to see that he could use a sparer style. Small drawings for a story called "Rodania the Magic Mare"—although not the large, heavily filled-in charcoals for the same story—exhibit the clean openness and concentrated focus that result from bareness of background (e.g., figure 4.03).

In 1909 Benda did the illustrations for Gene Stratton Porter's novel *A Girl of the Limberlost.* I have found no evidence of Cather's having seen these, yet certain of their stylistic elements together with her usual awareness of publishing events would seem to make it likely that she did.[12] There are four, including the frontispiece. All are line drawings and thus are similar, in that respect at least, to the *Ántonia* illustrations; that is, shading as well as outlines are done with distinguishable single lines, not solid modeling. Even so, they are considerably darker, more filled in with lines of heavy shading, than the drawings Benda would do for Cather's book. In subject matter they emphasize the romantic plot. Two of the four show no horizon line, but that may be only because the woods of the story's Indiana setting intervene between the viewer and the distant prospect. Of particular interest, as we think about the style of the *Ántonia* drawings, is a picture that is densely shaded on the right side and lower two-thirds of the page where two figures are shown in conversation, but with about half of the left side of the page left empty except for minimal indication of the horizon line and a distant scene (facing page 448). We can see hints in these *Girl of the Limberlost* drawings of a stylistic bent that might have led Cather to think of Benda for the *Ántonia* project,

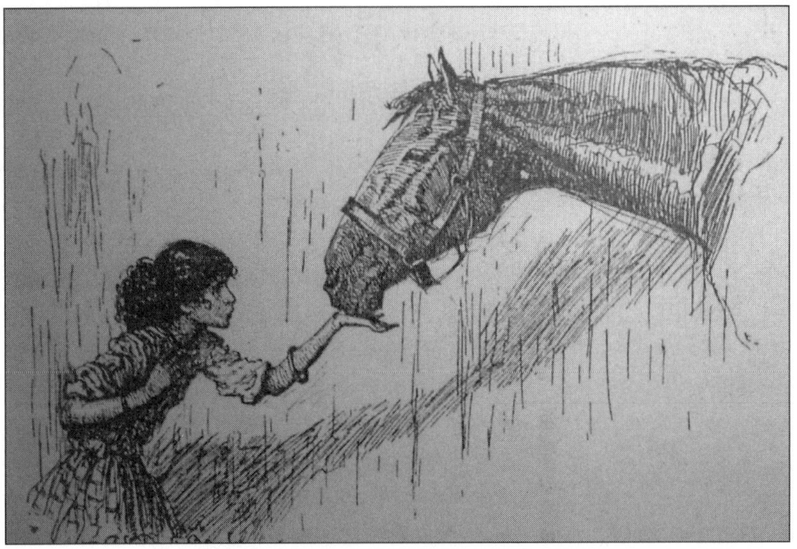

4.03 W. T. Benda, illustration for Lucille Baldwin Van Slyke, "Rodania the Magic Mare," *McClure's Magazine*, May 1911

but also elements that would have to be eliminated in order to produce the degree of spareness shown there. It is clear that Cather's direct involvement made a difference.

At the same time as she was working with Benda to rid his style of what she called, in "My First Novels [There Were Two]," the quality of "too much detail" (*On Writing* 97), Cather was also moving toward her own achievement of a barer style—the style she would attempt to define in her 1922 essay, "The Novel Démeublé." She had been insisting since at least 1913 that "art ought to simplify" (Bohlke 8), but part of her impetus for doing so now was the rejection of her 1915 novel *The Song of the Lark* by the distinguished British publisher William Heinemann, who had published *O Pioneers!* in England. Heinemann wrote to her directly telling her (so she reported in "My First Novels") that he was declining it because it was in the "full-blooded method" that "told everything about everybody," and in his judgment that kind of fullness "was not natural" to her (*On Writing* 96).

* * *

Cather's work with W. T. Benda as she was completing the writing of *My Ántonia* in preparation for publication is a striking and singularly well-documented instance of collaboration between author and illustrator. We know from her letters that it was she who conceived the idea for the spare pen-and-ink drawings; that she in fact tried to make suitable drawings herself; and that it was she, not her editors, who selected Benda for the project.[13] She met with him, discussed what she wanted, apparently showed him her own preliminary sketches, and approved his work before sending it to Houghton Mifflin. The resulting drawings are a superb example of complementarity between text and illustration. Cather herself said they caught the tone of the text and were one of those rare instances in which illustrations contribute to the telling of the story.[14] They have routinely been included in almost all subsequent editions, as Cather insisted they should be.

Why, we may ask, did she choose Benda? And why did she want illustrations of precisely this kind, which are actually quite different from his usual work? As we have seen, she was familiar with his work; it appeared in a dozen or more issues of *McClure's* between 1906 and 1912.[15] Charles Mignon states in his commentary to the scholarly edition that Cather selected Benda from among the many illustrators she had dealt with for the magazine "because he knew both Europe and the American West" (*MA* 512). He did indeed have familiarity with both; Polish by birth but an immigrant from Bohemia (as were the fictional Shimerdas), he had lived in the West and painted western subjects, though by no means was all of his work even for *McClure's* done for western material.[16] And Cather did state this reason in a letter to Ferris Greenslet dated November 24, 1917 (*Calendar* #399). In the same letter, however, she gave two more reasons: that Benda had imagination and that he was willing to work with her to get precisely the effects she wanted. My belief is that there was yet another reason that she did not mention.

In order to get the illustrations she wanted for her novel, Cather had to overcome her editors' initial preference for a frontispiece (Cather to Greenslet, November 24, [1917], *Calendar* #399). She was determined not to have so conventional a decoration and one that would necessarily have generalized, rather than being attached to specific moments or ideas in the text. What she was intent on having, instead, was a series of drawings in a style that would give the impression of the line techniques of old woodcuts. She may also have wanted to avoid the kind of romanticized frontispiece that had decorated her earlier Nebraska novel, *O Pioneers!*, which, though appealing, centers on female beauty of an idealized kind, and except for the evidence of strong wind in Alexandra's billowing scarf, gives no sense of place.[17]

Cather's correspondence with Greenslet and R. L. Scaife, the production editor, is striking in its revelation of how determined she was and the extent to which visual design was a part of her creative act of authorship. She conceived the appearance of the book while she was still writing it. As early as March 13, 1917, "even before she had completed a first draft," she was "thinking as a designer might about how to present her work" (Mignon, Textual Commentary, *MA* 483). In Jean Schwind's words, she "acted as artistic director of the project" (53). She specified the kind of paper that should be used for the illustrations, their sizing, their placement in the text, and even their placement on the page.[18] In a letter to Scaife on December 1, 1917, a week after she had told Greenslet why she wanted Benda for the project, she justified her determination not to have a conventional frontispiece and again explained why she wanted Benda, this time giving what appears to be a different reason than she had given only a week earlier: that she had seen his pen-and-ink drawings in Jacob Riis's 1909 book, *The Old Town* (*Calendar* #400). But this is in effect what she had already told Greenslet, that he understood Europe (as well as the West). *The Old Town* evokes a lost but nostalgically remembered European setting, a congenial theme as she thought about *My Ántonia.*

Significantly, in referring to Benda's work on Riis's book, Cather specified the drawings. She did not use the more general term "illustrations." Most of the illustrations in *The Old Town,* including the frontispiece and full-page glossies scattered throughout, are in fact not pen-and-ink drawings at all but charcoals reproduced in halftones. That is, they are Benda's usual kind of work. She explicitly stated that these were what she did *not* want: she considered them stilted.[19] What, precisely, she meant in her objection to stiltedness or conventionality in the halftones is not clear, but the example shown in figure 4.04 displays their cluttered, dark, and closed-in qualities.

The pen-and-ink head- and tail-pieces in Riis's book, however, are in a simpler, more open style.[20] Even these are more laden with details than the ones he would do for *Ántonia,* as we can see from the head-piece to Chapter IV, "Christmas Sheaf" (78) (figure 4.05) and a mid-chapter ornament from

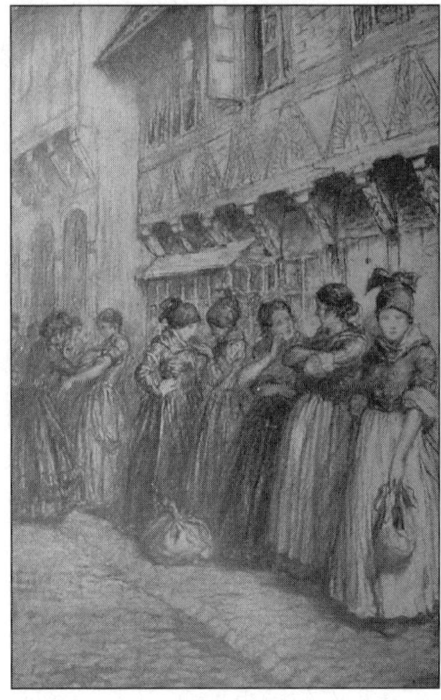

4.04 W. T. Benda, "The Girl Market" from Jacob Riis, *The Old Town* (following p. 118)

Chapter II, "Fanö Women" (21) (figure 4.06). Yet Cather might well have seen in these drawings the potential for achieving what she had in mind, through simplifying and un-cluttering them even further. It is worth noting, too, that unlike the glossy halftones in *The Old Town,* the pen-and-ink drawings were printed on the same rough-textured, cream-colored paper as the text—as Cather would insist the drawings in *My Ántonia* be done.

In his spare drawings for *My Ántonia,* Benda in fact captured much of the essence of Cather's narrative style. They offer a visual equivalent of her verbal clarity and selective focus on a few details set against a far prospect—the quality Welty designated as elimination of the middle ground. Benda captured these qualities not only because he read the text in typescript and as a capable professional was able to vary his style accordingly, but because Cather worked closely with him on his conceptualization of the drawings, going so far as to show him what she wanted by first trying to draw them herself (as Austin had done with E. Boyd Smith for *The Flock*). *She* was in control. And she was able to report to Greenslet that Benda was indeed seeking to capture her precise intentions.[21]

The novel was published with a total of eight drawings. Originally

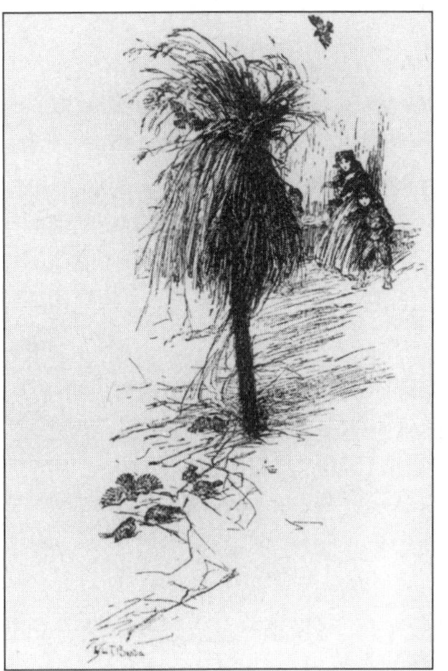

4.05 W. T. Benda, head-piece to "Christmas Sheaf," from Jacob Riis, *The Old Town* (p. 78)

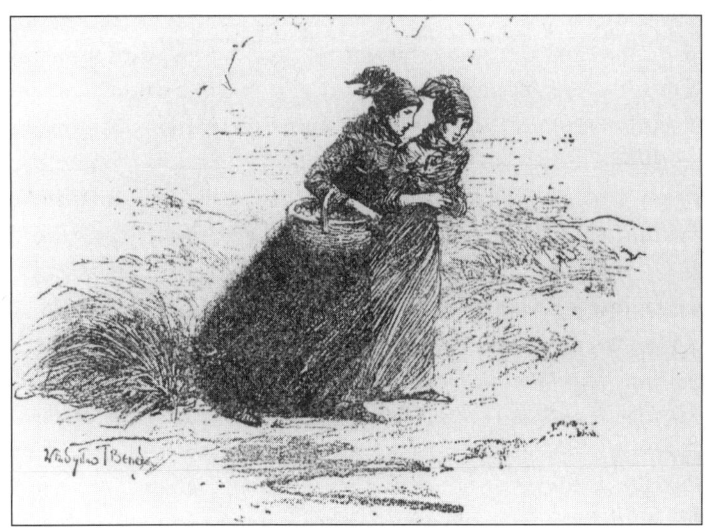

4.06 W. T. Benda, drawing of "Fanö Women," from Jacob Riis, *The Old Town* (p. 21)

there were to have been twelve, but Houghton Mifflin's skimpy production budget would not pay for more and Cather refused to ask Benda to execute four more drawings for the amount they were paying. This would seem to account for the concentration of the illustrations in the earlier half to two-thirds of the text. In calling the eighth drawing "Benda's final scene" and developing an argument that it reprises and revises the initial picture of the Shimerda family, thus bringing the series into totality (62), Schwind disregards the fact that Cather had not intended this to be the final one.

The first of the eight illustrations comes in the opening chapter, where Jim Burden tells us about his train trip to Nebraska. We see, much as Jim would have, an immigrant family waiting among their bundles on what we assume, from the textual context and the merest visual hint of the structure itself, to be a train platform (figure 4.07). The family is, of course, the Shimerdas arriving in Nebraska. The man's downward gaze and the overall darkness of the scene speak of discouragement. The girl whose bright eyes will later be celebrated in the text gazes out beyond the reader. Central emphasis is on the woman's cradling grasp of a treasured possession. Benda's practiced technique is greatly in evidence here both in mood and in composition. It is worth noting, however, that he does not simply render what the words say. Some of his drawings for *Ántonia* provide a visual extension, showing what the words imply but do not say. But in this first one, he not only refrains from sketching out the details of the shadowy train platform, instead leaving the space around the Shimerdas mostly blank, but omits some of what the words *do* say. The Shimerdas are not so much "huddled together" as grouped into a set of lonely individual figures. Their "encumber[ing] by bundles and boxes" seems to be minimal; of the "two half-grown boys and a girl" that in the text "stood holding oil-cloth bundles," one, in Benda's representation, is seated (providing the triangular structure that Schwind notes), and none is holding a bundle. The "little girl cl[inging] to her mother's skirts" does not appear at all (*MA* 5–6). But if the picture departs from details of the text, it nevertheless conveys in concentrated form the loneliness and anxiety that Cather's words imply but do not say—and appropriately so, since she is speaking in the voice of a child feeling his way toward an understanding of these unfamiliar people.

The Benda drawings have sometimes been seen not merely as departing from the text but as existing in tension with the verbal text. Schwind

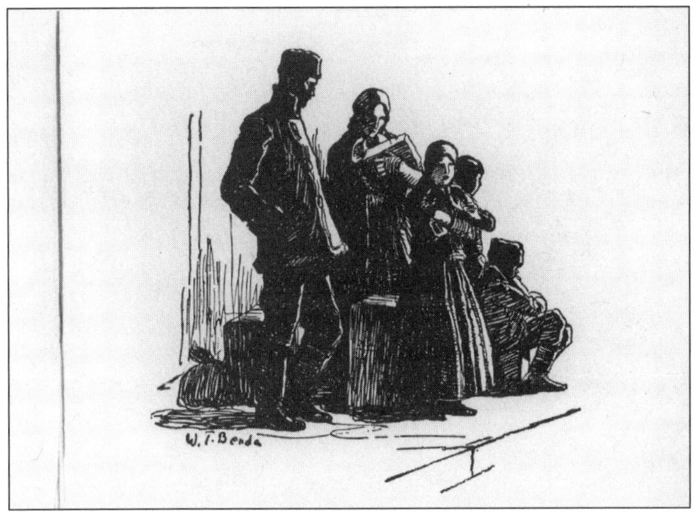

4.07 W. T. Benda, illustration #1 from Willa Cather, *My Ántonia* (facing page 6)

regards them as a deliberately ironizing strategy, Cather's own intentional undercutting of her narrator, Jim Burden. Woodress, citing this idea of Schwind's in his historical essay to the scholarly edition but considerably misrepresenting her argument, states that Cather "wanted [Benda's] stark black-and-white drawings to provide realistic balance to Jim Burden's nostalgic memory of his Nebraska youth" (*MA* 390). Although I agree with Schwind that *My Ántonia* is a self-ironizing text, I do not see the dissonances that undercut Jim Burden as being, for the most part, calculated, but rather as the evidence of Cather's own conflictedness.[22]

The second of the eight drawings again shows Mr. Shimerda, tall and lanky, still with bowed head suggestive of discouragement (figure 4.08). Ántonia and Jim have spied him out hunting, and Ántonia has confided to Jim that he is unhappy in the new country. Even as it conveys discouragement, however, this picture strikes the outdoor note that will characterize all the rest. For the first time we gain a visual impression of the vastness of the prairie and especially the spaciousness of its sky. Scattered curving lines indicate the prairie grass, and the sinking sun sends its long beams up into the sky, disappearing into blank page.

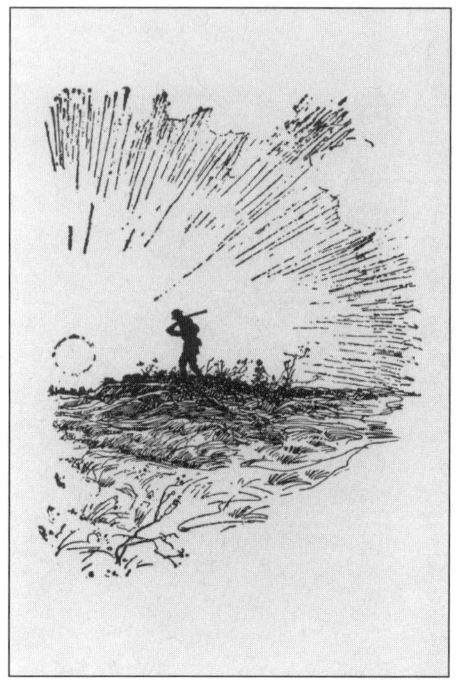

4.08 W. T. Benda illustration #2 from Willa Cather, *My Ántonia* (facing page 40)

The third drawing goes behind the text, in a sense, alluding to Mrs. Shimerda's giving Grandmother Burden some dried mushrooms brought from Bohemia but showing their source instead of the presentation (figure 4.09). It hints at far-off places, with a woman gathering mushrooms in the old country. The woman's figure is generalized; perhaps the clearest detail is her rolled-up sleeve, conveying the idea of physical work and peasant identity. A cluster of mushrooms is evident in the foreground. It is a scene of quiet and solitude. Having its most specific textual reference to a single elliptical sentence—"They [the mushrooms] had been gathered, probably, in some deep Bohemian forest . . ."—the drawing makes real what Jim Burden vaguely imagines.

The fourth drawing shows the Burdens' hired man Jake (who had accompanied Jim from Virginia and knew his fondness for Christmas evergreens) bringing home a Christmas tree (figure 4.10). With notable minimalism, the drawing indicates the empty countryside, the narrow trail, and a few weeds. The big, absolutely empty sky and the snow-covered prairie are

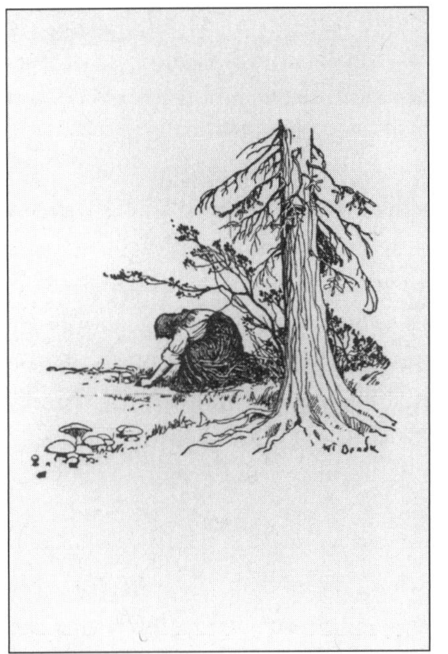

4.09 W. T. Benda illustration #3 from Willa Cather, *My Ántonia* (facing page 76)

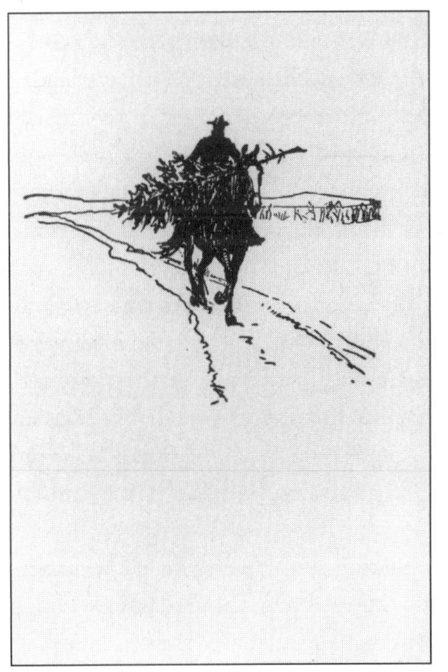

4.10 W. T. Benda, illustration #4 from Willa Cather, *My Ántonia* (facing page 80)

indicated by blank paper. Here, even more than in the second drawing, we see how effectively Benda solved the problem that had plagued early artists on the plains, how to depict what struck them as an emptiness or blankness and how to provide perspective in a space without landmarks to indicate distance.

Kinsey observes in *Plain Pictures* that many of the first Anglo artists on the Great Plains, including the sketchers who accompanied Major Stephen Long, sought out "views" and details to give their depictions focus, perspective, and interest. Benda's illustration avoids such devices. Like George Catlin, who traveled the Great Plains in the 1830s painting both landscapc and native inhabitants, he is "willing . . . to depict 'empty' scenes" (Kinsey 39). Catlin's *Nishnabottana Bluffs, Upper Missouri* (1832) shows only a slightly mounding green band—the prairie itself—with a big, broiling yellow sky (see figure 1.03). For Catlin, in this canvas at any rate, and for Benda, the emptiness is as important a component of the picture as the central image.

The fifth of the drawings, showing Ántonia plowing, offers another big sky (figure 4.11), an effect Cather sought to emphasize by having the drawing lowered on the page so as to create a sense of sunlight and air at the top.[23] Summer thunderheads are indicated, but only barely so, with a single meandering line. Again there is emptiness all around, with a strong central focus on Ántonia, the plow, the horses, and the heavy horse-collar. Benda's rendition of Ántonia herself is notably positive, with its erect posture, its open, forward- and upward-looking face, and its clearly indicated female curves. It may well be said, then, to undercut or at any rate offer an alternate vision to the repulsed terms in which a dismayed Jim regards her departure from his ideas of what she should be—"burned and brown as a sailo[r]," her neck "like the bole of a tree" (we do not see the objectionable neck in Benda's drawing), "sweaty" and "dust-plastered" (*MA* 117, 121). Here, the illustration does capture an ironizing intention on Cather's part. In its furthest extreme, when he states that "one sees that draught-horse neck among the peasant women in all old countries," Jim's reaction to the change in Ántonia is indeed "brutal" (Schwind 59), and the controlling narrative will lead him to modify his view.

The sixth illustration, with its radiating sun rays (figure 4.12), is reminiscent of the second, the one of a discouraged Mr. Shimerda out with his gun, hunting. In this case we see the sinking sun that will later magnify the

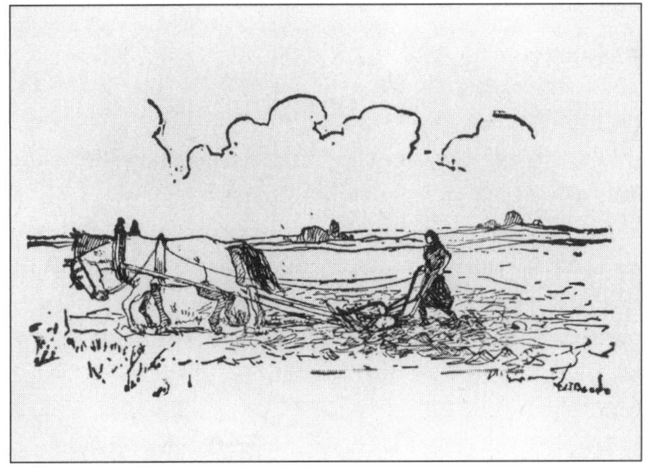

4.11 W. T. Benda, illustration #5 from Willa Cather, *My Ántonia* (facing page 120)

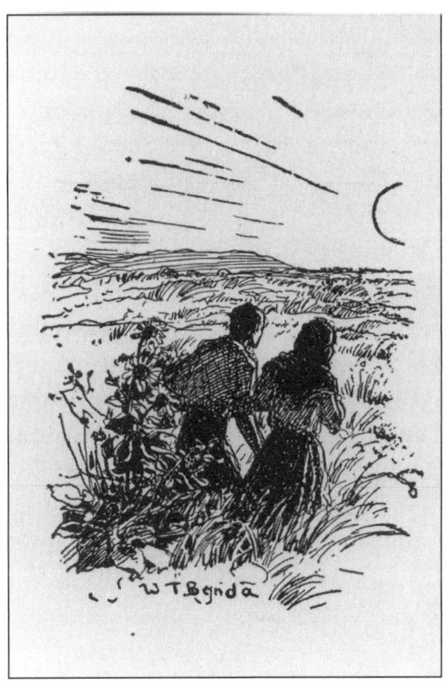

4.12 W. T. Benda, illustration #6 from Willa Cather, *My Ántonia* (facing page 134)

plow on the horizon, in the textual moment that for most readers is probably the single most memorable in the book:

> Presently we saw a curious thing: There were no clouds, the sun was going down in a limpid, gold-washed sky. Just as the lower edge of the red disc rested on the high fields against the horizon, a great black figure suddenly appeared on the face of the sun. We sprang to our feet, straining our eyes toward it. In a moment we realized what it was. On some upland farm, a plough had been left standing in the field. The sun was sinking just behind it. Magnified across the distance by the horizontal light, it stood out against the sun, was exactly contained within the circle of the disc; the handles, the tongue, the share—black against the molten red. There it was, heroic in size, a picture writing on the sun. (*MA* 237)

Whether such a phenomenon is scientifically possible I do not know; people well versed in physics have told me it is not. Certainly, though, the phenomenon of optical illusions on the plains and the difficulty of judging the distance of perceived objects or landmarks, as well as a peculiar magnifying quality, were noted by early (Anglo) visitors. Edwin James, biologist and geologist on the Long expedition to the Rockies in 1819 and 1820, observed that "nothing is more difficult than to estimate, by the eye, the distance of objects seen in these plains" because of mirage effects (quoted in Thacker 110). It was primarily from this account, Thacker argues, that James Fenimore Cooper derived the secondhand knowledge of the prairies that he drew on in his novel of the old age and death of Natty Bumppo, *The Prairie* (1827), including the optical illusion that occurs when Natty appears before the pioneering Bush family "backlighted by the setting sun," baffling them as to the true proportions of the figure they see. Thacker also points out that Hamlin Garland has a similar moment in *The Moccasin Ranch: A Story of Dakota* (1909): "As the sun rose, a kind of transformation-scene took place. The whole level land lifted at the horizon till the teams seemed crawling forever at the bottom of an enormous bowl. Mystical forms came into view—grotesquely elongated, unrecognizable. Hills twenty, thirty miles away rose like apparitions, astonishingly magnified" (3–4, quoted in Thacker 135).[24]

Wisely, Benda (and we assume Cather, as overseer of his work) did not try to show the plow itself. The mirage is left to the reader's imagination. Instead, his drawing generalizes by combining the textual moment when Jim and his "hired girl" friends see the plow with various other textual moments of Jim and Ántonia's ramblings on the prairie (figure 4.12). We see companionable young people, a head scarf implying immigrant identity, one sunflower plant, and empty prairie all around. Nothing intervenes between the close-up details and the far horizon.

Cather's heroizing verbal image of the outsized plow redefines the saga of the West from one of adventure and violence to one of cultivation and family survival. The passage is also a dramatic demonstration of the visual quality of Cather's writing. In the plow against the sun she creates a defining emblem—what Mary Austin would call a glyph—of her conception of the frontier as an agricultural and humane one. Moreover, the clustering of Jim and his hired-girl friends—or in Benda's drawing, one friend—asserts an inclusively gendered and also, to a point, an ethnically inclusive West.

The seventh drawing shows another big summer sky with the merest indication of cumulus clouds (figure 4.13). The rows of Lena's knitting are clearly indicated, along with her two knitting needles, her bare feet, and the line of a nipple inside her tight bodice—clear focus indeed! In a letter to Greenslet Cather gloated that Lena was fairly bursting out of her clothes (*Calendar* #411). The particular length of the skirt and the broad solidity of the bare feet would seem to support Schwind's reading (63) that this drawing is a purposeful allusion to Jules Breton's painting *Song of the Lark,* which Cather had drawn on for the title and jacket art of her previous novel (see fig. 5.1).[25] Again the effect is one of clear focus on a central figure placed within a surrounding spaciousness or near blankness (indicated by the white space of the page), with no distracting clutter—much as in the Breton painting, but with a far more marked factuality, cleanness of line, and openness.

The last of the series starkly shows Ántonia struggling through the snow into the wind (figure 4.14). The bent position of her head and the dark tones of her coat, hat, and boots (reproducing the text's "she wore a man's long overcoat and boots, and a man's felt hat") are reminiscent of the first picture, the one of the Shimerdas waiting on the train platform. Ántonia indeed appears, as Widow Steavens says, "lonesome-like" (*MA* 308), as the entire

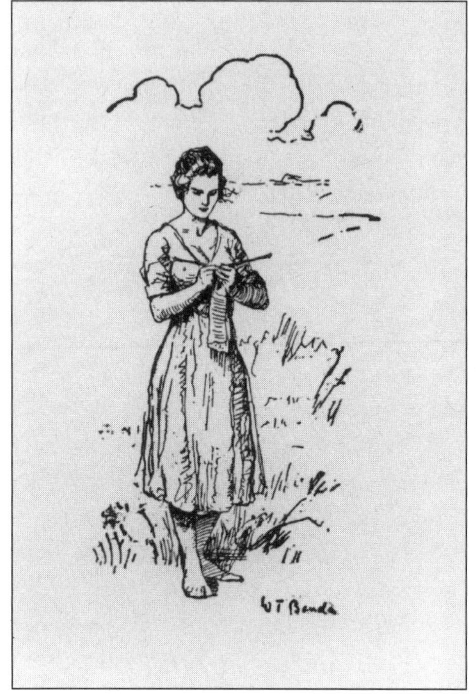

4.13 W. T. Benda, illustration #7 from Willa Cather, *My Ántonia* (facing page 160)

family did there. A single line outlines the top of the cloud, closing in the top of the picture in contrast to those in which either the clear sky or the hinted shape of cumuli opens the top. Again Benda captures the emptiness of the prairie, emphasizing it by isolating a few strong details: snow in the air, tracks, the whip in the hand. It is another masterful example of minimalist design executed with line techniques reminiscent of woodcuts.

When Houghton Mifflin issued the revised edition of *My Ántonia* in 1926 for which Cather shortened the introduction, the volume bore an illustrated dust jacket also done by Benda. The design of the original dust jacket had consisted simply of "heavy black" lettering on pumpkin-colored paper without a picture (Mignon, *MA* 493). The starkness of the image on the new jacket harmonized with the stark illustrations, but its glorification of Nebraskan agricultural life, drawing on though by no means replicating the "plow against the sun" image, is unsubtle, to say the least (figure 4.15). So far as I know, there is no record of Cather's opinion on this point.

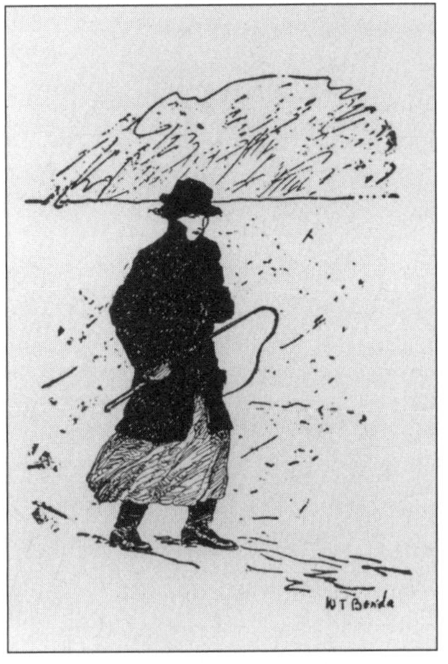

4.14 W. T. Benda, illustration #8 from Willa Cather, *My Ántonia* (facing page 308)

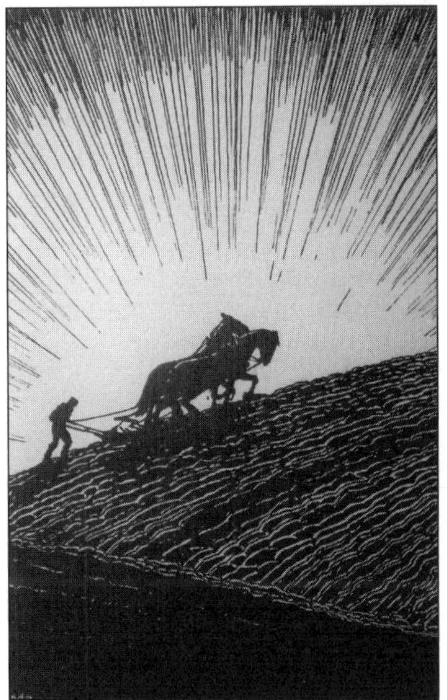

4.15 W. T. Benda, jacket design for 1926 *My Ántonia*

* * *

In interrogating Cather's reasons for selecting W. T. Benda as her illustrator for *My Ántonia,* we have cited several factors: his familiarity with both the Old World and the West, her prior acquaintance with him in connection with his work for *McClure's* (i.e., a reason partly of convenience), her admiration of some, though not all, of his work on Jacob Riis's *The Old Town,* and the fact that he was willing to work with her to execute her conception of the drawings. The question remains, where did she get that conception? My conjecture is that she had admired the illustrations in Austin's *The Land of Little Rain* and wished to emulate them.

The Austin–Cather connection has been recognized for some time. It is well documented that they knew each other personally, and connections between specific works have been demonstrated by several critics.[26] For the most part, it is *The Song of the Lark* and Austin's *A Woman of Genius* that have been linked, though in fact the connections extend much further, reaching both forward and considerably backward in time. To my knowledge, no one has suggested any connection of Cather's work with *The Land of Little Rain,* or even any indication that she was aware of it. Yet David Stouck has identified a likely borrowing even earlier, in 1893, in her story "A Son of the Celestial." She and Austin were personally acquainted by at least 1910, and in 1917, the year when Cather was corresponding with Greenslet and Scaife about the Benda illustrations, her awareness of Austin remained sufficiently keen to prompt a brief comment on Austin's newly published novel *The Ford* in a letter to Elizabeth Shepley Sergeant.[27]

Considering the mass of evidence that Cather was aware of Austin as early as the 1890s and that she remained both personally and professionally conversant with her up until Austin's death in 1934, it seems overwhelmingly likely that she knew Austin's very successful *The Land of Little Rain.* Keenly attuned to periodical literature as she was, she would likely have been aware of its serialization in *Atlantic Monthly.* More than once during her years as editor at *McClure's* she advised correspondents to send their manuscripts to *Atlantic Monthly,* and when she did, her clearly specified reasons show that she had more than a reputational acquaintance with that prestigious magazine. The publisher of *Little Rain* in book form, in 1903, was Houghton Mifflin, which in less than a decade would also be Cather's publisher and whose acquisitions editor, Ferris Greenslet, would become an acquaintance even sooner. The archive of correspondence between Cather and Greenslet reveals that they at times discussed Austin. There was ample and varied opportunity, then, for her to be acquainted with Austin's book and perhaps with behind-the-scenes information about its production history.

We know that Cather had seen Jacob Riis's *The Old Town* by at least December 1917. Probably she knew it much earlier; she may even have drawn on it early in the work on *My Ántonia* for the atmosphere of remembered European origins. Perhaps when she looked through Riis's book, Benda's pen-and-ink drawings reminded her of Smith's in *The Land of Little Rain.* As we have noted, the Benda drawings that she liked in Riis's book were only the head- and tail-pieces and a few small inserts; the full-page illustrations were the halftones she disliked. And in fact Benda's drawings in *My Ántonia* more closely resemble Smith's pen-and-ink drawings in Austin's book than they do his own earlier work. We recall that Cather initially meant to have head- and tail-pieces, not, emphatically, a frontispiece. The Smith illustrations of *The Land of Little Rain* are primarily of two sorts, full-page line drawings and head- and tail-pieces (although some editions also bore a halftone frontispiece, and some an additional three plates). Benda's illustrations of *My Ántonia* are most strikingly similar to the larger line drawings, especially in how they show a big sky by the use of white space.

When Cather and Greenslet were contemplating the new edition of *Ántonia* in 1926, Cather said that the Benda illustrations were one of the few instances she could think of in which pictures materially assisted the narrative.[28] She saw them as being essentially a part of the text—in Schwind's words, a "silent supplement." If my conjecture about the impact of Smith's drawings on Cather's vision for the illustrations of her book is correct, the critical judgment of at least one art historian that E. Boyd Smith "had few followers and made no major impact on American illustration" (Best 28) may merit revision.

Significant in their resonance of Cather's style and emphasis on dailiness in *My Ántonia,* the Benda illustrations are also significant in a biographical sense. If we consider them as a group, we can see a kind of balance between grimness or bleakness in the plains environment and sunniness or vitality. We can only wonder how this duality would have worked itself out had Cather been able to have the full twelve illustrations she wanted. As it is, at least two of the eight are distinctly dark in emotional tone—the picture of the Shimerdas' arrival and the scene of a pregnant Ántonia struggling through the snow, herding cattle. The one showing a stooped, depressed Mr. Shimerda might be added to this number. In these, reflecting the point of view of immigrants on the plains, Nebraska appears as a harsh, discouraging, and alienating place. That is also Jim Burden's point of view, initially. The night of his arrival he misses the "familiar mountain ridge" he had always seen against the sky, and feels as if he had fallen off the edge of the world into darkness where even his dead parents, watching from heaven, could not follow him (*MA* 7–8). He feels as if his very self were being "erased." But Jim quickly begins to respond to the sunniness and openness of his grandparents' farm, and the four drawings that emphasize spaciousness and brightness seem to reflect his increasingly positive, even idealizing view, especially in retrospect. At the end of the novel, of course, Cather's own pictorial language, as she looks through Jim's yearning eyes at the fertility and liveliness of the Cuzac farm, at the "goodness of planting and tending and harvesting," and views Ántonia herself as a "rich mine of life" (*MA* 342), seems to vindicate the positive view. The immigrants' initial sense of a hostile environment seems to have moved toward, and merged with, Jim's. Yet the text retains hints of dissatisfaction. Ántonia appears "battered" by life, and she insists that her daughters will never have to "work out" as domestics, as she did herself (*MA* 333). Benda's drawings capture both moods, the harshness and the love, just as they capture the sense of open space and big skies.

The movement that we see in Jim Burden from an initially harsh view of the plains to an idealizing bucolic acceptance was in fact Cather's own. In James Woodress's words, "Jim Burden's memories of his first months on the Divide are Cather's memories" (*Literary Life* 41). Her initial reaction essentially replicated the response of earlier settlers who felt oppressed by the prairie's vastness and lack of landmarks, making them feel "small and insignificant" (Thacker 37).[29] Accustomed as they were to wooded land, Americans who migrated from the settled East to the Great Plains did not "typically feel liberated as they came into the openness of the grasslands," but rather "complained of the heavy burden" of "vacancy and oppression . . . accompanying so much space" (Kinsey xii). In a 1913 interview Cather described her own initial impressions this way:

> I shall never forget my introduction to it. We drove out from Red Cloud to my grandfather's homestead one day in April. I was sitting on the hay in the bottom of a Studebaker wagon, holding on to the side of the wagon box to steady myself—the roads were mostly faint trails over the bunch grass in those days. The land was open range and there was almost no fencing. As we drove further and further out into the country, I felt a good deal as if we had come to the end of everything—it was a kind of erasure of personality.
>
> I would not know how much a child's life is bound up in the woods and hills and meadows around it, if I had not been jerked away from all these and thrown out into a country as bare as a piece of sheet iron . . . my one purpose in life just then was not to cry. (Bohlke 10)

It is clear from this interview and from other surviving recollections of her early impressions of Nebraska (importantly, a letter to Witter Bynner)[30] that Cather's response to her environment was already keenly visual. She especially comments on the absence of trees and recalls her joy when she could see some planted poplars or a few cottonwoods along a creek partway between the Cather ranch and town, as well as her disappointment when the first Christmas in Nebraska was observed with only a little shrub disguised as an evergreen with green tissue paper cut in strips. Like Mary Austin when she first arrived in California, Cather hated eating canned foods, resolved not to eat, and fell ill.

This alienated or "erased" response to the plains of Nebraska appears, in part, in an 1895 review of an art show in Lincoln in which Cather referred to the prairie sunlight as "glaring" and "shelterless" (Curtin 125). She would remain preoccupied with the quality of light in all her writings about the West, notably in a word-picture of the plains as seen through the eyes of Thea Kronborg as she returns from Chicago to her hometown in eastern Colorado (a version of the actual Red Cloud, Nebraska): "The train was crossing the Platte River now, and the sunlight was so intense that it seemed to quiver in little flames on the glittering sandbars, the scrub willows, and the curling, fretted shadows" (*SL* 174). Reflecting Cather's mature, benign view, Thea sees the plains here as "young and fresh and kindly, a place where refugees"—a term that wins such people more sympathy than the neutral term "immigrants"—"from old, sad countries were given another chance." The very spinelessness of the prairie soil, its "absence of rocks," seems to Thea to give it "a kind of amiability and generosity." Most emphatically, she thinks that "the absence of natural boundaries gave the spirit a wider range" (*SL* 174). Cather's linkage of topographical openness with mental freedom here adopts what Walter Hölbling calls a theory of a "'natural' symbiosis of open space and open mind" (147). Such a view of western spaces would remain with Cather through her writing of *Death Comes for the Archbishop.* The earlier anxiety about erasure of the self under the burden of blank skies over boundless land would never entirely leave her. Claude Wheeler's thoughts at a moment of discouragement early in *One of Ours* indicate such an anxiety: "Here [in the West] the sky was like a lid shut down over the world" (*One* 100). But the sunnier view, the view emphasizing release and openness, would come to predominate.

In her early stories of life on the Great Plains—works she later preferred to leave unnoticed, such as "Peter" (1892) and "On the Divide" (1896)—she emphasized the bleakness she initially perceived in the plains environment. Thacker calls these stories as "unremittingly grim" as Hamlin Garland's (148). Perhaps reflecting the fact that one of the first bits of local lore she heard when she arrived in Nebraska was the report of neighbor Sadilek's suicide, perhaps reflecting her later fear of being trapped on the plains far from centers of art and high culture, both works are preoccupied with loneliness, tawdriness, and death. Their color palette is dark. Unfortunately, it is difficult to explore interactions of text and illustration in these early stories, since they have never been reprinted with illustrations and their original venues are far from readily available.[31] Some of the stories she published after her career was well under way but prior to her emergence as a novelist—such as "El Dorado: A Kansas Recessional" (1901), "A Death in the Desert" (1903), "A Wagner Matinee" (1904), and "The Sculptor's Funeral" (1905)—show a continuing preoccupation with the darker view of the prairie West. None of these stories has the tone of ripe affection that predominates in *O Pioneers!* and *My Ántonia*—although to be sure, the opening chapters of *O Pioneers!,* much like Jim Burden's initial view, reflect a sense of bleakness, absence of beauty or comfort, and vulnerability to a punishing environment.

O Pioneers! opens with a wintry scene in a little town called Hanover "anchored on a windy Nebraska tableland . . . trying not to be blown away" (11). It is as unbeautiful a scene as one could well imagine, with its few haphazardly arranged, impermanent-looking buildings, its "frozen hard," "deeply rutted" road and a "pale, watery light" in a "leaden sky" (*OP* 11–20). Yet the harshness of this initial view is mitigated as the story develops (much as it is in *My Ántonia*) by an emphasis on fertility and agricultural abundance and a growing love of place, reflecting Cather's own softened retrospective view. It is significant that when she described the nature of the land to Elizabeth Shepley Sergeant, in comments about *O Pioneers!,* her governing metaphor had shifted from "a piece of sheet iron" (the phrase she used in describing her arrival in Nebraska) to one of fluidity and a yielding softness. Although she continued to extol the cottonwood trees that lined watercourses, despite their white cotton that many people regarded as a nuisance (Bohlke 146), she gave less and less attention to the treelessness of the prairies otherwise—to what they lacked—and more to the abundant grass, always in motion from the winds. "By the end of the first autumn," she said in an interview in 1921, "that shaggy grass country had gripped me with a passion I have never been able to shake. It has been the happiness and the curse of my life" (Bohlke 32). Like Austin in California, she had learned to love the environment she first found so unreceptive.

Perhaps the earliest of Cather's stories in which a tone of warm affection for Nebraska is felt, albeit still with hints of ambivalence, is "The Enchanted Bluff," published in *Harper's* in 1909. A story of childhood—specifically, boyhood—on the plains, it presents a Huck Finn version of Cather's memories of her early years in Nebraska along with a fantasized view of the Enchanted Bluff, or mesa, near Acoma in New Mexico. It thus serves as a particularly provocative transitional work between her writing about Nebraska and her writing about the Southwest.

The story opens in the voice of one of the boys. Through his eyes we see a vivid picture of a prairie sunset viewed from a sandbar in a river where they are camping overnight:

> We had our swim before sundown, and while we were cooking our supper the oblique rays of light made a dazzling glare on the white sand about us. The translucent red ball itself sank behind the brown stretches of corn field as we sat down to eat, and the warm layer of air that had rested over the water and our clean sand-bar grew fresher and smelled of the rank ironweed and sunflowers growing on the flatter shore. The river was brown and sluggish, like any other of the half-dozen streams that water the Nebraska corn lands. On one shore was an irregular line of bald clay bluffs where a few scrub-oaks with thick trunks and flat, twisted tops threw light shadows on the long grass. The western shore was low and level, with corn fields that stretched to the sky-line, and all along the water's edge were little sandy coves and beaches where slim cottonwoods and willow saplings flickered.[32]

Although Cather once said that she "hit the home pasture" in *O Pioneers!*, one senses that she had achieved her own voice here, in the combination of simple directness, highly visual perception, and affectionate memory of childhood and of Nebraska.

The boys who are spending the night on a sandbar in this unnamed river are at the end of their summer of play. Indeed, they are at the end of their sharing of boyhood. The narrator, the oldest of the group, will soon begin a job as schoolteacher and the others will return to high school. Already prospectively homesick, the narrator feels that he is leaving his boyhood behind as he leaves the "wilful and unmanageable" landscape of the river, always eating away its banks and washing its little islands downstream while it creates new ones, and that he is now entering a life of predictability and routine. The others, too, are pensive. They lie looking at the stars and a huge moon and speculating about matters from Columbus to the Aztecs to Coronado and hidden treasure. When they begin telling each other the places they dream of going some day, a boy named Tip names the Enchanted Butte and tells them what he has heard about it: that centuries ago there was a village "away up there in the air" on top of the bluff (not truly a bluff, of course, but the word builds on the "bluffs" of the opening paragraph), and while the men were down on the plains hunting a storm came and destroyed their dangling stairway. Caught with no way of getting back up, the men were slaughtered by an enemy war party, and the women and children stranded at the top starved. Despite this "dolorous" history (Faulkner 75), for the boys who have fished and camped and daydreamed together the mesa epitomizes adventure and escape from routine. They all declare that they will try to go see it, and whoever does will tell the others about it.

The visual language of "The Enchanted Bluff" is one of light and freshness and new growth. It is an idyllic setting, an idealized Nebraska of "slim cottonwoods and willow saplings" (trees native to Nebraska's watercourses) and stars in the unpolluted night sky:

> It was still dark, but the sky was blue with the last wonderful azure of night. The stars glistened like crystal globes, and trembled as if they shone through a depth of clear water. Even as I watched, they began to pale and the sky brightened. Day came suddenly, almost instantaneously. I turned for another look at the blue night, and it was gone. Everywhere the birds began to call, and all manner of little insects began to chirp and hop about in the willows. A breeze sprang up from the west and brought the heavy smell of ripened corn. (Faulkner 76)

The distant star becomes an emblem of the boys' aspiration to go and climb the mesa. Sadly, life carries them away from the freshness and wonder of their vision; none of them ever goes. But the idea of the Enchanted Bluff remains their emblem of escape and adventure, and twenty years later Tip has even passed the idea on to his son.

Accompanying "The Enchanted Bluff" as originally published were one full-page illustration and four small ones, drawn by an artist named Howard E. Smith. They succeed quite well in giving a sense of boyhood and freedom from adult constraints. What they do not give is a sense of the western landscape. Instead, they have the woodsy, shaded look of someplace farther east, perhaps Huckleberry Finn country. Only one, a small end-piece, gives the boys' fantasy of the Enchanted Bluff a pictorial place in the story's presentation, and it is all curves of gentle hills and hollows, from a vantage looking out of darkly shaded woods onto a vision of a more empty but still gentle-looking space with fluffy clouds hanging densely above the far mesa. An altogether too bucolic scene for New Mexico's arid plain and abrupt mesa, it has no flavor of the Southwest whatever (figure 4.16). Certainly the clouds in Smith's end-piece are a far cry from either Benda's minimally indicated clouds in *My Ántonia* or E. Boyd Smith's in *The Land of Little Rain.*

The scene of boys gathered around a campfire, enjoying the adventure of sleeping outside, away from home, was one that held a powerful emotional appeal for Cather. In *Alexander's Bridge* the doomed bridge builder passes such a scene on his train to Quebec, where he will have the fatal encounter with an emblematic crack in the structure that will carry him and his workmen to the bottom. Alexander's glimpse of the boys camping out serves as a reminder of a more innocent and natural life than his own has become.

It is imperative to note that Cather speaks, in "The Enchanted Bluff," as she would in numerous other works including *My Ántonia,* in the voice of a male. Not only personally but in her response to outdoor beauty and the idea of the West, she was already merging the feminine and the masculine. Essentially, she was constructing a gender-neutral aesthetic of the West. It would emerge only three years later in *O Pioneers!* in Alexandra's freedom to take a "man's" role in managing her farm and her sweetheart Carl's freedom to take on "feminine" traits of dreaminess and passivity and to feel unashamed of marrying into Alexandra's property. In addition, and of equal significance biographically, "The Enchanted Bluff" demonstrates that a "still farther West" was serving for Cather herself as an emblem of escape and adventure, even before her first trip to the Southwest.

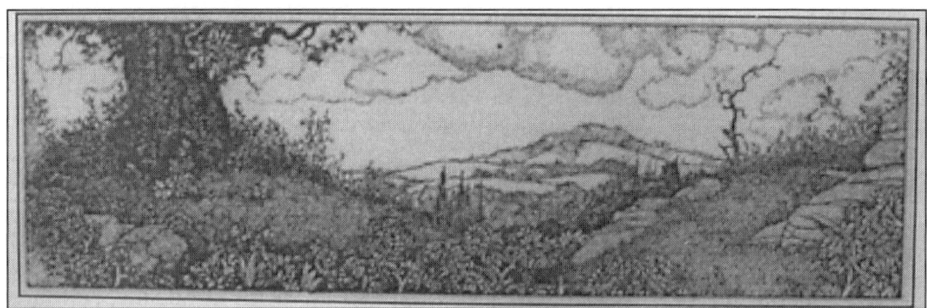

4.16 Howard E. Smith, footer for "The Enchanted Bluff," *Harper's Weekly,* April 1909

The phrase "a still farther West" comes from the *Cleveland Herald* of 1839, as quoted by Dawn Glanz (55). It occurs in a passage that remarkably, for newspaper rhetoric, constructs geography as a symbol for aspiration: "The tide of the past season has been setting toward the west stronger than ever, according to the newspaper sources on the various lines of travel towards the 'land of promise.' The upper Mississippi is no longer the utmost verge of that undefined territory—residents beyond talk of a still farther west." From the perspective of 1839, of course, Cather's writings about Nebraska already inhabit a "farther West." But when she wrote "The Enchanted Bluff" she was looking still farther, beyond the Great Plains to the West she would occupy in her later works, the Southwest of New Mexico and Arizona.

5

CATHER'S SOUTHWEST IN TEXT AND IMAGE

. . . a conception of clouds over distant mesas.

Willa Cather
"Light on Adobe Walls"

I thought I had never seen a landscape
reduced to such simple elements.

Mabel Dodge Luhan
Edge of Taos Desert

In 1925 Cather gave two interviews in which she made rather curious statements about the settings of her fiction. The July issue of *Century Magazine* quotes her as having said, "I write only of the Mid-Western American life that I know thoroughly" (Bohlke 85). Three months earlier she had told a *New York World* interviewer she did not want to become "too identified" with the "Western country," and added, surprisingly, that there was "little of the West in *The Professor's House.*" She then commented, "I love the West so much" (Bohlke 76).

These last half-dozen words would seem to convey more of truth than other parts of her statements about regional identification in her work. Certainly it was not true that she wrote "only" of the Midwest. By 1925 she had published *Alexander's Bridge,* set in Boston and London and ending in Quebec; *The Song of the Lark,* with early scenes in a small town in eastern Colorado, a version of Red Cloud moved west, and major sequences in Chicago, Arizona, and New York; *O Pioneers!* and *My Ántonia,* set in Nebraska; *One of Ours,* which begins in Nebraska before following its befuddled hero to France; and *A Lost Lady,* again set in a renamed version of Red

Cloud, and this is only the novels. Her short stories had roamed from Nebraska to Virginia to New York to Oklahoma, Kansas, Wyoming, Boston, and Pittsburgh, with New York holding primacy for the decade 1915 to 1925. Certainly *The Professor's House,* only six weeks from serialization in *Collier's* when the *World* interview appeared and still in serialization when the interview-article was published in *Century,* had far more of the West in it than merely a "little."[1] Her next novel, *Death Comes for the Archbishop,* already by July 1925 in its earliest stages of writing, would be set almost entirely in New Mexico.

We can guess that Cather's inaccuracy about the place of the West in *The Professor's House* may have been motivated by a desire to escape the limiting label "regionalist." As she said, she did not want to become "too identified" with any one region. But her equally inaccurate statement that she wrote only about the Midwest picks back up with one hand what she had thrown down with the other. Customarily labeled a Great Plains novelist, she is also correctly regarded as a writer of the Southwest, and that fact is of inescapable importance in the novel she was completing even as she misdescribed it. True though it is that in her letters she used the phrase "the West" to refer ambiguously, from a New York perspective, to Nebraska and points west, Cather also left abundant evidence that she thought of the real West as that farther territory. Certainly the boys of "The Enchanted Bluff"—wishful projections of Cather herself—would define it that way. We must finally reject, even while we find in it an element of truth, Bernice Slote's claim that "the real West to Willa Cather was the West of settlement, of the immigration of peoples" (96).

It is well known that Cather first went to the Southwest in 1912 to distance herself from her hectic work for *McClure's* and consider what sort of change she would make in her life. In doing so, she was participating in what can only be called a trend in tourism—surprising as it is to think of Cather as trendy. Anne Farrar Hyde calls "American pride in the western landscape" a "twentieth-century phenomenon" (6–7)—a slight exaggeration, since interest in the West and pride in its scenery were strong by the later nineteenth century. *Picturesque America* alone indicates as much. Hyde's emphasis on descriptive language and tourism, however, goes far toward justifying her claim. Nothing in the experience of nineteenth-century travelers, she writes, "equipped" them to meet the "challenge" of describing or even understanding the western landscape; essentially, they lacked an appropriate vocabulary until, around mid-century, they found a suitable frame of reference in the aesthetic of the sublime. It was this invocation of the sublime, rather than the earlier use of a language of comparison to European models, that allowed the development of a "scenic nationalism" (Hyde 7, 19, 21). Yet even when interest in the West surged, tourists were slow to follow, since explorers' accounts emphasized "hostile" or "threatening" qualities of the environment to be encountered there. The Southwest, in particular, was perceived as "barren, dirty, and backward" even after the more northerly Mountain West had begun to attract admirers of its quasi-Alpine vistas. By 1900, with widespread emphasis on evidence of early civilization on American soil as a counter to Europe's claims to antiquity, the Southwest came to be regarded as "charming and antique" and became a "popular tourist spot" (Hyde 212, 215).[2] It would become more popular yet in the wake of World War I.

In 1912 Cather went to visit her brother Douglass in Winslow, Arizona, where he was stationed with the Santa Fe Railway. Using his house as headquarters, she traveled to nearby attractions including Walnut Canyon (near Flagstaff), which became Panther Canyon in *The Song of the Lark.* In 1915 Cather and Edith Lewis visited Taos and—importantly—Mancos, Colorado, and Mesa Verde National Park, not an easy bit of tourism at the time.[3] Shortly afterward she proposed to Houghton Mifflin to write a travel book of some sort about the area. In keeping with both the visual nature of her imagination and her sense of the market, she intended it to be illustrated.[4] She did in fact write an article about Mesa Verde, which appeared in the *Denver Times* in January 1916, but the proposed travel book, which she seems to have thought of as being in competition with work by Mary Austin, never materialized.[5] Instead, drawing on her encounter with architectural remains of Native culture in Mesa Verde, she wrote a short story that she then called "The Blue Mesa," which remained unpublished, probably because the materials of the story were as yet so fresh. Well-ripened memory was always the main wellspring of Cather's work. She set "The Blue Mesa" aside in order to take up work on *My Ántonia,* but later incorporated it into *The Professor's House* as "Tom Outland's Story"—a staggering accomplishment and an extraordinarily significant product to have come out of a tourist visit.

Yet the importance of the 1915 trip to southwestern Colorado goes even further. An episode that Edith Lewis narrates in her memoir *Willa*

Cather Living indicates just how rigorous the excursion was and gives us a glimpse of its great rewards. The inexperienced guide who led Cather and Lewis in through a deep canyon to see an as yet unexcavated site took them down a dangerously precipitous cliff where they sometimes had to "hang from a tree or rock and then drop several feet to the next rock." Becoming disoriented, he was unable to find a way back up from the canyon floor that could be climbed without ropes. Lewis and Cather wound up sitting on a rock for several hours, waiting for their guide to go find help, as night fell. It was an adventure to remember and one that was reported in newspapers, but the main importance of these hours of being "lost" was the visual treasure Cather found in them. "We did not talk, but watched the long summer twilight come on, and the full moon rise up over the rim of the canyon. The place was very beautiful" (Lewis 97).

Let me pause for a moment over the word "beautiful." In *Birthing a Nation,* Susan Rosowski identifies the catchall descriptor "beautiful," when used by Cather's father in letters written during his western rambles, with "conventions of a masculine West." Judging his statements that pronghorn antelope were "the most beautiful thing you can imagine" and the prairies themselves "beautiful beyond description" to be "comically self-conscious," Rosowski seems to say that any "description of place or landscape in the conventional sense" is a masculine convention (33). In this connection, I think of Tom and Roddy in the mesa country in *The Professor's House.* Many aspects of their approach to the landscape—its adventurous quality, their readiness to lay claim to what they find—replicate a stereotypical masculinist westering. But in my reading, their pronouncing the place "beautiful" does not. When Cather wrote these scintillating landscape descriptions of the mesa she was of course assuming Tom's voice, but we see an at least equal willingness to write landscape description when she was looking through the eyes of Thea Kronborg in *The Song of the Lark.* As the phrase I have quoted about their hours sitting on a rock indicates, we also see such willingness on the part of Edith Lewis. Elizabeth Shepley Sergeant remembers Cather herself writing "vivid" descriptions of Arizona and sharing Sergeant's own "passion" for "landscape and weather" (89, 168). Rather than the adoption of a stale masculine convention, the landscape descriptions in her western and southwestern fiction might be regarded as evidence of that "intimacy with nature" that Sergeant sees as lying "at the very root" of her creativity (130), and thus as a much more complexly gendered habit of perception and expression than Rosowski implies in her objection to the word "beautiful."

To borrow Lewis's words about a later trip to the Southwest that provided misadventures of a different sort, the quiet and unstructured times that Cather spent in these rugged, open spaces "heightened the special character of a journey" by "fix[ing] the light, the colours, the whole mood" in her memory (141). Light, colors, mood: these are the primary elements of Cather's writing about the Southwest.

The year after Cather visited Mesa Verde, she returned to New Mexico, to Taos, which she praised enthusiastically in a letter to Elizabeth Sergeant. In 1925 she and Lewis visited the Grand Canyon, the San Gabriel Ranch near Española, and again Taos, where they stayed at the "formidable" Mabel Dodge Luhan's compound (Woodress 363). Although Cather insisted on a good measure of privacy while there, we can well believe that when she returned from her rambles with Tony Luhan in his Cadillac at dinner time she would have discussed the beauties of what she had seen with Mabel, whose own writing during the 1920s and 1930s was "inspired" by the "image of Taos as a garden of Eden, inhabited by an unfallen tribe of men and women" (Rudnick, Introduction xii). The traces of such conversations may, indeed, have contributed to *Death Comes for the Archbishop,* the masterwork that Cather conceived that summer—as we know that Tony Luhan's manner and name did.[6] That is, Cather's seeing may have been enriched by Mabel Dodge Luhan's seeing—another point of connection in the network I see as an alternative western tradition of Austin's and Cather's own.

For all their differences in temperament and persona, and what would have been a real difference as to whether Taos was home to unfallen humanity, Cather's and Luhan's responses to the Southwest had much in common. Luhan writes in *Edge of Taos Desert* that when she left New York for New Mexico in 1917 "no one ever went" there and "hardly anyone had ever even heard of Santa Fe" (3). Perhaps she meant hardly anyone in her own circle. She speaks of what she found in New Mexico in terms of visual and mental clarity and of authenticity. For her it was a fulfillment of the "yearning for fundamentals" that Lois Rudnick sees as having drawn Cather, D. H. Lawrence, and Georgia O'Keeffe as well (Introduction xii). Describing her initial impressions of Santa Fe, Luhan exclaims, "How *good* this fresh air, this clear simplicity." On her first morning she sat on a slope above the town, noting "how everything was intensified for one—sight, sound, and taste," and felt "more awake and more aware" than ever before (*Edge of Taos Desert* 10, 18). It was a sense of awakening to a clarified view of life that characterized the response to New Mexico of many literary and artistic visitors, Cather and Austin not least among them. Luhan's delight in the absence of clutter, in particular, resonates Cather's avowed and Austin's intermittently practiced minimalist aesthetics: "There was no disturbance in the scene, nothing to complicate the forms, no trees or houses, or any detail to confuse one. It was like a simple phrase in music or a single line of poetry, essential and reduced to the barest meaning" (*Edge* 59).

Despite her joy in the natural setting of Santa Fe, Mabel quickly moved on to Taos. There, in addition to a "vibrant and revealing light" and clear, "shining" air that "brought out every height and depth of tone and color in the natural world" (*Edge* 59, 32), she found the Pueblo people (and specifically Tony Luhan) whom she credited with bringing her to a kind of rebirth, despite the "illimitable distance between us [Anglos] and them" (58). Inverting the traditional captivity narrative to make it, instead, a redemption narrative, she wrote of being "captured" out of a life of inauthenticity. We can doubt the sincerity of her avowed wish that she belonged at the pueblo, given her continuing patronage of Art with a capital A, but she did demonstrate its genuineness to the extent of building a house and adjacent cottages near enough to the pueblo that Tony, whose personal presence was so powerfully attractive for Cather as well as for many others among Mabel's guests, could readily go back and forth. We can see simply in the physical arrangement the spatial diagram, as it were, of a new and more irenic racial dynamic in the West.[7]

Luhan's vision of a biracial community in the West was unquestionably tinged with exoticism. In claiming that she had been "redeemed" or had regained paradise (Rudnick, Introduction xiii), she went much further into an orientalizing vision of the Native than Cather or even Austin ever did. Speaking of the people of Taos and Santo Domingo (another pueblo of special significance to her), she employed tropes of mystery and occult knowledge that effectively othered them and maintained the very "distance" between white and dark that she purported to wish to bridge. Impervious to this aspect of her own response, however, she could only rejoice that her "heart grew clear" and she felt "befriended" by the world (*Edge* 12, 32).

I am not aware if Cather ever commented on *Edge of Taos Desert.* She did praise the earlier volumes of Luhan's memoir, especially its achievement of a sense of reality of the place itself (*Calendar* #1036). In a letter of 1930, when she was in Paris, she seems to have counted on Mabel to understand when she expressed weariness of festive occasions and said she missed New Mexico (*Calendar* #1014). At the moment she jotted that letter, and when she wrote of the Southwest in much the same way elsewhere, she was conceiving of the landscape and way of life as a retreat from busyness and artificiality—much as Mabel conceived it.

In the summer of 1925, while staying at La Fonda in Santa Fe after her two weeks with the Luhans, Cather found a copy of William Howlett's biography of Father Joseph Machebeuf, assistant and friend of Bishop Lamy, first bishop and archbishop of Santa Fe, and her conception of *Death Comes for the Archbishop* crystallized. The next summer, deeply engaged in the writing of the book, she made what was to be her last trip to the Southwest. During this visit she spent several days or part-days writing in the living room of Mary Austin's new house while Austin was away for medical reasons. She especially enjoyed working beside a big open window in the library of the quiet house, but flared into anger when Austin started telling people she had written her noted book there. Sergeant gives an account of Austin's pointing to a certain chair and saying that Cather sat there to write *Archbishop.* Cather, Sergeant writes, was "exasperated" when she told her about it (236). Cather and Austin had a great deal in common, including their deep joy in the Southwest and its people, but their friendship suffered after this violation, as Cather considered it, of her privacy. It suffered further when Austin proclaimed in her autobiography that Cather's celebration of things French in *Archbishop* was a "calamity" for the local culture (*EH* 359).

As with Quebec, after publication of *Shadows on the Rock,* and even her native Virginia, after publication of *Sapphira and the Slave Girl,* Cather seemed to lose interest in visiting the place she had loved so much after she had drunk up its use for her writing. Perhaps the places she had written about in a way that satisfied her existed for her thereafter so totally in her books that she no longer needed their geographic reality. Her years of travel in the Southwest had resulted in three major novels. She never returned.

* * *

In writing about the Southwest, Cather produced word-pictures of extraordinary clarity and vividness. This visual quality of language in *The Song of the Lark, The Professor's House,* and *Death Comes for the Archbishop* would seem to lend itself well to illustration. Photographer Laura Gilpin thought so, at any rate. She "hoped to interest Cather in collaborating on an illustrated edition" of *The Professor's House* but failed in efforts to reach her (Sandweiss 66). Yet all three novels, in their original book form, were published without pictures. The serialization of *The Professor's House* in *Collier's* was stylishly illustrated, however, and the Knopf second edition of *Archbishop,* in 1929, which I will consider at some length, featured illustrations by Harold von Schmidt.

Even though *The Song of the Lark* was never serialized or illustrated in book form, it nevertheless raises a significant question of picture–text interaction. The dust jacket of the first edition featured a reproduction of Jules Breton's painting *The Song of the Lark* (figure 5.01), which Cather had seen and admired at the Art Institute of Chicago and had drawn on for her title (Woodress 259, March 719). Clearly, the painting does not convey either Thea's appearance or the landscape of the decisive scenes in the Southwest when she reconceives her musical identity. Despite having initially promoted its use on the jacket (as her correspondence with Ferris Greenslet during April 1915 demonstrates), Cather later came to feel that both the jacket and the title had been a bad idea in that they were essentially misleading, implying that the "song" was Thea's own, in the person of the open-mouthed peasant girl.[8] She had intended a considerably more subtle connection. The girl in Breton's painting is supposed to be looking up with open-mouthed wonder upon hearing a lark singing above. The representation, then, is of Thea's "hearing" the call of beauty and aspiration—probably too abstract a conception to be conveyed pictorially.[9]

If it is true, as Cather told an interviewer, that *The Song of the Lark* was the greatest pleasure to write of any of her novels up through *One of Ours* (Bohlke 31), the reason may lie in the opportunity it afforded her to shape her own development of artistic vocation into a mythic form through the story of Thea Kronborg and to relive the transforming impact of her 1912 trip to the Southwest. The sequence of Thea's retreat to the ranch owned by Fred Ottenberg's father and the empty cliff dwellings located there is told

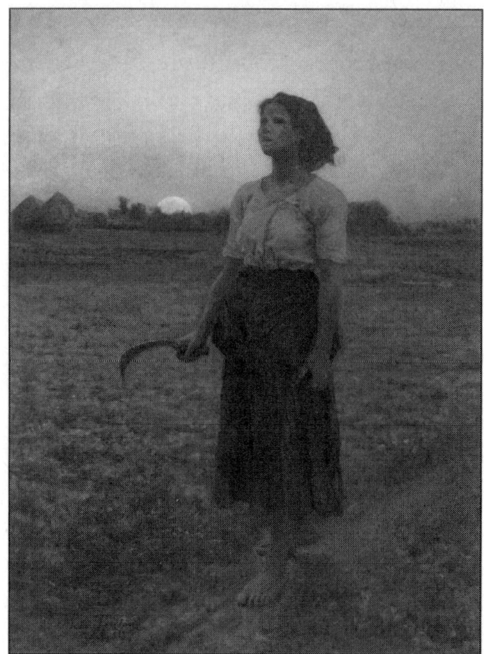

5.01 Jules Breton, French (1827–1906), *The Song of the Lark,* 1884, oil on canvas, 110.6 x 85.8 cm (Henry Field Memorial Collection, 1894.1033. Reproduction, The Art Institute of Chicago. Photography copyright © The Art Institute of Chicago)

with a sense of exhilaration in the dramatic landforms and the clearness of the air, and a sense of release and boundlessness.

The southwestern sequence of the novel, Part IV, begins with a magnificent, albeit brief, description of the "blue slopes" and "snowy summit" of what Cather calls San Francisco Mountain, actually Humphreys Peak *in* the San Francisco Mountains, standing in "inexorable reserve" just to the north of Flagstaff (*SL* 233). Lying "about its base," the passage continues, are

> the pine forests of the Navajos, where the great red-trunked trees live out their peaceful centuries in that sparkling air. The piñons and scrub begin only where the forest ends, where the country breaks into open, stony clearings and the surface of the earth cracks into deep cañons. The great pines stand at a considerable distance from each other. They do not intrude upon each other.

These solitary trees become a metaphor for the Navajos themselves, a people who have traditionally lived in widely scattered familial groups rather than in the pueblos that Anglo observers of southwestern Indians found so preferable. It is a splendid and expressive opening paragraph to the sequence, but one unfortunately marred by a groundless assertion that the Navajo language itself "is not a communicative one," along with a curiously nonvisual and essentially meaningless statement that each tree in that forest "has its exalted power to bear" (*SL* 233). What, one wonders, would a noncommunicative language be? And how would a tree "bear"—in the sense of having to bear a burden, not in the sense of producing or conveying an implication—an "exalted power"? What would that power be? It is not her attempt to attribute portentous meaning to the landscape, then, that makes the description of the mountain and its forest so magical, but its sense of "sparkling air," deep contentment (trees living out "peaceful centuries"), and the drama of the land's "break[ing]" and "crack[ing]" into canyon country. These are attributes of place that will continue through Cather's textual scene-painting in *The Song of the Lark* and into the equally visual landscape sequences of *The Professor's House* and *Death Comes for the Archbishop.*

The phrase "sparkling air," with the added adjective "high," will come in again in the third paragraph of Part IV, while the "blue slopes" and "snowy summit" of the initial word-picture are elaborated by the accrual of details and dynamic motion. It is as if the picture were made into a moving picture, tracing Thea's shifting views of the mountain as she rides southeast from Flagstaff in a democrat wagon, with the scene off to the north being obscured or revealed by the undulating slopes and the thickening or thinning tree branches. Once again scene becomes metaphoric for human presence:

> Old Biltmer followed a faint wagon-trail which ran southeast, and which, as they travelled, continually dipped lower, falling away from the high plateau on the slope of which Flagstaff sits. The white peak of the mountain, the snow gorges above the timber, now disappeared from time to time as the road dropped and dropped, and the forest closed behind the wagon. More than the mountain disappeared as the forest closed thus. Thea seemed to be taking very little through the wood with her. The personality of which she was so tired seemed to let go of her.

> The high, sparkling air drank it up like blotting-paper. It was lost in the thrilling blue of the new sky and the song of the thin wind in the piñons. (*SL* 233)

The "blotting-paper" action of air here recalls the "erasure of personality" Cather felt when she first went to Nebraska, reworded in Jim Burden's anxious plaint that "between that earth and that sky I felt erased, blotted out" (*MA* 8). But now the connotation is altogether different. Thea's constructed self (which is what I take "personality" to mean) has become a burden to her real self, and it is a relief when the seemingly endless ("high") reservoir of dry air—literally, Arizona's low humidity, in a place seen with eyes able to perceive beauty—soaks the falseness off of her as if blotting up wet mold. Part of that falseness is an artificially constructed notion of feminine gender that Thea redefines by giving vent to her "underlying masculinity" (Sivils 13), or her "androgyny" (Rosowski, "Female" 237). During her time at the canyon, she enjoys the kind of muscular exercise conventionally seen as masculine, while at the same time, in her imagination she identifies with a female presence in the landscape lingering on from the lives of Native women long ago.

Throughout her time at the ranch, with many days spent in the cliff-side rooms at the canyon, Thea continues to exult in the dramatically vertical landscape, especially its spaciousness and its light and colors. Cather captures the visual impression of these canyons and cliffs as "abrupt fissures," "great fold[s] in the rock," "wrinkle[s] of the cliff," "perpendicular" assemblages "made up of ledges and boulders." Her descriptions often use a language of architecture—"jagged" walls with "platforms," "ledges," and alcoves (*SL* 234, 235, 241, 251). These forms are also challenges to Thea's and Fred's athleticism as they hike and climb, and thus become—as we have seen Cather's settings do repeatedly—emblematic projections of life's challenges, beckoning Thea on to greater achievement as an artist. "I'm not going to stop now until I get there," she insists, as she and Fred try to climb to a group of very high cliff dwellings by an eroded trail. "I'll go on alone" (251). Her insistence on reaching so high a goal by so difficult a route prefigures her determined pursuit of her professional goals. It prefigures, as well, the austerity and isolation of her success. Cather refuses to define Thea's refusal to depend on Fred, either when climbing or when pursuing her career, as unwomanly.

These rugged cliffs and the hollowed dwellings they hold are equally austere. Little wonder Thea finds her real self in this environment! They are "clean with the cleanness of sun-baked, wind-swept places," "full of sun"; a "river of blue air" flows between them, a "great wash of air" that is richly invigorating (*SL* 235, 252). (A motif of blueness runs throughout the section from its salute to the "blue slopes" of what Cather erroneously calls San Francisco Mountain.) Like the cliffs and hollows, Thea is able to let herself become, for the time being, "a mere receptacle" for the essence of the place. She could "become" a color, "like the bright lizards that darted about on the hot stones outside her door," the opening of her chosen cave, or "become" a "continuous repetition of sound, like the cicadas" (*SL* 237). This emptying of herself so that she is fully open to "sustained sensation" allows her to develop an experiential sense of her art, and thus the capacity to move it to a higher level. Even the colors around her deepen in richness and nuance.

In what Cather probably intended to be her ultimate word-picture of the place, the set-piece of the sunrise when Thea and Fred have hiked out to the cliff dwellings early to cook breakfast there, descriptive richness perhaps overreaches, but is undeniably luscious in its rendition of color and light, with the "red sun" touching the edge of the rim with "coppery fire," "thin red clouds" beginning to "boil" as the warmth increases, and moist brush and piñon trees "glittering and trembling, swimming in the liquid gold" (*SL* 247). Touches of gold, purple, red, and tan chase each other through the chapter until even the air itself, with the approach of a storm (a set-piece in descriptions of desert places and the Rocky Mountains familiar from Ferde Grofé's *Grand Canyon Suite*), turns a "turbid green" that grows "murkier and murkier" and at last even "change[s] to purple" (*SL* 254). The words evoke a sense of atmospheric drama. As Rosowski correctly and insightfully observes, "the air may be at least as important as the land in Cather's idea of the West, and breathing freely may be a defining feature of her frontier" (*Birthing a Nation* 56).

Cather would later conclude that the lushness of her visual representation in *The Song of the Lark* as well as other over-elaborated aspects of the novel made it an example of undisciplined writing. In part, this judgment was a response to the criticism offered by William Heinemann when he rejected *Lark* on grounds of its being too ample in style and scope. This rejection must have hurt at the time; she was still struggling to establish herself as an artist, as well as to make a living. But it would prove as constructive as Sarah Orne Jewett's advice to write what she knew, from her own "parish." Rarely, after *The Song of the Lark,* would she convey the visual character or emotional impact of a landscape through extended description.

Like *The Song of the Lark,* so *The Professor's House,* set mostly in indoor spaces within distant sight of Lake Michigan, turns on a central episode set in the Southwest, "Tom Outland's Story." In both, Cather's visual language is one of cleanness, dryness, big skies, and soaring spaces, with an emphasis on color and light.

In her article "Mesa Verde," published in the *Denver Times* in January 1916, Cather called the area that would serve as the model for Tom's Blue Mesa a "land of sharp contours, brutal contrasts, glorious color and blinding light."[10] When she came to write *The Professor's House* less than a decade later, she would economically particularize the "sharp contours" but leave the contrasts unasserted, to be realized by the reader, and colors would show themselves "glorious" rather than be labeled as such. It is a distinction New Critics used to call showing rather than telling. Cather would drop trite descriptors like "blinding," leaving the word-pictures in *The Professor's House* in a sense more literal. Colors, for example, are established almost solely through naming, usually without modifiers. At the same time, they are more synesthetic—as in Tom Outland's reference to his time on the mesa as "that summer, high and blue" (*PH* 252). He does not tell us the meaning; he does not describe its affective quality except in words that do not literally describe "summer"; he simply posits it: "there was that summer, high and blue." The plain descriptors "high" and "blue" indicate more than a literal referent. (How can a summer be "high"?) It is an enormous advance in Cather's evocative powers over the fuller, more embroidered style of *Lark,* and certainly over her article about Mesa Verde, significant though it is. Even so, the central idea of the place would remain essentially the same as in the 1916 article.[11]

We can see from her language, in both the article and the novel, at least some part of the reason why Cather so loved the Southwest: an integrity of overall structure, as seen in the little still city Tom first glimpses through falling snow, and an "absence of clutter" that serves as "a reproach to the messiness in which we live" (*PH* 331). On this point of bareness versus clutter, as well as with respect to the interest they shared in the traditional

Spanish religious art of New Mexico, Cather, Mabel Dodge Luhan, and Georgia O'Keeffe shared an aesthetic, the minimalist aesthetic Cather enunciated in 1922, three years before *The Professor's House,* in "The Novel Démeublé." Of course, she would not always adhere to the principles she enunciated there. Certainly she did not do so in *One of Ours,* also published in 1922.[12]

The *Professor's House* was serialized in *Collier's* in June, July, and August of 1925. In a notice that appeared the week before the first number, the magazine touted both Cather's reputation, as evidenced by her Pulitzer Prize, and the "amazing pictorial beauty" of the new work. The ensuing serialization was lavishly illustrated by the recognized magazine artist Frank Street (1893–1944). Yet given the "essential and reduced" nature of Cather's word-pictures of Tom Outland's Southwest, Street's illustrations seem almost incongruous. They are lively and competent but for the most part heavy and enclosed. Thirteen of the twenty drawings (including the cover of the issue in which the first number appeared) are indoor scenes, mostly of social occasions. Of the seven outdoor scenes, one (on the cover) shows Professor St. Peter in his swim cap; another shows him swimming, wearing the same cap; one shows Tom Outland arriving at the professor's walled garden, so closed-in a space that the picture has a decidedly indoor feel to it despite the hoe in the professor's hand; and one shows St. Peter sitting on a grassy bank, thinking. That leaves only three of the twenty for outdoor scenes on the mesa—even though it was the mesa section, Book II, that Cather famously referred to in pictorial terms as the window opening onto the sea in a Dutch painting. Perhaps one could say that this distribution echoes her structural design, which was to make the atmosphere "rather overcrowded and stuffy" and then "open the square window and let in the fresh air that blew off the Blue Mesa" (*On Writing* 31). If so, it is overbalanced; the "overcrowded and stuffy" effect stifles the breath of "fresh air."

Even in the three illustrations showing the mesa there is little sense of spaciousness and openness, and thus a failure of complementarity to the text. Probably the most striking of the three, first showing the deserted cave houses (figure 5.02), appeared on the title page of the July 11 number (a slight oddity, since the number actually begins with a continuation of Book One, "The Family," with "Tom Outland's Story" coming a page later). In the upper right corner we see the "little city of stone, asleep . . . in the face of the cliff"

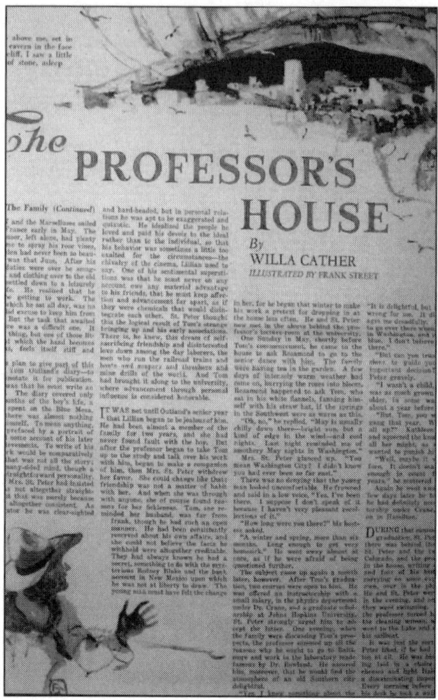

The PROFESSOR'S HOUSE

By WILLA CATHER

ILLUSTRATED BY FRANK STREET

5.02 Frank Street, illustration for *The Professor's House*, *Collier's Magazine*, July 11, 1925 (p. 24)

(*PH* 199), and in the lower left Tom gazing up at it, his hand lifted in astonishment. The paragraphs of print, as well as the title and Cather's and Street's names, become the intervening landscape across which he looks—the same device as the E. Boyd Smith drawing of the coyote looking at the full moon across a hillside of print in *The Land of Little Rain.* White space, although not extensive, gives some impression of openness. In that same number, a second illustration shows a dark, cramped interior with Tom watching while Roddy Blake sleeps. If there is any hint of the West, it is Tom's wide-brimmed hat.

In the July 18 number, the illustration surrounding the title shows Father Duchene standing with Tom in front of the cliff dwellings in an attitude of reverence. Rather unaccountably, both are positioned with their backs to the ruins and there is no hint of the landscape except as we can infer it from the dark mouth of the cave. The secondary illustration in this number is again an indoor scene, Tom at lunch with the helpful government worker in Washington, when he goes to seek government funding for preserving the

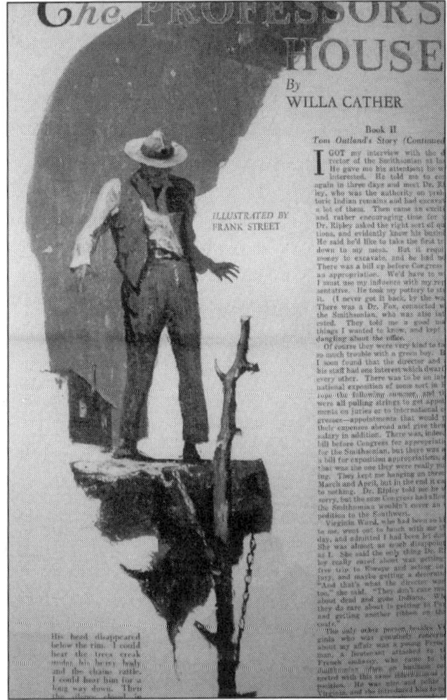

5.03 Frank Street, illustration for *The Professor's House, Collier's Magazine,* July 25, 1925 (p. 22)

relics he and Roddy have found on the mesa. The last of the three pictures on the mesa is the title illustration of the next-to-last number, on July 25 (figure 5.03). It shows Tom, recognizable only by his hat (for his torso and limbs look heavier and older than we probably imagine), gazing down over the side of a ledge after (as we know only from the words excerpted as a caption) the departing Roddy, after they have quarreled. It is night; there is a hint of blurry stars; and again we get no sense of the expansive southwestern landscape except as we can infer it from the rocky ledge.

Cather seems not to have cared greatly about the serialization of the novel except as it made good business sense. Even so, it is hard to imagine that she could have been very pleased with Street's illustrations. One especially wonders what she thought of the distinctly Mephistophelean representations of Professor St. Peter.

In contrast to the mere glimpse of spaciousness in the *Collier's* illustrations, the text itself opens up a large window through which we see an austere but expansive world. Like early settlers on the Great Plains, Cather acknowledges the overwhelming and potentially disorienting nature of the flat prairie in Tom Outland's observation that "the Blue Mesa was one of the landmarks we always saw from Tarpin—landmarks that mean so much in a flat country" (*PH* 185). But the mesa serves as far more than merely a landmark. Tom is fascinated by its color and its air of mystery—a "naked blue rock" that "nobody had ever climbed . . . set down alone in the plain, almost square, except that the top was higher at one end" (*PH* 185). He and his friend Roddy plan to climb it when their employer sends them to tend cattle on their winter range, near the mesa. It quickly becomes, for them, an emblem of adventure and challenge, while retaining its value of scenic beauty.

The most frequently noted descriptive passage in the entire Tom Outland section of the novel is the moment when Tom first glimpses the cliff city. Beautifully realized in prose as crystalline as the air itself, it is intensely visual:

> I wish I could tell you what I saw there, just as I saw it, on that first morning, through a veil of lightly falling snow. Far up above me, a thousand feet or so, set in a great cavern in the face of the cliff, I saw a little city of stone, asleep. It was as still as sculpture—and something like that. It all hung together, seemed to have a kind of composition: pale little houses of stone nestling close to one another, perched on top of each other, with flat roofs, narrow windows, straight walls, and in the middle of the group, a round tower. (199)

The passage conveys a sense of having named the essentials—walls, windows, tower—while more affective language catches the emotional impact: "nestling," "perched," "asleep." But it is the phrase "veil of snow" that most gives the passage its ineffable quality. These words are repeated, but compressed, verbatim from Cather's newspaper article "Mesa Verde," where Richard Wetherill also first glimpsed the Mesa Verde ruins "thru a veil of lightly falling snow" (*PH* 330).

In the seventy-six pages of "Tom Outland's Story," clear air and quality of light are explicitly singled out for notice in at least eight passages, and color in at least five more, not counting the synesthetic attachment of "blue" to the word "summer." Days at the winter pasture, near the foot of the mesa, are "blue and gold" and the nights "clear" and "frosty" (*PH* 189). Blue, gold, and lavender or purple are the predominant palette throughout, giving the language here a kind of splendor that has nothing to do with wordiness. Tom's first approach to the mesa, on a winter morning, is rendered in clear and briskly sensuous writing:

> The bluish rock and the sun-tanned grass, under the unusual purple-grey of the sky, gave the whole valley a very soft colour, lavender and pale gold. . . . It may have been the hint of snow in the air, but it seemed to me that I had never breathed in anything that tasted so pure as the air in that valley. It made my mouth and nostrils smart like charged water, seemed to go to my head a little and produce a kind of exaltation. (*PH* 198)

The coldness, combined with the clearness of the air, makes the passage almost astringent. When Tom and Roddy are living up in the stone city, exploring and excavating its treasures, they look out onto "an ocean of clear air" (*PH* 211). And when Tom returns to the mesa after his months in Washington, with all their frustrations, it is the air that most stirs him. His response is again conveyed within a palette of gold and violet:

> And the air, my God, what air!—Soft, tingling, gold, hot with an edge of chill on it, full of the smell of piñons—it was like breathing the sun, breathing the colour of the sky. Down there behind me was the plain, already streaked with shadow, violet and purple and burnt orange until it met the horizon. (*PH* 239–40)

The light, in this place of clear air, is of a quality that has intrigued more visitors than Cather, both before and since. At daybreak, she writes, it turns the mesa top red and the cedar trees and rocks "gold," a "metallic" color "like tarnished gold-foil" (*PH* 190). Things "fairly swim" in the light (239), which at certain times of day produces a sharpened clarity so that Tom sees lines and shadows more clearly than even his observant eyes have caught them at other times. "Playing into" the "still yellow" rabbit-brush, the "horizontal rays of light . . . brought out the contour of the ground with great distinctness" (*PH* 191–92).

Tom Outland has in fact come to the mesa country precisely for its air, having been advised by his physician to "live in the open all summer" after a bout of pneumonia (*PH* 184)—a reflection of a widespread belief that the dry air of the Southwest was a curative for respiratory problems. According to Weigle and Fiore, "convalescents" began arriving soon after the Treaty of Guadalupe Hidalgo in 1848, "seeking dry, clean air and sunshine," and Santa Fe was "proclaimed to have the ideal weather for sufferers from consumption and other lung ailments" (Weigle and Fiore 5).[13] Sunmount Sanitarium, established in Santa Fe in 1902 under the name Tent City as a pulmonary hospital, was also promoted more generally as a "health resort" (Weigle and Fiore 10). Alice Corbin Henderson, co-editor of *Poetry* magazine, came there in 1916 seeking a cure for tuberculosis. Cather would have known her, or at least known of her, from her position at *Poetry* as well as through Mabel Dodge Luhan, who came to Santa Fe the same year. Corbin Henderson's 1922 anthology *The Turquoise Trail* included a poem by Cather, and in that same year Cather's onetime fellow editor at *McClure's,* Witter Bynner, came to visit Corbin Henderson at Sunmount, where she was again in residence as a patient (Weigle and Fiore 18). Quite apart from these specifics, it seems self-evident that Cather would have been aware of New Mexico's image as a place of resort for health seekers. Such an image would have held special meaning for her since one reason her own family went to Nebraska from damp Virginia was the recurrence of tuberculosis in the family. One of her poems about the Great Plains, "Macon Prairie (Nebraska)," dramatizes the death of her "Westward-faring" aunt Jennie, who died of tuberculosis not long after migrating to Nebraska in 1877.[14]

It is not surprising, then, that this idea of the restorative quality of the dry air in the Southwest is important in both *The Song of the Lark* and *The Professor's House.* Thea goes to Arizona after wearing down her health in Chicago and is revitalized; we see her restored vigor in her hiking, climbing, and playing at sword-fighting with Fred. When Tom spends a summer alone on the mesa he feels a "vitality . . . too high to be clouded"—language that evokes the quality of the air itself (*PH* 251). We can see in Cather's emphasis on visual delight, quiet, and the restoration of health a turning away from the Western's traditional interest in violence and conquest. Conquest is not entirely absent, however; Tom and Roddy relish the physical adventure of their exploration and have no hesitation about expropriating the relics of Native civilization that they find. Yet that very fact contributes to the sense of tragic solemnity that hangs over the entire novel. It is not celebrated.

In addition to its clear air, the altitude and vertical planes of the mesa are particularly noted. In terms of its steepness and crevices, the landscape at times takes on a threatening quality, which we see fulfilled when the donkey carrying "Mother Eve" falls from the trail. Tom warns Roddy about the danger of climbing down at night, especially in a state of anger. This land has none of the softness and yieldingness Cather celebrated in Thea's perception of the Great Plains from the train window. But the unfamiliar jutting heights of the mesa also give it majesty. The dangers of falling and of storms that would "pounce on us like a panther without warning" (*PH* 191) are inseparable from the mesa's awesome beauty. "No wonder the thing bothered us and tempted us," Tom exclaims, being "always before us" and "always changing," standing up against the horizon at sunset like "one great ink-black rock against a sky on fire" (*PH* 191). But what is important in this rugged setting is not conflict or adventure but an image of protected tranquility—the sleeping stone city hangs "like a bird's nest in the cliff, looking off into the box canyon below" (*PH* 211). Not only does Cather's presentation of Tom's Blue Mesa appropriate a language of the sublime and of the long expanses of time that Americans longed for in their land, but it folds a language of shelter and nurturance ("like a bird's nest") into the steepness and rockiness. The impact of her sense of place here comes from its combination of peril with wonder and with an implicitly female enclosure. It is a powerful mix.

In considering the complementarity between the Benda illustrations to *My Ántonia* and Cather's visual language, we saw how involved she was in shaping the total experience conveyed to a reader through the physical object of the book. The record of her interactions with her editor is extraordinarily full. It shows her not only working to develop the illustrations she wanted, but insisting that they be printed on the same paper as the text and in the same ink, specifying the kind of paper that should be, and as early as March 13, 1917, when the manuscript was still far from complete, specifying the font and the color of binding she wanted.[15] She demanded to see the resulting "visual effect" as soon as Houghton Mifflin had a dummy set. Even her decision to have her name shown without her customary middle initial was a visual one, based on her impression of its appearance in conjunction with the title just above it.[16]

In this history of Cather's involvement in the total communicative product that constituted *My Ántonia,* we see an author's shaping of what Jerome McGann calls an "iconic" text (53). Indeed, in light of this history (supported by an extraordinarily full archival record) we might question McGann's statement, in his truly magisterial book *The Textual Condition,* that William Blake is "unique in the history of English literature precisely because of his effort to bring every aspect of the signifying process, linguistic as well as bibliographical, under authorial control" (57). Perhaps that is true in the most literal sense, since Blake was the master workman on every aspect of his books of poems, whereas Cather proved unable to execute her own drawings satisfactorily. But she moved very far along the continuum of authorial control. McGann himself mentions, as a similar example to Blake, Ezra Pound's collaborative involvement in the production of an iconic reading field in *A Draft of XVI Cantos* in 1925, eight years after the publication of *My Ántonia* and in the same year as *The Professor's House.* When we read about Pound's designation of papers, colors of ink, and page arrangement, with a similar invocation of the history of bookmaking (McGann 122–23, 130, 138), we may feel that we have stepped back into the world of Cather's correspondence with Houghton Mifflin.

A similar level of involvement on Cather's part is evident in the publication of an ornamented second edition of *Death Comes for the Archbishop* in 1929, after the first edition, in 1927, was published with no illustrations except on the dust jacket. In turning to this last and, in her own mind (as well as the minds of many of her readers), greatest of her fictional engagements with the Southwest, we again see her shaping the "bibliographical signifiers" that make up its visual "reading field" (McGann 57). In this case the documentary record is not nearly so complete as for *My Ántonia.* Even so, it is sufficient to demonstrate once again how visual Cather's imagination was and how important to her was the total physical package in which her verbal text was conveyed to readers.

Unlike the usual experience of reading *My Ántonia,* for which the Benda drawings are normally retained, readers of *Archbishop* almost inevitably encounter some variant of the unillustrated first edition. Even scholars quite familiar with her work are likely not to have seen the second edition and its illustrations. Most, like myself, may not even have been aware of its existence prior to Charles Mignon's work on the printing history of the novel.

Mignon states in his textual essay to the scholarly edition that Cather herself "preferred the illustrated edition" (523). Perhaps so, but there is conflicting evidence. A notation in the Knopf company's records quoted by Mignon does indicate that in 1940 at any rate, Cather was "insist[ing]" that the illustrated edition be reprinted (Mignon 534). But in September 1929, just prior to its release, she had written to Blanche Knopf that she did *not* like the illustrated version, but since it had been done, she hoped it would be out in time for the Christmas trade (*Calendar* #980). It was. In a letter to Alfred Knopf in 1933 (dated only "September 24," but with the year clearly visible from its processing into the Knopf office) she confessed to becoming persuaded of the soundness of his plan for the illustrated edition (*Calendar* #1194). This statement is probably not an endorsement of the second edition as a whole, however, but a reference to Knopf's plan to issue the "December Night" section as a separate publication with decorations elaborating upon those of the second edition. Clearly, she was pleased with the little booklet that resulted. She sent a copy to Zoë Akins as a Christmas present and said in the accompanying note that she thought the pictures were quite effective (*Calendar* #1207). Still, an expensively decorated gift booklet intended for Christmas trade is a very different matter from a novel.

I find Cather's preference for the illustrated *Archbishop*—if she did prefer it—surprising. She had often objected to the illustrations published with her works in the past, and in 1937 would reject in the most emphatic terms a proposal by Houghton Mifflin to reissue *My Ántonia* with color illustrations by Grant Wood (*Calendar* #1385).[17] In any event, if she did want the illustrated *Archbishop* to become standard, she was disappointed. Because of wartime paper shortages, Knopf reset the book in 1944 following the *first* edition rather than the second, which not only had been designed with oversized pages but ran forty pages longer (Mignon, Textual Essay 552). The available record is silent on Cather's reaction to this decision; she seems to have accepted it, if not out of preference for the original, then out of her awareness of wartime hardships and her enormous trust in Alfred Knopf's judgment and goodwill. Some years earlier she had told Knopf that she liked the typeface of the second edition, its wide type block, illustrations, and heavy paper because she believed they gave the book a "handmade look . . . as if it had been printed on a country press," as she wished it to look (Mignon, Textual Essay, 555)—a statement that firmly links her thinking about the illustrated *Archbishop* to her thinking about the physical properties of *Ántonia,* since she also saw Benda's pen-and-ink drawings as an allusion to earlier modes of bookmaking.[18] Her statement demonstrates, once again, her sensitivity to the appropriateness or inappropriateness of the visual "reading field" to particular texts. In 1934, when Knopf proposed using the same font as in the second edition *Archbishop* for *Lucy Gayheart,* she rejected the idea on grounds that it was unsuitable for that more modern and romantic novel (*Calendar* #1229).

Harold von Schmidt (1893–1982), the illustrator for the second edition, had already done the dust jacket for the first edition as well as illustrations for the serialization of *Archbishop* in the *Forum.* According to his own statement, he was selected to do the second edition at Cather's insistence. Von Schmidt would also do the "lavish" ink illuminations for the excerpted "December Night" issued separately in 1933, 1934, and 1935 (Mignon, Textual Essay, 520, 522). Just as W. T. Benda might have, von Schmidt described his work with Cather in terms of collaboration (Mignon 520): "I worked for two years on these sixty-odd drawings for Willa Cather's beautifully written story of old New Mexico. She had insisted with her publisher that I do the illustrations, and my dealings were all with her directly. I made pencil roughs, and we talked over the approach to take" (quoted in Reed 206). Since we have only his word for this, and indeed only his word for Cather's having "insisted" that he be given the assignment, we might be inclined to wonder whether he is exaggerating. But there is every reason to believe him. Considering that he had already done the dust jacket and the serialization, and given that Alfred Knopf was accustomed to deferring to Cather's wishes, it is very unlikely that he would have been engaged for the second edition if she had not been pleased with his work. Moreover, granted her long-standing interest in the physical design of her books, we can well imagine that she worked closely with him, as he says.

Yet I remain puzzled by her apparent enthusiasm. Von Schmidt was strongly associated with the West, to be sure, but with an image of the West that she was resisting and revising. His drawings and paintings were primarily given to furthering clichés of violence and fighting, the masculinities of the cowboys-and-Indians vision. And indeed such elements are far more prominent in his illustrations for *Archbishop* than they are in the text. Moreover, his style in black-and-white drawings is heavy. He himself explained that he found working in pen and ink uncongenial ("for me, it runs and slops away"). He preferred "lampblack tempera with a small amount of opaque white added to it," producing a "rich flat black." In his comments on his "black and whites," he insisted that he "tr[ied] to get the most from the least" and if he could "do without a line" he "eliminate[d] it" (quoted in Reed 205). Yet very few of his fifty-eight drawings for *Archbishop* seem to bear out that statement; very few can well be described as minimal. Nor do they often make significant use of white space, despite his avowed devotion to the "aesthetics of type combined with black and white pictures" and the way in which paper becomes "a part of the picture." Recognizing that "white in a dark area can create great brilliance and the illusion of intense light" (quoted in Reed 205), von Schmidt did at times use such techniques to good effect in the *Archbishop* decorations. They are singularly appropriate to the intensity of southwestern light. On the whole, however, his "rich flat black" drawings scarcely bear comparison with the spare pen-and-inks by Benda in *My Ántonia* or by Smith in *The Land of Little Rain.* What is more important, their heaviness, clottedness, and closed-in composition do not accord well with Cather's light touch in narration and verbal images.

The choice of von Schmidt is especially surprising in view of his dust jacket for the first edition (figure 5.04). Its darkly blackened boldness conveys a muscular masculinity little in keeping with Cather's characterization of Latour. Moreover, it belies von Schmidt's own statement about his conception of the illustrations for the second edition—that he believed her characters to be "so well realized in words" that he should not risk confusing readers by depicting them himself, and therefore "did the pictures as decorations that would set the background for the story and help the audience get to know the old New Mexico as she knew it and as I knew it." Cather, he says, did not at first agree but later thanked him for "insisting on doing it the way I wanted" (quoted in Reed 206–207). This seems to imply that she wished him to picture her characters in close-up detail and he resisted doing so. But

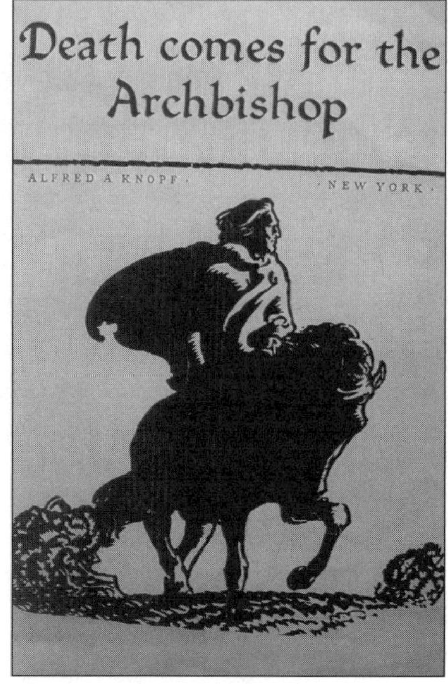

5.04 Harold von Schmidt, dust jacket image for first edition of *Death Comes for the Archbishop* and half-title page of second edition

on the dust jacket of the first edition he had already shown Father Latour with considerable specificity. And his rendition does indeed "confuse" this reader.[19]

The image of Latour shown on the dust jacket, re-used for the half-title page of the second edition, has a swashbuckling look. Except for the lack of armor we might take him to be a knight out on adventure. The muscular good looks and dramatically flowing hair are far from any word-picture Cather ever draws of Latour and very far from the historical Bishop Lamy's appearance in surviving photographs reproduced in the scholarly edition (although Cather did state in a letter to President Thomas Masaryk of Czechoslovakia that the cover illustration was derived from an actual image of Lamy in his youth).[20] The billowing cloak is romantic and self-dramatizing, and even the horse—heavily muscled like horses ridden by medieval knights, because only an animal on the scale of a draft horse could support their armor—seems strikingly unsuited to the time and place. Its head is not in a position one would expect of a horse being ridden across the plains, and if one supposes that the lowered head is meant to indicate the dire straits of the thirsty animal in the novel's opening chapter, the vigorousness of the neck and legs would seem to deny that.

Von Schmidt's stated preference for "decorations that would set the background" of the novel strikes me as a wise strategy, wiser by far than his depiction of Latour on the dust jacket. Indeed, his term "decorations" captures very much the sense of Cather's own intentions with the Benda drawings for *My Ántonia;* she used that very word in at least two letters to her publisher. When von Schmidt emphasizes, in stating his understanding of the task of an illustrator, that an image should "set the mood and the character of the story, establish the time, the place, and the kind of individuals involved" (quoted in Reed 45), he virtually restates her earlier statements of her expectations. Their standards, then, seem to have been perfectly in accord. Our task here as readers of the illustrated edition is to ask how Cather's text functions pictorially and whether von Schmidt achieved complementarity in his illustrations.

Much of Cather's attention to setting in *Archbishop* is taken up with topography—large land masses—and in particular the contrast between the vertical landforms and the flat desert spaces across which Fathers Latour and Vaillant toil and the fleet-footed Indians run, leaving no trace (*DCA* 248). In that sense it is a more geometric book than her earlier writings of the Southwest. The opening chapter of Book One, "The Vicar Apostolic," announces this geometric vision. As Latour wanders thirstily among miles of "conical red hills," nearing exhaustion, the arid landscape strikes him as a "geometrical nightmare" (*DCA* 17). Never again after this point is the topography of New Mexico described in such revolted terms. A man "sensitive to the shape of things" (*DCA* 17), Latour comes to love his diocese and its people and to regard the environment he once thought nightmarish as, instead, invigorating. To be sure, the arid plain west of Albuquerque around Laguna and Acoma, with its widely spaced mesas, is a far cry from the "disorder" of the Jornada del Muerto, the "Way of Death," where he wandered in confusion in the opening chapter. The mesas strike him as possessing a great dignity—perhaps reminding us of the "great pines" north of Flagstaff, in *The Song of the Lark,* which "stand at a considerable distance" apart and courteously "do not intrude upon each other" (*SL* 233). Unlike this human metaphor in which Thea's perceptions are couched, Latour's perception of the dignity of the mesa landscape is given in architectural terms, with the high mesas resembling large public buildings or "vast cathedrals" (99)—an ennobling metaphor indeed, in the mind of a priest and future bishop.

The geometric or structural motif is even extended to patterns of timbering on a mountain near Taos, so sharply outlined that it "had the sculptured look of naked mountains like the Sandias" (which are indeed naked and sculptured in appearance, especially when seen from the west or north). The verbal brilliance of this passage using geometric terms to describe vegetation lies in its effect of sharply defined patterns of color following the sculpting of rocks into ridges and hollows: "The general growth on its sides was evergreen, but the canyons and ravines were wooded with aspens, so that the shape of every depression was painted on the mountain-side, light green against the dark, like symbols; serpentine, crescent, half-circles" (*DCA* 159). Many painters have caught, or have sought to catch, the appearance of mountainsides in the Sangre de Cristos and Manzanos, with their long, rounded folds or pleats in linear, fanning-out ridges and hollows, as if the palm of a great hand were set on the top with its fingers spreading downward. This linearity of the landscape is beautifully caught in Father Vaillant's sight of "hills close about [Santa Fe] like two encircling arms" when he is leaving for his ministry in Colorado (*DCA* 267). In the passage quoted above, Cather paints these folded shapes with colors. Later she shows her readers "sharp red sand-hills spotted with juniper"—as precise and minimally rendered a verbal equivalent of the actual slopes, as well as of a number of painterly representations, as one could find (*DCA* 267 and again 276–77). Stuart Davis's 1923 canvases *New Mexican Landscape* (figure 5.05) and *New Mexico Gate* show the juniper-spotted hillsides in precisely the same way.

As in *The Song of the Lark* and *The Professor's House*, Cather's visual language in *Archbishop* emphasizes quality of light, clearness of air, and colors. The sky itself possesses a kind of vitality, with a "constant change of accent" and "ever-varying distribution of light":

> [I]n the vast plains of Kansas, Father Latour had found the sky more a desert than the land; a hard, empty blue, very monotonous to the eyes of a Frenchman. But west of the Pecos all that changed; here there was

> always activity overhead, clouds forming and moving all day long. Whether they were dark and full of violence, or soft and white with luxurious idleness, they powerfully affected the world beneath them. The desert, the mountains and mesas, were continually re-formed and re-coloured by the cloud shadows. *(DCA* 101*)*

When his feeling about his mission is positive and hopeful, Father Latour delights in the sunlight rendering distant mountains so "bright" that he thinks the "first Creation morning might have looked like this" (*DCA* 104). But when he is discouraged and apprehensive—as he is during his first visit to Acoma, where he celebrates the Mass perfunctorily and feels oppressed by "a sense of inadequacy and spiritual defeat"—he experiences it as a "blindin[g] . . . glare" (*DCA* 105). In much the same way, Acoma's doomed

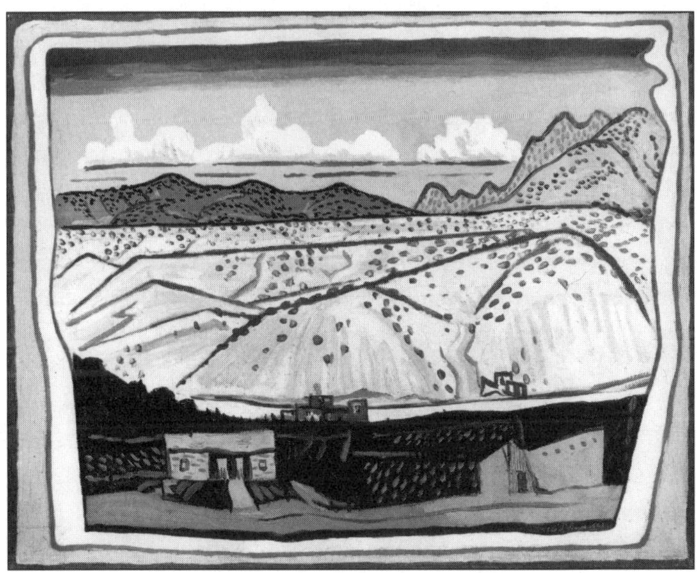

5.05 Stuart Davis, *New Mexican Landscape,* 1923, oil on canvas (accession number 1972.49, Amon Carter Museum, Fort Worth, Texas)

priest Baltazar had seen the sunlight as a "bak[ing] . . . fire" (*DCA* 119) when he was wishing he could escape the consequences of his own actions. If the landscape shapes the lives and emotions of those who live in it, their emotions also shape their perceptions of it. We see much the same projective process in *My Ántonia* when a tired and apprehensive Jim Burden feels in danger of being "erased, blotted out" by the empty Nebraska sky, whereas only a day later, reassured by his grandparents' care, he lies under that same sky as content as an expanding pumpkin (*MA* 8, 18).

Cather's own delight in the high desert is evident in the resplendent colors of her word-pictures. She proves herself indeed, as Woodress calls her, a "verbal colorist" (*Literary Life* 403). The red ball of the setting sun painting the edges of storm clouds "with molten silver" (*DCA* 126); the multitiered houses of Taos Pueblo "gold-coloured in the afternoon light, with the purple mountain lying just behind them" (*DCA* 158); the top of the hill south of Santa Fe where Latour finds the rock for his cathedral glowing in the "last rays of the sun" as if it were "melted gold" (*DCA* 255); the rosy purple of wild verbena forming such thick mats that it is like a "great violet velvet mantle thrown down in the sun" (*DCA* 279); and the old town of Santa Fe itself colored in "tawny adobe" (we are reminded of Austin's fondness for that adjective) "with a few green trees, set in a half-circle of carnelian-coloured hills" (*DCA* 282). She dwells on this improbable rosy-red of the Sangre de Cristos, the Blood of Christ Mountains, exploring how it varies according to atmospheric conditions from "intense lavender" with "all their pine trees strokes of dark purple" to a "more and more intense rose-carnelian" like the "dried blood of saints and martyrs . . . which liquefies upon occasion" (*DCA* 284–85). Liquefied color.

When we collect such word-pictures together as I have here, it might seem as if *Death Comes for the Archbishop* were descriptively over-written, like a travel book designed to lure tourists. Of course, that is not true. It is not by any means a book filled with lengthy descriptions. As Cather said she aspired to do, she "touch[es] . . . the note" of landscape description and "pass[es] on" (*On Writing* 9). Much of the text is, in fact, notably abstract, given to Latour's or Vaillant's meditations on their spiritual goals and responsibilities rather than to visual delight. The clearness of the dry New Mexico air, affording clarity of perception, contributes to these meditations but also ironizes them, since the priests (especially Latour) are often far less clear in their purposes and their sense of how they should respond to their parishioners' needs than the image of visual clarity might imply. Even when they penetrate the unfamiliarity of their surroundings and grasp a clear sense of what they are about—let alone when they do not plumb these depths of mystery—their vision is often far less clear than the mountain air. Cather's language celebrates the "clean . . . bareness" of Jacinto's room at Pecos Pueblo—an acknowledged anachronism, since the pueblo had actually been abandoned in 1838, ten years before the Treaty of Guadalupe Hidalgo that brought the historical Lamy and the fictionalized Latour to New Mexico. It celebrates the "lightness" of the air at this "bright edg[e] of the world" and the fact of there being "so much sky" (*DCA* 288, 245). In the moonlight the clear air gives the towers of Latour's church a sharp definition and allows him to see quite clearly the "line of black footprints" poor Sada has left in the snow (*DCA* 221, 230). Yet the ultimate ambiguity of a sinister cave lurks at the center of the novel. Many readers are finally unable to determine whether Cather intends to show her archbishop as being drastically limited in his perception of and response to the persecution of the Navajo and the persistence of de facto if not de jure slavery in the Southwest, and unable to decide whether she herself inveterately ameliorates such problems.

Von Schmidt's illustrations for the second edition consist of ten full-page pictures, thirty-two headers, and sixteen footers. The full-page illustrations are placed on the verso of the half-title page to each of the nine sections or books, plus the prologue; that is, at the start of each section they appear on the page on the reader's left, facing the beginning of the first chapter of that section, on the reader's right. Each chapter also has a one-third page header. The effect, then, is of great simplicity when one looks at the half-title pages, since they are blank except for the words of the title, but with the turn of the page one sees a cluster of pictorial decoration, the full-page illustration on the left and the header on the right, above the first line of type. The sixteen footers vary from a one-inch strip across the bottom at a chapter's end to two-thirds of a page, depending on the flow of the type.[21] It is indeed a lavishly decorated volume.

Each of the ten full-page illustrations takes its subject matter from a dominant idea or episode in the section it opens, though not necessarily in the first chapter of that section. In the case of the prologue, "At Rome," the link is proleptic; both the main illustration and the header are scenes of New

Mexico, not of Rome. Eight of the ten, including the prologue's drawing of a massive butte (reproduced in the scholarly edition), are outdoor scenes. For Book I, "The Vicar Apostolic," the full-page illustration is of Father Latour kneeling before the cruciform tree; for Book II, "Missionary Journeys," it is a generalized scene of the mesa country; for Book III, "The Mass at Ácoma," the church at Acoma looming massively up from its mesa-top; for Book V, "Padre Martinez," one of the two great houses at Taos Pueblo (a familiar image, from numerous paintings); for Book VII, "The Great Diocese," two tiny mounted figures, the two priests, moving across a desert plain toward a massive butte; for Book VIII, "Gold under Pike's Peak," a prospector panning for gold; and for Book IX, "Death Comes for the Archbishop," Latour's (Lamy's actual) cathedral. The two full-page illustrations of indoor scenes are the mysterious cave of Book IV, "Snake Root," showing Jacinto pressed against the wall, arms outstretched, like the reverse of a crucifix figure, and for Book VI, "Doña Isabella," showing the lady herself playing her harp in a crowded parlor.

In the eight outdoor scenes the indications of sky are of particular interest; they are done in heavy parallel lines. These nonrepresentational lines (it is not always clear whether they are intended as clear sky or clouds) either partially or wholly enclose the tops of the pictures, delimiting the openness that we might expect. Only in VII is there a strong sense of New Mexico's big sky (figure 5.06). Indeed, this drawing is almost all sky. The smallness of the figures riding across the plain and the great distance to the mesa convey the hugeness of the territory for which Latour and Vaillant are responsible and also, perhaps, the courage and commitment that impel them to persevere in their pastoral journey. Despite the immense openness of sky here, the top is fully closed in with black lines, rather than the partial closure of most of the others.

More typical are the skies of Book I (figure 5.07) and Book II (figure 5.08)—where the little sky in evidence is once again indicated by heavy lines, with a relieving focal point of blankness. With the downward perspective of this drawing (the view is from an upper slope into a narrow, enclosed canyon), the emphasis seems to be more on depth than on height. This is typical of von Schmidt's representation of the New Mexico landscape; he tends to choose enclosure over openness.

The emblematic cruciform tree of Book I might better have been left

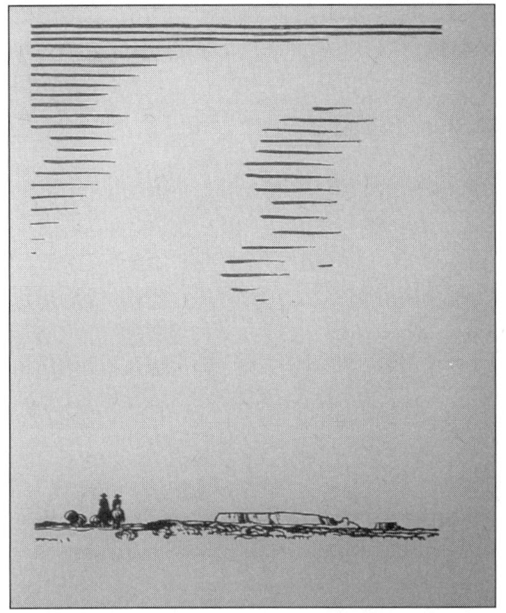

5.06 Harold von Schmidt, full-page illustration for Book VII, "The Great Diocese," showing Father Latour and Father Vaillant riding across the plain west of Albuquerque, from *Death Comes for the Archbishop*, second edition (p. 224)

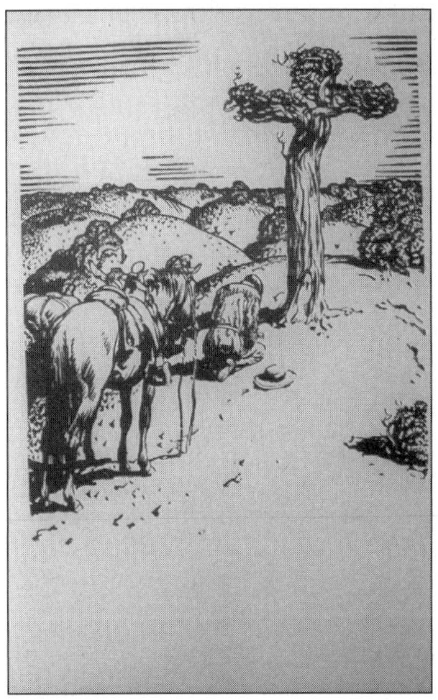

5.07 Harold von Schmidt, full-page illustration for Book I, "The Vicar Apostolic," showing Father Latour kneeling before the cruciform tree, from *Death Comes for the Archbishop*, second edition (p. 18)

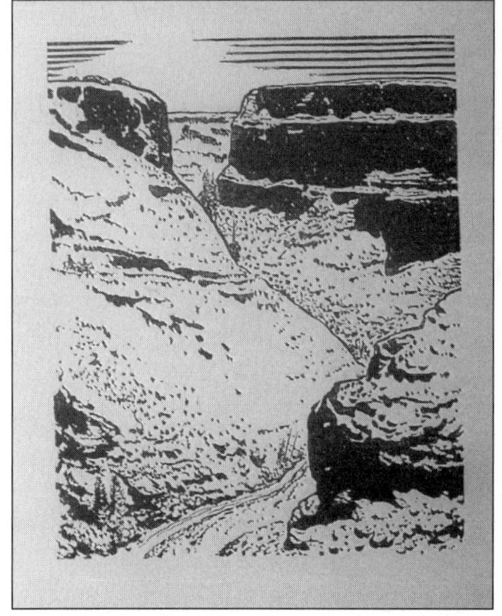

5.08 Harold von Schmidt, full-page illustration for Book II, "Missionary Journeys," showing canyon landscape, from *Death Comes for the Archbishop*, second edition (p. 60)

to the reader's imagination, since it necessarily strikes the viewer (especially one acquainted with New Mexico's junipers) as improbable. Cather's description is improbable enough:

> . . . one juniper which differed in shape from the others. It was not a thick-growing cone, but a naked, twisted trunk, perhaps ten feet high, and at the top it parted into two lateral, flat-lying branches, with a little crest of green in the centre, just above the cleavage. Living vegetation could not present more faithfully the form of the Cross. (*DCA* 17–18)

Not being a horticulturalist, I cannot say with certainty that it is impossible for a juniper to look like that, that there has never been and will never be one, but as a former resident of the area whose five-acre homesite was covered with piñon and juniper, I can say that I never saw a juniper that even approached such a shape. Junipers do have twisted trunks with twisty branches that come off at a variety of angles, usually slightly upward-

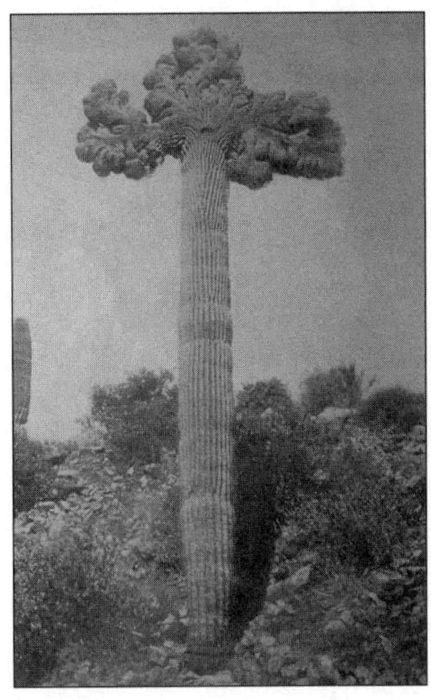

5.09 Photograph of cruciform "Coxcomb Cactus," *Out West* 29, no. 1 (July 1908): 2

reaching and turning more upward as they extend out but sometimes reaching downward. Usually the branches are in clumps beginning very near the ground.

Curiously, von Schmidt's rendition of the cruciform tree closely resembles a photograph of a cruciform cactus, rather than juniper, with ornately braided crown (labeled an example of a "rare variety" known as "Coxcomb Cactus"), that appeared in Charles Lummis's *Out West* magazine in 1908 (figure 5.09). The resemblance is so close that one wonders if von Schmidt had seen this picture. Or perhaps Cather saw it, remembered it when she began to write *Death Comes for the Archbishop,* and later brought it to von Schmidt's attention. I raise this possibility simply because of the visual oddity of a tree in cruciform shape and the fact of her thorough acquaintance with periodicals, especially during her *McClure's* years. Perhaps she remembered the image but misremembered it as a juniper. This entire conjecture is rendered the more plausible by the fact that the title of the *Out West* article to which the photograph served as an introductory plate, on the facing page, was "God's Country—the Desert," an idea of obvious pertinence to her conception of *Archbishop.*[22]

Von Schmidt's head-pieces and tail-pieces are mostly given to typical

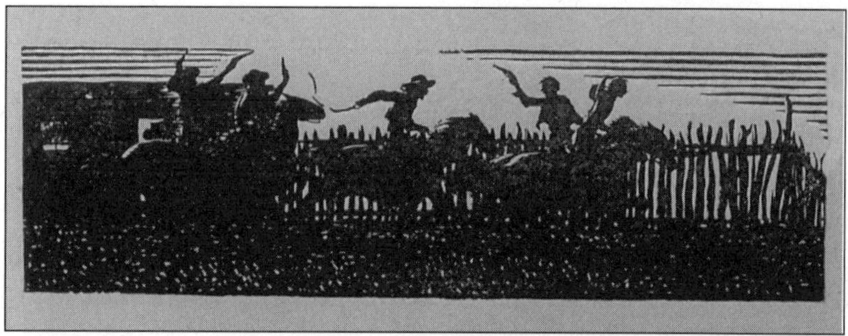

5.10 Harold von Schmidt, tail-piece for Book I, Chapter 3, "The Bishop Chez Lui," showing riotous cowboys, from *Death Comes for the Archbishop,* second edition (p. 48)

regional scenes. As head-piece for the first chapter of Book I, for example, "The Cruciform Tree," he provided a picturesque adobe wall with a ristra of peppers, a man in sombrero, a shawled woman, and two burros. At the end of the same chapter, transitioning to the second chapter, "Hidden Water" (which begins on the same page, so that the drawing serves as both tail-piece of the one and head-piece of the other), he showed a young herder with his goats, against a backdrop of sparsely vegetated hills. Horizon lines in these small drawings (about two inches high and the width of the block of type) are almost always high, and the effect is often rather crowded.

These small drawings of the goatherd and the village scene harmonize well with the text in that they show either specific references (the goatherd is mentioned, the Indian runner in the head-piece for "The Legend of Fray Baltazar" is mentioned) or typical scenes evoked in the novel (an adobe wall in an unnamed village, and a Navajo weaver at the start of the chapter called "Eusabio"). Several of these head- or tail-pieces, however, show the kind of conventional western action that, although referred to in passing, is scarcely Cather's emphasis. An example is the drawing of mounted men shooting up a town shown in figure 5.10. Here a disadvantage of von Schmidt's mode of indicating sky becomes obvious, since the parallel lines with which he shows sky in this night scene look the same as his daytime skies. The action scene of Latour and Vaillant outside Buck Scales's hovel, the head-piece for Book

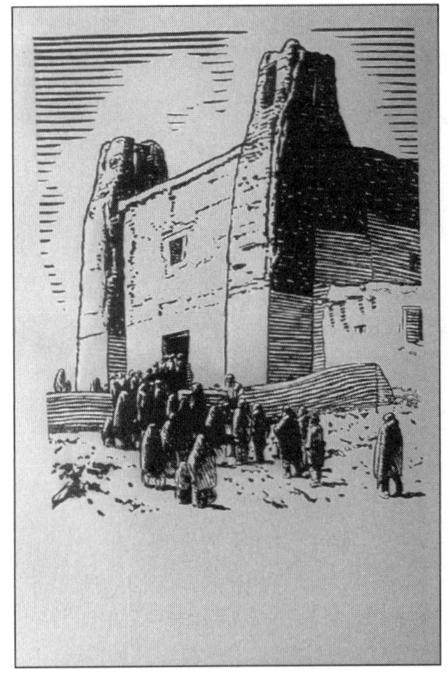

5.11 Harold von Schmidt, full-page illustration for Book III, "The Mass at Ácoma," from *Death Comes for the Archbishop,* second edition (p. 92)

II, Chapter 2, "The Lonely Road to Mora," does, of course, represent an episode of great significance in the text. It is not as though von Schmidt invented his action scenes out of whole cloth. But action is overrepresented in the illustrations as compared to the text. A head-piece of stereotypical cowboys on galloping horses (at the start of the second chapter of Book V, "The Old Order") represents no moment in the text at all, while a lively roundup scene not of cattle but of goats (the tail-piece of Chapter 6 of Book IX) has only the loosest of connections. The illustrations pull Cather's book closer to the masculine Western than it is in its original unillustrated version.

Churches are featured in several drawings, in each of which their massiveness is emphasized, as in the fine full-page illustration showing the church at Acoma (figure 5.11). As in the tail-piece of the cathedral at the very end of the book, the church structure dominates the scene. The stream of worshippers approaching the door gives a strong sense of social density, also felt in several other street scenes and interiors. Some of these are indeed quite crowded, such as a full-page picture of Doña Isabella entertaining her guests (the verso of the half-title page of Book V, "Doña Isabella") and also

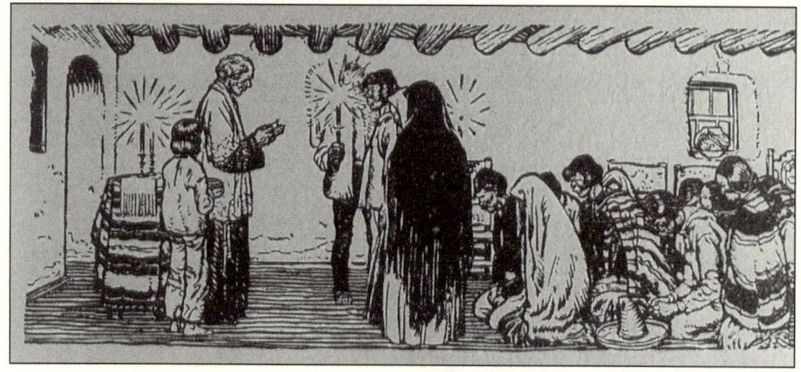

5.12 Harold von Schmidt, head-piece for Book II, Chapter 1, "The White Mules," showing Father Vaillant marrying a series of couples, from *Death Comes for the Archbishop,* second edition (p. 61)

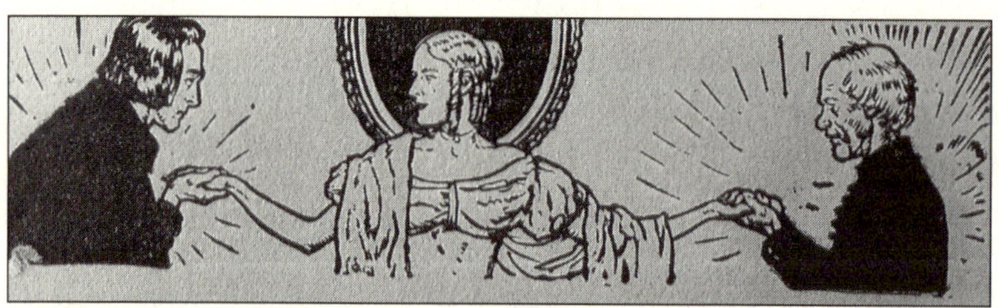

5.13 Harold von Schmidt, tail-piece for Book VI, "Doña Isabella," Chapter 2, showing her between Father Latour and Father Vaillant, from *Death Comes for the Archbishop,* second edition (p. 222)

the rather cartoonish drawing of Father Vaillant saying Mass in the head-piece to Chapter 1 ("The White Mules") of Book II (figure 5.12). Vaillant is caricatured again in the tail-piece to Chapter 2 of Book VI (figure 5.13), where his stated lack of comeliness is emphasized.

The drawing so clearly showing the imagined features of both Latour and Vaillant, like the one of Vaillant conducting a sequence of marriage ceremonies (figure 5.12), definitely violates von Schmidt's stated intention of providing "decorations that would set the background for the story" without "depict[ing]" the characters and thereby "possibly confus[ing] the reader whose interpretations of her words might be different" (quoted in Reed 206–207).

Only sporadically do von Schmidt's illustrations capture Cather's tone and her light touch—her desire to do "something in the style of the legend, which is absolutely the reverse of dramatic treatment"; "not to hold the note . . . but to touch and pass on" (*On Writing* 9).[23] On the whole, that quality of legend is conveyed far better by the Holbein woodcut that provided her title or by the Puvis de Chavannes murals which she said were an inspiration. Again, I am at a loss to account for the positive response to von Schmidt's illustrations she sometimes—but not always—indicated.

A more startling pictorial image in the second edition of *Death Comes for the Archbishop,* with a significance all its own, appears in only a single copy. Directly beneath the title of Book I, "The Vicar Apostolic," in her own copy, Cather pasted a snapshot of herself on horseback (figure 5.14).[24] Not in words but in a visual image of herself in riding trousers, an image that emphasizes her vigor and androgynous evasion of conventionalized femininity, she avows her personal identification with the idealized hero of what she considered her finest work.

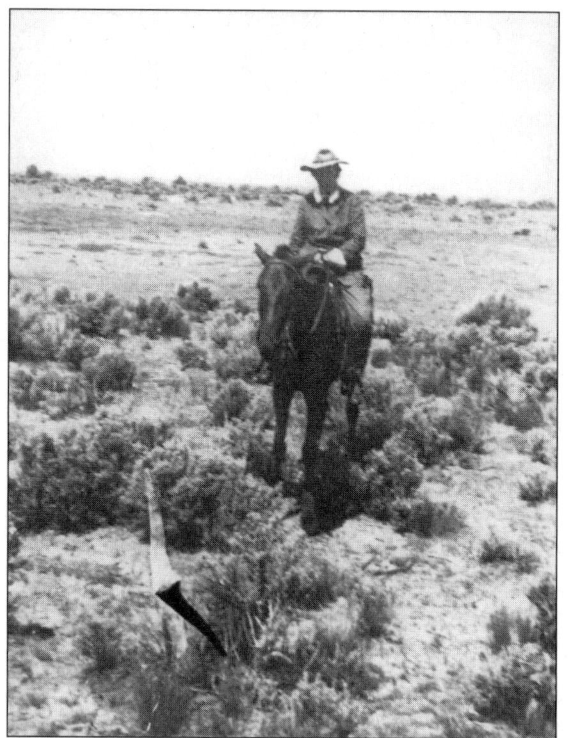

5.14 Snapshot of Willa Cather pasted into her personal copy of *Death Comes for the Archbishop*, second edition, on the half-title page of Book I, "The Vicar Apostolic"

6

FROM SEEING TO VISION

Out West, the west of the mesas and the unpatented hills,
there is more sky than any place in the world.

Mary Austin
The Land of Little Rain

The great fact was the land itself.

Willa Cather
O Pioneers!

In *Birthing a Nation,* her revisionist study of women writers committed to "freeing women from the alterity of the Western's scripts" (113), Susan Rosowski offers a compelling example of the persistence of such scripts: a 1971 anthology, *The Literature of the American West.* Published by Austin's and Cather's own first publisher, Houghton Mifflin, it includes nothing at all by Austin or by Jean Stafford, an unduly neglected writer that Rosowski importantly reclaims. By Cather there is only "Neighbour Rosicky," which is labeled "charming." The introduction to the anthology is a symposium of male writers' understandings of the West and the Western. Among other notables represented, Rosowski quotes Frederick Manfred, who muses that the West offers "enough left of wild nature to *subdue*" and that what still matters is "*men* who are ruggedly individualistic" (*Birthing* 113, emphases mine).

The narrative field through which Austin and Cather approached their writing of the West was littered with such detritus as Manfred's pronouncement. It was a field made up of historical, political, and fictional celebrations of masculine and national acts of subduing. There can be no doubt that the public discourse of the West was an important force against which they shaped their resistant versions. At least equally important, as we have seen, was their approach to their conceptions of the West by way of visual experience, both their own and the mediated visual experience afforded by artists and photographers. All this was absorbed, to reemerge in a language of visual imagery conveying a vision of the West in which gender was no longer a matter of absolutes. The word "vision" thus takes on multiple meanings, from conventions of museum and magazine art, to personal seeing and how it might be captured in words that help readers also see, to pictorial images printed alongside those words, to the more abstract conceptual sense.

Both Austin and Cather left abundant evidence of the visual nature of their experience of the West, including evidence of their revulsion at the unsightly litter and the general ripping up that accompanied white migration and industry, marring its spacious unclutteredness. Visual cleanness or starkness is one of the primary components of how they saw the West, becoming for both a powerful metaphor for ethical and writerly cleanness. Similarly, spaciousness of vistas became emblematic of a wideness of mind. The pictorial mode in which they wrote served, then, both as description and as the ground on which to construct a moral and social vision. And it is clear that Austin, at least, saw the West as the model for America's future.

Bruce Jackson defines the West as not so much a geographical place as an "idea" and a "portable dream." By "portable" he means not only a dream that migrants could carry with them but a dream whose geographic siting moved across the continent as the tide of white settlement swept inexorably westward. The idea of the West, Jackson writes, "promised you weren't really trapped after all" (3–5). Rosowski, too, ponders how escape, the lure of personal freedom, became a "staple" of the literary West in dreams of "lighting out for the territory, leaving civilization behind, and embracing a life of wandering." Such a notion entailed, however, not only the "pervasive cultural arrogance" of assuming that westering Anglos had an inherent right to such a life, regardless of the interests of those who happened to be in the way, but also the "pain of displacement" experienced by those who went west and found that they missed their homes, or the corresponding pain of being left behind (*Birthing* 177, 190, 132).

Both Austin and Cather experienced that pain of displacement but refused to accept it with the passivity assumed to be women's nature or lot in life (the passivity assumed in the trope of woman as earth available for plowing, explored by Annette Kolodny in *The Lay of the Land*). Instead, they set about reconstructing their lives on their own initiative. In their writing of the

West, they rejected such "staples" of male freedom as ruggedness and subjugation of the land and its creatures, but also rejected the alternative of a traditional feminine gendering based on assumed domestic contentment. Rather, they showed that women might find in the West the space to live freely and vigorously just as men did, but without the violence and urge to conquest of conventional masculinity. Of course, they were not alone in claiming male freedoms for women, and thus freeing women from the constraints of conventional gender roles. Vera Norwood identifies a number of women's writings about the West (diaries, memoirs, sketches, stories) that provide "glimpses of women turning to nature for relief from the restrictions of gentility"—that is, from repressive notions of propriety ("Crazy-Quilt Lives" 84).

When men went west for freedom (in some cases the freedom of lawlessness), they were fulfilling conventional notions of gender. When women did so, they were challenging those conventions. In seeing the West as a space for gender liberation, Cather and Austin sought both a new womanness and a new masculinity. They reconceptualized the West and Southwest not so much by feminizing them as by envisioning a kind of dual gendering. In doing so, they became central forces in the establishment of an alternative western tradition.

More obviously in Austin's writing than in Cather's we see a vision of the West and its meaning growing out of the land itself. In part this is because Austin devotes more of her creative effort to close description. The value of seeing and understanding geological and biological forms is more often foregrounded in her work than in Cather's. Austin is also far more interested in indigenous people—real, living indigenous people, not merely the lost peoples of archaeological record that Cather wrote about in *The Song of the Lark* and *The Professor's House.* When Austin writes about Seyavi, the Paiute basket maker who served her as a model for both self-sufficiency in a harsh natural environment and an artistry using materials the place itself provided, she shows us Seyavi's very hands, gathering and weaving the reeds that her baskets are made of. Austin claims to have herself gone out with Seyavi and other Paiute women and not only observed but participated in their gathering of herbs and other plant-life from which they gain their necessities and the materials of their handcrafts. When Cather shows us the remains of native women's pottery they are always just that, *remains,* relics of the past, not an ongoing art she can observe in progress, let alone participate in. Her connection with these women's lives and art is made through the imagination rather than direct personal contact—very compellingly, to be sure, as Thea instinctively perceives in her own body the weight on the cliff-dwelling women's backs as they carried their babies down and up the steep trail, but never with immediate, living presence. Mike Fischer has convincingly argued that Cather similarly "managed to believe" that the Sioux of Nebraska belonged either to a distant past or, if still living, to a geographically distant Someplace having nothing to do with her idealized presentation of, and her family's participation in, white pioneering (33).

Fischer raises a troubling issue. Cather's blithe minimizing of the real presence of Native peoples and her mitigation of the history of their decimation by whites are indeed objectionable. On the other hand, it would seem that she needed to do just that if she was to eschew the violent plots of the Western in order to create a new kind of western writing with more irenic emphases. It is difficult to reconcile the two imperatives.

At any rate, Cather's evasion of the fact of Native presence does not mean she lacked a strong interest in the real Southwest of her actual experience. I do not for a moment accept John Murphy's assertion that New Mexico and its long human history served her, in *Death Comes for the Archbishop,* only as "a pretext for thoughts about God and Christianity" ("Holy Cities" 65). Ann Moseley's analysis of her precise ecological writing in *The Song of the Lark* demonstrates that Cather's involvement in her geographical and archaeological subject matter was both literal and respectful, that she respected the Southwest enough to take pains to set it down correctly. The record she left us in her own words—in letters and in her article about Mesa Verde, let alone her fiction—is its own testament to the honesty of her investment in the Southwest in and of itself. That she saw the region as aesthetically inspiring would have been reason enough for her investment of so much creative energy, let alone that she took its landscape aesthetic as a paradigm for a writerly aesthetic. She also saw it as a locus of bodily health, mental refreshment, and freedom from professional and personal pressures. We will return later to the question of whether Cather's values, in her books about the Southwest, were derived from her sense of place or were attached or ascribed to it through a process we might call opportune emblematizing.

For now, let us pursue the real presence of the Southwest as a locus of being and an emblem of freedom.

Biographically, both Austin and Cather defined their first achievement of freedom from stereotyped notions of how girls should live in terms of free movement and independent vision in the West. Such freedom of movement brought them release from states of depression attendant on their sense of displacement from familiar homes. For Austin, as she remembers it in her autobiography, this came in the moment she discovered wild grapes to eat while rambling by herself in the California desert. For Cather it was found in her liberty to ride her pony about the countryside, fetching the mail and visiting neighbors. During these solitary rides, she said, she and the country "had it out together" (Bohlke 32). What both describe is a degree of autonomy and mobility greatly exceeding the supposed bounds of propriety for girls or young women, who were expected to content themselves with a state of domestic confinement. Austin's family reacted by invoking normative behavior directly and judgmentally: "It was so *like* Mary, her family remarked, to almost starve to death on a proper Christian diet and go and get well on something grubbed out of the woods" (*EH* 195). In Cather's case, the family seems to have tacitly accepted not only her rambling but her unconventional—and surely quasi-masculine—dress and hairstyle during adolescence. What it was that led them to do so remains a mystery.

After these early breakthroughs into freedom from a range of constraints based on assumptions about gender, Austin and Cather continued to find liberation in the West both biographically and in their fiction. Austin asserted her freedom from her prim birth family's expectations and also from the restrictive conventions of marriage by tramping the mountainsides, fixing her attention on her natural environment (a way of telling husband and family where they rated in her scale of priorities), and associating with people at or beyond the limits of respectability.[1] These included both sheepherders—workers of low social class who, according to prevailing assumptions, might have been expected to constitute threats to her virtue—and Native Americans, the very people targeted for elimination in the process of settlement being carried out by her own race and class. Later, she further asserted her freedom from gender conventions by leaving her husband, shaking off her responsibility for providing direct maternal care for her mentally disabled daughter, and dressing in flamboyant, sometimes quasi-masculine and quasi-western ways whenever she chose. Her display of personal freedom in disregard of gender expectations and her sense that the West provided a fit space for such freedom can be seen in *The Land of Journeys' Ending* when she makes her "siesta" outdoors in the shade of a saguaro (*LJE* 123). As Ann Zwinger correctly observes, society still carried a lot of "Victorian baggage of 'nice girls don't,' and one of the things nice girls didn't was camp out alone" (xviii). But Austin enjoyed camping out (except when her husband was dictating every detail). As her siesta among the saguaros demonstrates, she literally slept around, perhaps for the very purpose of mocking the kind of assumptions usually expressed by that phrase in our own time.

Cather does not usually seem so resistant to social norms as Austin. Although her early assumption of a quasi-masculine persona in dress and other aspects of self-presentation is often noted, she developed strategies for accommodating herself to social expectations as a part of her career progress. As late as 1906, when she left her job as schoolteacher in Pittsburgh to join the staff of *McClure's* in New York, she was still attracting comment by students about her dandyish (meaning both sharp and quasi-masculine) appearance, but the workaday attire they noticed was clearly in accord with the role of New Woman and she had learned that it was advantageous to dress for social occasions in ways generally regarded as appropriate. When she went to the Southwest she enjoyed dressing in trousers that accommodated her strenuous—many would have said unwomanly—hiking and climbing. Her trips also entailed feats of horseback riding through rugged country. We have already seen a visual record of her assured and certainly not side-saddle horsemanship in the snapshot pasted into her own copy of the illustrated *Archbishop.* All of this is in sharp contrast to her urbane self-presentation in New York. It demonstrates a remarkable fluidity of gender roles.

A similar fluidity, moving toward androgyny, is demonstrated by various of Cather's western fictional personas. Contrary to the prevailing style of showing women in repose, in art of the late nineteenth and early twentieth centuries, her female heroes in the West live vigorously, moving freely between conventional gender roles.[2] Alexandra, in *O Pioneers!,* a woman who challenges her brothers' would-be limitations on female land ownership, dresses in a man's coat while retaining feminine beauty and makes bold decisions about livestock rearing and crops while continuing to enjoy quiet days in the kitchen with women friends. Jim Burden, in *My Ántonia,* a male narrative persona whose childhood reflects Cather's own, directs his lifelong admiration toward a woman who works in the fields "like mans" (*MA* 118) and bears children like the earth itself (not that he approves of her manly behaviors when she works outdoors, but in those moments he is regarded with at least a tinge of irony). In *The Song of the Lark,* Thea climbs mountains better than her male lover. In *The Professor's House,* the career of the male writer-professor parallels Cather's and the story of the cowboy amateur archaeologist is based not only on Richard Wetherill's discovery of the Mesa Verde ruins in 1888 but in part on her own experiences there. And in *Death Comes for the Archbishop* a male religious imperialist who is in some ways feminized was implicitly claimed by Cather as a version of herself when she pasted her own picture beneath the words "The Vicar Apostolic." We see in these various characters Cather's willingness to project her female self in the guise of a male and to imagine characters who display the supposed gender characteristics of the other sex. And she places these androgynous characters in the West.

Thea Kronborg, fashioned after both Cather herself and the singer Olive Fremstad, finds herself artistically when she experiences two epiphanies in the Southwest, both directly connected with the landscape and its ecology. In the first of these she identifies with the physical sensations of cliff-dwelling Native women and her throat, the reservoir of her voice, with the containing forms of their pots. In the second she identifies her soaring aspirations with the freedom and strength of a high-flying eagle. After these epiphanies, the text emphasizes Thea's freedom. She stands "straight and free"; she becomes "freer and stronger under impulses"; and she and Fred are together "exceptionally free" (*SL* 256, 259)—the word "free" appears three times in as many pages. To be sure, much of the rest of the novel is devoted to showing that, ironically, Thea is not free, but limited in her choices by the demands of the arduous discipline she has chosen. But the discipline would be of no value without freedom and self-empowerment, and she gains these in the West.

It is characteristic of Cather that her strong female artist-figure comes *to* the West to find freedom and self-validation. Austin's strong women are *of* the West. This is merely one among many manifestations of Austin's greater directness of acquaintance with the region and its people. She shared—indeed, more than shared—Cather's vision of the West as a locus of gender liberation. Examples of strong, self-reliant western women in her fiction who challenge gender conventions include "El Zarzo" of *Isidro,* the Walking Woman, Seyavi the basket maker, the oddly named William of *Santa Lucia,* Anne of *The Ford,* and Dulcie Adelaid of *Cactus Thorn.* Except for Seyavi, these women also demonstrate the performative construction of gender in their attire.[3] Yet Austin's association of the West with opportunities for gender equality and freedom for women to determine their own lives is complicated by irony in a way that Cather's is not. The West *should* provide such an arena, because its spaciousness readily implies mental spaciousness, thus freedom from narrow ideas, and because Anglo society is relatively unformed there. The Walking Woman, for one, is able to gain fulfillment as a lover and mother as well as fulfillment in work as the equal of a man, and she is able to live her life with full freedom of movement—as the evidence of her strong footprints shows. But it is not easy for a woman to do so, even in the West. Notions of propriety and of male supremacy are so deeply held among Anglos that they continue to assert their presence even in a comparatively unformed and unregulated society. Even so, Austin argues implicitly, it is more nearly possible for women to gain freedom from gender expectations in the West than elsewhere.

In many of her works, most evidently in the short stories of *Lost Borders,* Austin seeks to develop an analogy between strong but mistreated women and the harsh desert country itself. This analogy is, however, far from logically consistent. The equivalence is loose in multiple ways. The desert is rarely (not quite never) described as beautiful, whereas its harshness seems patently evident, awaiting only a special person indeed (Austin, for example) to think it beautiful. It would seem by analogy that an unbeautiful but inwardly strong and supportive woman merely awaits a man who will see her real beauty. And indeed "The Walking Woman" bears this out, although it is not a male but rather the female narrator who discerns that "the track of her two feet," supposedly lame, "bore evenly and white." (Why "white," a term with unsettling and apparently irrelevant connotations, I do not know.) In the opening sketch of *Lost Borders,* she posits that if the desert were a woman she would be a beautiful and alluring, though "tawny" and strong-featured one. That is, in setting up the two terms of the analogy, she proposes beauty, not kindness, as the given. None of the stories ever makes the point that pretty women are in fact not kind, unless it is the pretty girls in "Bitterness of

Women" who are so horrified by Louis Chabot's disfigurement that they will no longer flirt with him.

Austin would not work out the instabilities of the woman–desert analogy and its shifting terms until *Cactus Thorn,* and then only by dropping the idea of men's foolishly supposing that pretty women are also kind and supposing the same of the desert. Instead, she demonstrates that *both* desert and woman are in fact *both* beautiful and deadly harsh. In the case of neither woman nor desert is the beauty obvious or easy, and what passes for kindness (or nurturance) in both is also far from facile. The image of thorns around the cactus blossom brings both twofold analogous ideas together by way of the beautiful Dulcie Adelaid's "thorn," the dagger with which she kills a faithless man who did not treat her as a moral equal. (That the "thorn" itself is morally neutral is demonstrated by her having earlier used it to save his life from a rattlesnake.) He had acted unilaterally in going on to court another woman, rather than regarding the sexual tie as one to be broken only by mutual consent.

Austin's fervor on this point goes back to her own affair with, or romantic fixation on, Lincoln Steffens around 1910–1911.[4] She regarded their relationship as a mutual commitment and was bitterly shocked when she found that Steffens had moved on to another relationship without discussing it with her first. For the rest of her writing life, she persisted in arguing the necessity for women to have an equal say in the ending of a sexual relationship. Her fixation on this principle and the unacceptability of a man's unilaterally severing a relationship enters into and shapes her novel *No. 26 Jayne Street* as well as *Cactus Thorn.* It is a measure of how profoundly she regenders life in the West that she reverses the sexes of the two parties in returning to the idea in *Starry Adventure.*

In Dulcie Adelaid, the terms of the equivalence between woman and desert at last fall into place. By developing a desert aesthetic within which to position her beautiful, "tawny," and environmentally adequate heroine, Austin is able to show that in both woman and environment what seems like unforgiving harshness is actually strength, and both desert and woman demand to be taken seriously. Woman and place alike are starkly beautiful and are fully the equals of the man. Similarly, Cather's Thea, in *The Song of the Lark,* becomes the equivalent of the rugged high desert where she comes to a realization of her own strength. Staying alone in the "cleanness of sun-baked, wind-swept places," she "could become a mere receptacle for heat, or become a colour, like the bright lizards that darted about on the hot stones outside her door; or she could become a continuous repetition of sounds, like the cicadas" (*SL* 235, 237). Although we must recognize that, as Mary Louise Pratt argues, the gaze from an elevated position can be a commanding and appropriative act, in Austin's and Cather's writings of the West both vision and hearing are presented as receptive openings of the self to the beauty and significance of place. Like Dulcie Adelaid, Thea draws strength from the austere landscape and feels sufficiently self-assured to kiss her man "without constraint or embarrassment . . . straight and free" (*SL* 256) when he relates to her directly, or to administer a quick push (but not a stab) when he toys with her.

Certainly Cather was never so overtly and explicitly feminist in her values as Austin, nor was she so direct as Austin in asserting that the West was the proper arena for regendering of conventions. As we see in these parallel passages from *Cactus Thorn* and *Song of the Lark,* they both—Austin explicitly, Cather implicitly—"suggested that western women are liberated from the restrictive norms of femininity by the vast and undominated scale of the land," and both found that the desert had an "ability to breed equality" (C. Taylor 122).

Writing about *The Land of Little Rain,* in particular, Elizabeth Ammons states that Mary Austin's "unbordered territory" represents both "geographically and literarily" a space "beyond or, at the very least, on the edge of white patriarchal control" (*Conflicting Stories* 89). Ammons's interest here is primarily in a feminist conception of literary form; her emphasis is on Austin's rejection of the Western's linear plot, her "refus[al] to participate in the most conventional western paradigm of narrative" (93). In many of her writings, of course—in some of the *Lost Borders Stories,* but in several of her novels as well—Austin did "participate" in plotted writing, but still in a way resistant to "white patriarchal control" of a "western paradigm." In her plotted works, she continued to write what Ammons calls "an antimasculine version even of very masculine territory" (96). That masculine territory entailed, in large part, plots based on conflict aimed at white male domination of land as well as of women. The strain of Austin's effort to adapt a patriarchal form to feminist purpose shows in moments of implausibility, wrenched language, and a troubled logic such as that we have brushed against in *Lost Borders,* the two-part analogy between woman and desert. Perhaps this is why, with only a few exceptions such as "The Walking Woman," Austin has been more admired as a writer of nonfiction.

If her location on the margin of a patriarchically controlled literary landscape led to problematic strains in Austin's writing, however, it was also a principal source of her power. Benay Blend recognizes this in stating that she "favored the desert" because she "saw that austere landscape and its creatures as a nonconformist world" that "refused to comply with the requirements of American materialism" (18). By turning her affection and appreciation to the vast landscapes of the desert and mountain West rather than the more domesticated ones of her native Illinois (which she came to regard as bland), Austin found the perfect site for figuratively as well as literally sustaining her resistance to the status quo on numerous issues, not feminism alone. She resisted the trashing of the West by settlers and industrial interests; she resisted preservationists such as Muir who wanted the West to remain a place for Anglos to visit rather than a place for agrarian communities (which she tended to idealize even when writing about them very persuasively); she notably resisted the urban water grab by Los Angeles that resulted in desertification of the Owens Valley; she resisted avocational violence against animals; and she resisted Anglo exclusivity. Her outspokenness on all these issues was not always easily reconciled with a fictional mode, but they gave her nonfiction—and at times her fiction as well—a memorably sharp edge. The austere, often unaccommodating beauty of the Southwest (including arid California) became an emblematically appropriate spatial referent for her unaccommodating social criticism, implying that only the equally hardy need enter.

Willa Cather also found coherent plot structures difficult to construct, given the incompatibility of patriarchal conventions of western narrative, but in general was more successful than Austin in finding ways to avoid the violence and female submissiveness to heterosexual love plots that such conventions entailed. She accomplished this largely by eliminating conflict plots through interrupting linearity with what Jo Ann Middleton has called vacuoles—silences or skips in time that entail a refusal of cause-and-effect sequencing. It is largely this refusal of narrative conflict that gives her books (she tended to resist the term "novel") their quality of meditativeness as well as subtlety. Conflicts that would result from linear plotting or easily typecast characters are buried beneath the misleadingly tranquil surfaces of her "narratives." The depth that results is one of Cather's greatest strengths as a writer. But such techniques also mean that she rarely gains anything like Austin's cutting edge of directness. This can be frustrating for the reader who sees real issues of right and wrong (which the history of the West provides in such abundance) that Cather simply refuses to address, or addresses in only the most modulated tones. In *Death Comes for the Archbishop,* for example, although the brutal subjugation of the Navajo is acknowledged, it is softened by being positioned within the archbishop's valedictory musings. His harshest term of judgment against Kit Carson is "misguided" (*DCA* 308).[5] Austin forthrightly calls the same episode "a disgrace to America" (*LJE* 221).

Like this matter of the driving out of the Navajo, much of the difference between Austin and Cather relates to cultural diversity. Both saw the Southwest in its character as home to ethnically diverse population groups and viewed that ethnic richness with interest and delight. At that point their responses diverge. Precisely because of its multiculturalism, Austin saluted the Southwest as a model for America's future. She began *The Land of Journeys' Ending* with an avowal that it would be "a book of prophecy" and ended it by exclaiming exultantly "*hasta mañana,* . . . 'until tomorrow'!"[6] Cather looked toward the past and spoke of the Southwest in elegiac terms. It would be easy to drape Austin in the robes of enthusiast for cultural diversity and equality and Cather in those of the Europhile who cared little for any other group (as Austin herself charged in her comments on *Archbishop*). But the contrast is not quite so simple as it appears.

As we know, soon after Austin went to California she befriended, or was befriended by, Native Americans, in particular Seyavi, the Paiute "basket woman," as well as by Anglo prospectors, Basque shepherds, and members of the Spanish-speaking community who had settled in California generations earlier. From the evidence of her autobiography as well as her fiction and nonfiction, we can see that she valued this variety in her circle of acquaintances despite their being on if not beyond the fringes of gentility. She writes of Native Americans, in particular, with respect. It is no surprise, then, that in *The Land of Journeys' Ending* she treats the multicultural nature of the history of the Southwest as one of its beauties. Of course, she does not romanticize the Spanish to the point of exculpating them; on the contrary, she recognizes bluntly that Coronado "burnt two hundred hostages at the stake" when he and his men wintered near the present Bernalillo and that Spanish sovereignty was "forced" on the indigenous inhabitants. She tells of the Pueblo Revolt of 1680 without the least imputation of guilt on the Natives' part, instead seeing in their resistance to Spanish domination "futile heroisms" (*LJE* 236–37). If the pueblo-dwelling tribes are easy heroes here, at the expense of the nomadic and seminomadic tribes—as they almost always are in the eyes of Anglos, whose favor habitually goes to settled agricultural folk—she at any rate does not dismiss Native groups as a whole as if they were less worthy than people of European origin. Indeed, she views the pueblos, where Native people were living prosperously and well when the Spanish came, as ideal "republican . . . commonwealths" whose rebellion against colonizers was motivated primarily by that supposedly most American of virtues, a "predilection for worshiping God after the dictates of their own hearts" (*LJE* 236–37). The earliest Americans, or at any rate the pueblo-dwelling of them, are defined here as the politically truest Americans—a pattern of thinking, by no means Austin's alone, which Walter Benn Michaels deplores in *Our America* as a ploy justifying nativism and the Immigration Act of 1924 (45–47).

We do not have to maintain Michaels's view of the speciousness of such views of Native American life in order to see that Austin was indulging a degree of idealization here. Like other "antimodern feminists" (a term coined by Margaret Jacobs), she held Pueblo culture up as an alternative model by which to critique industrial America. But when placed against the vicious Anglocentrism of prevailing views associated with all we refer to as Manifest Destiny, her maintaining of clear distinctions of guilt and innocence in the invasions of the Southwest strikes one as a considerable gain in historical honesty. If she also falls into sporadic romanticizing of Spanish and mestizo settlers, she is at any rate clear-eyed and plainspoken in her assessment of the American takeover of the Southwest and the role of Christian (or she might prefer to say "Christian," in quotation marks) churches in both major waves of Euro/Anglo invasion. With the arrival of the "gringo," she writes, the fullness of oppression closed about the "terraced towns": "It was not until they fell into the clutch of this most Christian but un-Christlike civilization of ours, that with anguished certainty our Ancients fel[t] close over them the Left Hand of God" (*LJE* 235–36). Her skepticism about even the sincerity, let alone any measure of tolerance or gentleness, of Christian missionizing is clear, emphatic, and by no means limited to the Americanization effort that brought such atrocities as enforced attendance at "Indian schools." She regards the Spanish missionaries with an equal dubiousness: "Whatever the urge that compels great populations to sow themselves to all four quarters of the earth, the desire to spread the blessings of Christianity was, in the sixteenth century, a popular way of rationalizing it" (*LJE* 26).

Those of us inclined to admire Austin's forthrightness and her respect for diverse peoples are disappointed, then, to see that she sometimes slipped into the very mire of Anglocentrism that she deplored. As Melody Graulich writes in her introduction to a recent reprinting of *The Land of Journeys' Ending* (one that fortunately, unlike the 1987 reprinting of *Lost Borders,* preserves the illustrations), some of Austin's racial attitudes expressed there, particularly about African Americans, are "indefensible today" (xxii). They were in fact indefensible then, if only as measured against her own consciously maintained principles. To be sure, that is scarcely surprising; we are all of us shaped by our time, even if that means (as it did for Austin) being shaped into an oppositional frame of mind, and we are all better able to see the lapses we deplore in others than in ourselves. When we read of Austin's bossiness in telling Indians in New Mexico how to revive their own arts, we are probably merely amused. But when we see, in the story "Bitterness of Women," her description of Marguerita's unattractiveness cast in terms pointedly linked with her Mexican origins, we are and ought to be uncomfortable.

At some points *Starry Adventure* is also a betrayal of Austin's own best principles, despite the compelling strength of such elements in the book as its linkage of landscape with a new and mutually liberating vision of gender. The problem relates to Austin's use of the word "native" without adequate specificity. Gard, her Anglo center of consciousness, whose family moved to New Mexico because of his father's tuberculosis (a historically accurate reason for much migration to the area from the East in the early years of the twentieth century), repeatedly uses the term "native" for any of the darker-skinned people whose ancestral home is New Mexico, including Native Americans and Hispanos alike. Not only does this mean that for Gard the distinguishing characteristic must be skin color, thus throwing the undercurrent of social relations into a brown–white polarization, but such a grouping, without recognition of their specificity, would be offensive to all concerned.

At first Gard is the transparent perceiver of social distinctions he does not understand, but prejudice seeps into his mind as he grows. He refers mentally to "dirty natives" and to a former business associate as a "Mex." Given the mastery with which Austin uses the naive third-person point of view, one keeps waiting for her to bring Gard to a point of recognition and change, but that narrative moment never arrives. It is as if she is so intent on her treatment of landscape as a power for mental expansion, her demand for honesty and equality in gender relations, and her redefinition of western adventure into an inward process analogous to gestation, that she forgets to empower her treatment of race. Reading scenes such as the one near the end that is apparently designed to demonstrate the maturation of Gard and Jane's androgynous relationship—when he "whistled up a native boy" and "told" him to ride Jane's horse home (*SA* 411)—we can only remind ourselves that we all bring our personal and societal limitations to our art, try as we may to envision something better.

Austin did, in her personal migration and subsequent returns, experience the West as a place of new beginnings, as did Cather in her encounters with the Southwest. But being a newcomer carries its own quandaries. Gard ponders with bemusement the alienness of the ideas Easterners bring with them to the New Mexico highlands, such as Jane's parents' notions of class distinction and another visitor's expectations of a "bronco-busting, steer-dogging, gay señorita sort of affair" (*SA* 206, 268). The real West is not amenable to such ideas, and most people who bring them don't stay long. As Austin puts it, they "skid through" (*LB* 79). Those who submit themselves to the largeness and openness of the place, who try to learn its traditions rather than impose their own, find their views broadened accordingly. Gard observes that since the end of the war (that is, World War I), people have come to New Mexico "looking for fresh beginnings, for a frame of life which had no taint of the war sickness" in the hope of getting it "out of their systems" just as "lungers" had come hoping to rid themselves of tuberculosis (*SA* 186). Over the many years of their maturation as shown in the novel, New Mexico provides that kind of healing and tutelage to Jane and Gard. Like "a father you never had" (*SA* 191)—or in Austin's case, the mother she never had but kept searching for in the western landscape—it brings them gradually to new understandings of their shared life to be lived there.[7]

Unfortunately, Gard's optimistic belief that the land will reject alien or unworthy ideas and the people who hold them does not always prove true. Eudora Ballintin, who arrives with notions of a personal glamor to be enhanced and enriched by the "glamorous light" of New Mexico and its old system of patronage, stays. Like Mabel Dodge Luhan, she keeps bringing in new batches of friends from the East, giddy visitors who have "no knowledge of human backgrounds produced out of the soil." These fashionable people avid for "props" go away again unchanged (*SA* 245, 334). It is sadly ironic, then, that while Gard ponders the inappropriateness of such eastern visitors' expectations of Wild West excitement, he himself mentally refers to a group of indigenous laborers as "Greasers" (*SA* 268). Even Austin's most exemplary Anglo, freed from irrational notions of gender, has a lot to learn about ethnicity.

Like Austin, Cather conceived of the West in terms of a geographic spaciousness and beauty that afforded enlargement of vision. Its clarity of air allowed "breathing freely" (Rosowski, *Birthing* 56) in both physical and mental, or spiritual, ways. We see the expansive and sturdy-ing impact of the western environment in Cather herself and in various of her characters. The prairies give rise to a kind of giganticized vision in Alexandra's dream figure of the male muse who is able to carry her when she feels weak (an agriculturalizing as well as a reassigning of the usual genders of muse and creative agent) and also in Jim's and the immigrant girls' sighting of the outsized plow on the horizon. Similar moments of enlargement of personal, as well as literal, vision are found in her novels of the Southwest as characters encounter the equally spacious but grander landscapes of the mountains and desert.

Just as obvious in Cather's as it is in Austin's work, however, is the persistence of old ways of seeing and thinking. Perhaps the most glaring example is Jim Burden's lapse into Anglocentrism when he accuses a frightened Ántonia of "jabber[ing] Bohunk" (*MA* 44), but at various other narrative moments he behaves condescendingly toward her for being foreign and female. He sloughs off the vision of the West that he had formed from reading a dime novel about Jesse James on the train coming to Nebraska, but he can't entirely slough off the limitations of ingrained patterns and prejudices that he brings along as surely as he carries the book. How much of Jim's limitation of vision is attributed to him by Cather for ironic purposes is difficult to say, but a similar limitation of vision despite the mind-expanding experience of the West is evident in her own proclivity for ignoring the living presence of Native Americans.

This returns us to what Murphy praises as Cather's use of the West as a "pretext" for writing about "God and Christianity" in *Death Comes for the Archbishop,* or what I would term her imposition of imported ideas onto the Southwest. We see such an imposition very clearly, I think, in the image of the "cruciform tree" before which newly arrived Vicar Apostolic kneels in prayer (see figure 5.07). It is hard to imagine a cruciform juniper, although a confused traveler giddy with thirst might imagine one, particularly if that traveler were a priest whose most treasured image is the cross. In such a case his wishes might well be imposed on what he sees around him.

Father Latour's more general perception of his enormous new parish similarly reflects his viewing it with a stranger's eyes and, as a result, sometimes imposing alien interpretations. Understandably yearning for "his own kind, his own epoch, for European man and his glorious history of desire and dreams," he regards his parishioners at Acoma—a spot inhabited for hundreds of years, probably since AD 900—in demeaning "reptilian" terms as "rock-turtles on their rock" (*DCA* 109). His reaction is strangely unpastoral, despite his feeling a degree of sympathy for the Acomas when he realizes that every stone in the imposing church, even the enormous beams that span its nave, must have been carried not only up the sheer sides of the mesa but, in the case of the timbers, for forty or fifty miles (from the mountain known to Anglos as Mt. Taylor) "on the backs of men and boys and women" (*DCA* 107). We can read the chapter that immediately follows this passage, "The Legend of Fray Baltazar," as Cather's acknowledgment of the injustice of the Spanish oppressors, clerical as well as governmental, that led to the Pueblo Revolt of 1680. Indeed, Father Latour himself thinks of the church at Acoma, usually seen as one of the most beautiful treasures of the Spanish Colonial period, as "warlike" (*DCA* 106)—surely an indictment of the Spanish, not the Natives.

These passing criticisms of the Spanish do not extend to a questioning of the entire missionizing and colonizing endeavor, however, but only of the failings of specific individuals. Neither in her own voice nor in Latour's (of course) does Cather ever express such broad reservations. She seems to accept with tranquility—the tranquility that readers often sense in her prose style itself—the idea that a foreign religion and social system should be imposed on the native peoples of the Southwest and most of their land taken away from them. To be sure, there are moments, such as her reference to the harrowing of the Navajos, when it is hard to tell whether she has intentionally or subconsciously sewn "dock burs" into the textual "pants" to make us uncomfortable with what she seems to accept so smoothly (Urgo 25–28).

Austin, by contrast, questions very directly both the Christianizing mission that entailed such repression for Native Americans and the later Americanizing mission, with all its Anglocentrism:

> When the gringos came, they despised the Spanish-speaking even more than they did the Indian. And the Protestant missionary, with the Indian Bureau behind him, has made a dull, debasing smear over the lovely and aesthetic culture of the pueblos. Looking back, shall we come at last to see Christianity marching across the world as it marched along the Rio Grande, with dull, effacing foot, always confusing the teachings of its Founder with the particular obsession of the time in which it is expressed? (*LJE* 197)

Disregarding the later Protestant missionizing, Cather saw a thrilling gorgeousness and moral splendor in the spread of Catholicism. She seems never to have questioned the propriety of trying to "make good Americans" of the Native Americans and Mexicans whose homeland the United States took over, even though she indicated in letters and other writings that diversity was one of the beauties that attracted her to the Southwest.

Cather's attitude toward the multicultural makeup of the Southwest and people of color in general remains a puzzle. In large part they seem to have remained merely accessories to a picturesque scene. The place itself she made morally emblematic but, with rare exceptions, not the people. Her letters from Arizona in 1912 convey an orientalizing fascination with a bronze-skinned Mexican identified only as Julio who may briefly have fluttered her romantic interest. Clearly, she saw this man as beautiful. Similarly, in a noted passage of *The Song of the Lark* when Thea goes to a dance in Moonstone's "Mexican town" and sings for the group afterward, Cather pays tribute to the beauty and graciousness of these brown-skinned people, but does so in romanticizing ways while showing them as being worshipfully deferential to Thea's whiteness.[8] It is clear that she participated, even if in relatively benign ways, in the racism of her time, specifically by perceiving the West as an exotic but backward place that white people would find interesting but scarcely suitable for habitation. This would go far toward explaining her celebration of the American takeover of the Southwest in 1848 as a redemption—the celebration Austin labeled a disaster for local culture.

In *Land of Enchantment, Land of Conflict,* David Caffey presents a more extended argument supportive of Austin's point. Observing that "the earliest contacts among Indians, Hispanics, and Anglos in the Southwest were recorded by fiction writers as encounters of violence and hostility," he finds such "accounts of violent conflict" in two groups of novels: "the early novels of the Southwest, including dime novels," in which there is "nothing subtle about the nature of race relations," and "historical novels written and published in the twentieth century but set in earlier times" (35). "Without shame," Caffey writes, the writers of early Westerns "characterized the rivals of their Anglo heroes as red savages, bad Injuns, sneaking assassins, swarthy Mexicans, and worse" for reasons of "racial prejudice, a rampant nationalistic spirit, and the novelist's need for a menacing antagonist" in order to sell books. Such racial portrayals, he continues, "served to justify the aggressive exploits of the heroic frontiersmen who 'civilized' the West" (36).[9] We can readily see, by comparison, how revisionist Cather's writing was. Rosowski, in *Birthing a Nation,* is right on target in seeing that Cather's project of regendering the West poses a challenge to the defining Westerns of the early twentieth century. Her choice of the Catholic Church, rather than Indian wars or the cattle industry or any of the other violent stories that make up the typical stuff of Westerns, as "the most interesting of all [the West's] stories," as she said in a published letter to the editor of *The Commonweal* (*On Writing* 5), could scarcely be more revisionist. Except for Captain Forrester in *A Lost Lady,* she did not write about heroic frontiersmen civilizing the West through violence; she rarely wrote about violence at all, although her esteemed bishop in *Archbishop* carries a revolver. In her short story "The Dance at Chevalier's" she does have a "swarthy Mexican"—one of the racial types mentioned by Caffey—who is in fact a sneaking assassin, but her portrayal of race can rarely be called prejudicial in such unnuanced or unambiguous ways.[10]

Continuing his argument of the racist and repressive nature of

Westerns, Caffey points out that "following on the heels of the Americans" who took over New Mexico—the event in 1848 with which the prologue to *Death Comes for the Archbishop* begins—came "a conqueror of a different sort" (39), Jean Baptiste Lamy, the original for Latour in *Archbishop,* and the ultramontane church. Caffey sees Cather's treatment of these events as being marred by "denigration of native priests and native culture in favor of the European refinements introduced by Latour." The "eastern literati" who praised the novel, he concludes, seem to have been "largely oblivious to the way her views struck many residents of the Southwest" (39–40). The reaction in New Mexico, in fact, still reverberates, particularly the reaction to her stating as fact the disputed canard that Padre Martinez "was one of the leaders of the rebellion" against Governor Bent, the first American governor of the New Mexico Territory, and "himself planned the massacre" (*DCA* 11). Even her physical description of Martinez reflects a revulsion that is especially striking when we realize that her sketch of his appearance resembles the cave Latour finds so revolting in the chapter "Stone Lips."[11] Clearly, in the dispute between the historical Lamy and the local priests, Cather is correctly seen as having taken the newcomer's side, just as she anchored her narrative perspective in the newcomer's point of view in all three of her southwestern novels. To be sure, adopting the perspective of the newcomer allowed Cather to write of the Southwest with freshness and wonder, as well as with a directness fueled by her own sense of discovery. As we have seen, her visualizing descriptions of the "great country of desert and mountain ranges" (*DCA* 82), with its clear air and rich coloration, has a tangy deliciousness. Her descriptions of mountain landscapes have celebratory and inspirational qualities.

Cather also endorses in *Archbishop,* as in no other work, a desert aesthetic. No more than Austin—or Gilpin or O'Keeffe—does she mitigate the harshness of the desert. Hers is not a romanticizing presentation. When Latour wanders lost somewhere south of Albuquerque he faces an "interminable desert of ovens" (hills shaped like Native and Mexican *hornos,* or outdoor ovens; *DCA* 20). The "hundreds of square miles of thirsty desert" in which Latour and Vaillant seek to bring European Catholicism to their parishioners are a forbidding land of extremes of heat, cold, storm, and dryness and of great loneliness as they pursue their journeys (*DCA* 33, 69, 71). Cather's use of this environment as a test of her two priests' manhood and determination is, indeed, one way in which her writing of the Southwest is not revisionist at all, but quite traditional (Tompkins 71–72). At the same time, she uses her harsh setting as a stylized visual world of cleanness and bareness implying both ethical and aesthetic stringency. When Latour walks in the desert while visiting his Navajo friend Eusabio, he savors the "crystal sharpness" of the air toward evening (*DCA* 243). To the more vigorous Father Vaillant, the desert and its "yellow people" are "the dearest" of "all the countries he knew" (*DCA* 260). Vaillant's willingness to think of the desert people as children and to take advantage of their ready generosity in order to raise money for the church may temper some readers' warmth toward him, but his eagerness to serve his flock, even to the point of learning to preach in Spanish, fixes him as indeed, as he himself asserts, "*their man*" (*DCA* 217).

David Teague, in writing about "the rise of a desert aesthetic" in the late nineteenth and early twentieth centuries, provides a useful context for both Cather's and Austin's development of such an aesthetic. Another extremely popular book, not mentioned by Teague, which was first published during the period he surveys (in 1925) was a book of daily religious devotionals compiled by one Mrs. Charles E. Cowman called *Streams in the Desert.* The title bears witness to America's interest in its arid regions during those years. So wide was its readership that by 1945 it was in its twenty-fourth printing. Reading *Archbishop*'s scenes of refreshing streams in the desert, one wonders if Cather knew of this book. Her care and persistence in developing the visual beauty, as well as harshness, of the desert allows her to achieve concentrated effects of physical and spiritual refreshment when she shows streams in those deserts. In the opening chapter when Latour is lost in the desert, his horse's ability to sense the nearness of water leads him to Agua Secreta, Hidden Water:

> Below them, in the midst of that wavy ocean of sand, was a green thread of verdure and a running stream. This ribbon in the desert seemed no wider than a man could throw a stone, and it was greener than anything Latour had ever seen, even in his own greenest corner of the Old World. But for the quivering of the hide on his mare's neck and shoulders, he might have thought this a vision, a delusion of thirst.

Running water, clover fields, cottonwoods, locust trees, little adobe houses with brilliant gardens, a boy driving a flock of white goats toward the stream—that was what the young bishop saw (*DCA* 24).

Even the goat, an animal stigmatized in the Bible as well as in the Greek and Roman mythology that Cather knew so well, is transformed into an animal of innocence in this New World scene, as if that is part of its newness. Here, along the banks of the "life-giving water" in the clean and cleansing desert, Latour demonstrates his fundamental respect for the humble Spanish speakers who receive him. His self-introduction is equally unassuming: "'Blessed child,' he replied in Spanish, 'I am a priest who has lost his way. I am famished for water'" (*DCA* 31).

In scenes such as this Cather shows us her vision of the possibilities of the Southwest as a place of beauty and discipline within which a literate Frenchman can serve both the interests of Rome and an aggressor nation and the interests of a presumably illiterate villager. Within this space the newcomer and the hereditary inhabitant can greet each other as equals and fulfill their common needs. Taking up the trope of geographic space equated with mental space, she writes in *The Song of the Lark* that in the wide vistas of the West "the absence of natural boundaries gave the spirit a wider range" (174). That is the possibility Cather sees the West as offering America. Not conquest, but peaceful mutual acceptance. Not a supremacy of masculine brawn, but the opportunity for male and female alike to choose the way of living that most appeals to them. The tragedy is that she could not maintain such a vision. Like every other newcomer, she brought her own and her culture's shortcomings with her.

7

A CONTINUING TRADITION: LESLIE MARMON SILKO, MARGARET RANDALL, AND BARBARA BYERS

> She was intensely alive to the country—as a musician might be
> alive to an orchestral composition he was hearing
> for the first time. She did not talk about it much—
> but one felt that she was deeply engaged with it always,
> was continually receiving strong impressions
> from the things she saw and experienced.
>
> *Edith Lewis*
> Willa Cather Living

In writing about the West in a pictorial mode that described what they saw there and also proposed a moral and social vision, Austin and Cather were adapting a literary practice in which they had grown up, the use of landscape as an emblem or occasion for spiritual meditation.[1] In this sense, their approach was a traditional one, with deep roots in the nineteenth century. It was also traditional, as Krista Comer argues in *Landscapes of the New West,* in its eschewing of urban experience in the West. As we know, however, Austin and Cather did not merely continue traditional practices of landscape writing, any more than they perpetuated the conventions of the Western, but engaged it in a way that contested many of the established implications of the spacious, rugged West.

Mary Hallock Foote, a generation earlier, had envisioned a West gentled by the presence of domestic femininity. Although she pointed out, especially in her fiction, the harshness and perils women faced in the West, she emphasized nurturance and the quotidian in a series of pictures that avoided such staples of western imaging as barroom fights and armed conquest. Helen Hunt Jackson, too, had written a feminized story of the West, in *Ramona,* with a genteel domestic heroine saved by a female herbal healer. Austin and Cather continued Jackson's and Hallock Foote's revisionism but in very different ways. Eschewing their way of presenting gender, they constructed, instead, a less conventional, more inclusive androgynous gendering. This vision of the West not only redirected attention away from violence and conquest but challenged one of the favorite plots of the Western, the ruining of masculine adventure by the arrival of genteel femininity—a scenario Wallace Stegner typecasts as the plot of "civilizing" women taming "roving" men.[2] Austin's and Cather's women were free to engage in their own roving or work, to dress as they liked and live as they liked, to cross barriers of class (and for Austin ethnicity as well), and to open themselves quietly to the beauties of the western landscape, rather than appropriate it for dominion.

By bringing together several contemporaries of Austin and Cather who shared their recourse to the Southwest as an escape from restrictive social assumptions—Elsie Clews Parsons, Mabel Dodge Luhan, Georgia O'Keeffe, and Laura Gilpin—we have been able to see not only shared experiences and at times direct interactions among them, but also commonalities in their ways of picturing the West. It was these commonalities—not uniformly shared, to be sure, but variously recurrent—that established an alternative, anti-Western western tradition. For these modernist women of the Southwest the new tradition differed from the old in its construction of gender. It also differed (and here I think especially of the pacifist Elsie Clews Parsons) in being a tradition of peace. Judith Fryer writes that World War I was seen as revealing a "pronounced need to return to forms of the past" (35). Making a rare approach to an explicit argument, Cather seems to propose just that when Father Duchene, in *The Professor's House,* points out that the pre-Pueblo cliff dwellers seemed to have been a people who "declined in the arts of war" and built a culture "worthy to be a home for man" by developing "the arts of peace" (*PH* 217–19). Here and in *Death Comes for the Archbishop,* Cather juxtaposed wars and their aftermath against the peacefulness of southwestern settings and cultures as an argument for a new and quieter social order—as did Austin in *Starry Adventure.*

That both Austin and Cather were entirely conscious and deliberate in their contesting of the established "scripts" of the Western is beyond doubt.

We can infer this from the alterity of their works, of course; as Rosowski writes, such elements in Cather's fiction as "girls who can ride faster . . . than boys" contribute to "shattering the Western code" (*Birthing* 67). But they also made explicit statements about their own writing that show the self-awareness of their shaping of an alternative tradition. Cather's use of quotation marks in calling *O Pioneers!* a "slow-moving story, without 'action,' without 'humour,' without a 'hero'" and her definition of its subject as "heavy farming people" and "pig yards" bespeaks her revisionist aim (*On Writing* 94). In *My Ántonia* she sets up a model of the conventional Western (in the form of the Jesse James novel young Jim reads on the train going west) and shows it to be false. And in her essay "My First Novels [There Were Two]," she avows that when she turned to writing novels of the Great Plains she "ignored all the situations and accents that were then generally thought to be necessary" (*On Writing* 93). The essence of the drama of the Southwest, she wrote, was the church (*On Writing* 5)—that is, not cowboys or cattle drives or Cavalry charges or wagon trains beset by Indians. Mary Austin was even more explicit in stating flatly that although her books were "always of the West" (which is not quite the case), they were "never what is known as 'Westerns.'" In that, she claimed, they were "always a little in advance of the current notion" (*EH* 320).

The alternative tradition Austin and Cather led in establishing did not by any means end with their careers. Both Georgia O'Keeffe and Laura Gilpin, for example, remained active for several years after Austin's death in 1934 and Cather's in 1947. Unlike Anglo visitors who brought to their encounters with the desert preestablished notions of what a hospitable world should look like and used those notions as a basis for seeing the desert in terms of lack, or "what it was not" (Solnit 67), Gilpin and O'Keeffe, much like Austin and Cather, saw it in terms of a positive unclutteredness and integrity. In their art of the Southwest, O'Keeffe's in paint and Gilpin's with a camera, we see a modernist vision immersed in a powerful geographic vision, one equally rejecting of both a stereotypically masculine and a stereotypically feminine aesthetic. It is an equalitarian vision rooted in the Southwest and rendered in a strong, minimalist style.[3]

Another thread of connection can be seen in the work of photographer Nancy Newhall. Newhall, who later collaborated with Paul Strand on the book *Time in New England* (1950) and with Ansel Adams on *This Is the*

American Earth (1960), first saw western landscapes in 1940 and was "genuinely surprised to be so deeply affected" by them (M. Wilson 51). In the summer of 1944, her attention having been directed by Adams's wife Virginia to the desertification of the Owens Valley, she read Mary Austin, who had collaborated with Adams earlier (on *Taos Pueblo,* 1930) and had fought against the diversion of water from the valley to Los Angeles. Newhall was spending the summer in the arid high valley of south-central California where Austin herself lived for much of her early adulthood. It was under these circumstances, then, of direct experience of Austin's own place as well as her highly visual prose that Newhall made the photograph *Dead Tree, Owens Valley,* showing the starkness of a dead tree still retaining some of its intricacy of pattern, standing against the shape of a distant mountain and against a sky that takes up the top two-thirds of the picture (see Norwood and Monk 60). We can well believe that Austin would have been interested and pleased. Later, with collaboration by Ansel Adams, Newhall would write an article about Austin published in *Arizona Highways* in 1968.[4]

Edith Lewis's words used as the epigraph to this chapter refer, of course, to Willa Cather and to New Mexico, but they might equally well have been written about Newhall or O'Keeffe or Gilpin. Perhaps they would not so well have suited Austin or Mabel Dodge Luhan, both of whom *did* talk about their aliveness to the country, and did so a great deal. Lewis's words do seem particularly well suited, however, to Leslie Marmon Silko and Margaret Randall, writers of the pictured West among our own contemporaries who continue a female tradition providing an alternative to the overdecorated and frequently violent traditions of the Western. Both New Mexicans, Silko and Randall—the one very well known, the other less so—are "deeply engaged with [the Southwest] always" and are "continually receiving strong impressions" from the things they see and experience there. In this concluding chapter, I want to indicate some parallels and implicit connections of both Silko and Randall, as well as Albuquerque artist Barbara Byers, with Austin and especially with Cather.

I have chosen these figures in part because they demonstrate the opening of southwestern art and letters to women of new voices and visions—in Silko's case Native, in Randall's and Byers's case matter-of-factly uncloseted lesbian. In particular, I want to underscore Krista Comer's argument, in

Landscapes of the New West, that Silko is indeed a western writer and thus provides demonstration that western regionalism is not merely a "white thing" (8–9). The continuance, by writers and artists such as Silko, Randall, and Byers, of Austin and Cather's tradition of a reconceived, regendered West has been facilitated—has been made possible, in large part—by enormous changes in American society with respect to the status of ethnic minority groups, assumptions about women, and a greater openness of discussion not only of gender roles but of sexuality. It has been facilitated, too, by the persistence of a deeply rooted environmental concern, despite governmental and industrial inattention or even hostility. In the 1930s that concern especially occupied writers and artists of the Southwest in the form of indignation over erosion, often seen as quasi-sexual violations of the mother's body. Environmental concern has continued to occupy artists and intellectuals and citizens of all sorts up to the present.[5] That concern is yet another thread of commonality with Cather and especially with Austin.

In 1925 Willa Cather wrote two short letters to Mabel Dodge Luhan mentioning an incident that was later retold at greater length by Edith Lewis in her memoir about her partner of so many years, *Willa Cather Living.* The two accounts comprise a kind of collaborative telling. Together, they establish a curious and coincidental link with Silko, as well as an indirect but very important link or parallel between Cather and Lewis, on the one hand, and Randall and Byers on the other. And curiously enough, by way of a passing reference to canned food, their three-part account also reaches back in our story to both Austin's and Cather's first arrival in the West.

In the first of Cather's two notes to Luhan, written some time in July 1925 (*Calendar* #790), she mentioned that she and Edith would soon be going to Laguna—that is, to Leslie Marmon Silko's home pueblo. In the second, written August 7 (*Calendar* #792), she reported that they had been there and had unexpectedly stayed over for three nights, despite the lack of accommodations they would usually have considered suitable, because heavy rains had made it impossible to get on to the place they most wanted to see, Acoma. Lewis's account, published almost thirty years later, adds that their stay at Laguna was "a curiously interesting and memorable experience," and one that found its way into *Death Comes for the Archbishop* in the same way that many of Cather's stored-up memories were incorporated into her writing, by being "drawn on when they were needed" (144, 146, 101–102). In this case, her memories did not remain stored up very long; she was already hard at work on *Archbishop,* with its important Acoma sequence, when they made their visit. Here is Lewis's account in full, with a few comments of my own:

> At that time the Santa Fé trains stopped at Laguna, where the beautiful Laguna pueblo is. From there one had to hire a car to go to Ácoma, about thirty miles away. When we got off the train, there was no one to help us with our suitcases except two little girls, about eight and ten years old. They told us that "two ladies"—their mother and the cook—ran the hotel. The hotel turned out to be the roughest and dirtiest we had ever stopped in. The poor, overworked woman who kept it never had time to sweep it—there were great clods of earth on the carpets. The windowpanes in our bedrooms were broken in jagged holes, and burnt matches and cigarette papers were scattered all over the floor. The only bathroom was down a flight of stairs and at the end of a long, dark corridor. All the food in the hotel came out of cans, including the milk and butter.
>
> Behind the hotel was a wretched "tourist's camp," where families in old cars crusted with mud, and with mattresses tied to them, often stopped for the night. Sometimes they would try to leave before dawn, so as not to have to pay the 50 cents fee.
>
> We had intended to stay in Laguna overnight, drive to Ácoma, and go on the next day. But it turned out to be a season of cloudbursts.

They had in fact arrived in the early part of the region's annual monsoon season.

> Every day there were heavy rains, and the road to Ácoma was impassable for a car. We had to stay in Laguna a week.

> Yet during that week, in those very uncomfortable surroundings, Willa Cather often said afterwards she got the most constructive ideas for her story that she had in the whole course of writing it.

This is a surprising assertion and one we are free to doubt, as we are often free to doubt statements in Lewis's loving memoir. The "most constructive ideas" would seem to have come from the biography of Father Machebeuf that Cather came across while in Santa Fe. Even so, the visit to Laguna and Acoma was undoubtedly important. Cather told Luhan that she didn't for a moment regret the enforced stopover.

> The hotel was almost empty. One guest I remember, a prosperous Mexican named Mr. Narcissus, who arrived in Laguna with a flock of fifty prize rams, with wonderful curling horns—each ram valued at $500. The food at the hotel was so bad that we often bought crackers and cheese at the Indian trader's, taking it out to eat on the ledges behind the pueblo. A very interesting little French family kept the railway station—the daughter was the railway telegrapher, and used to throw the messages to the engineers of the fast trains, as they ran through without stopping. It was pleasant to sit on the bench outside the station house and watch the life that came and went. The Laguna Indians seemed to travel a great deal, and were always getting on and off trains. They were an unusually handsome tribe, and the women wore very pretty costumes.
>
> Finally a day came when our driver, a Carlisle College Indian named Mr. Sarascino, announced that he could get us to Ácoma. There is no need to tell of that journey—Willa Cather has told it in the *Archbishop*. In a sense, she had been looking forward to it all her life. As we passed the Mesa Encantada (the Enchanted Bluff) we stopped for a long time to look up at it.

So the "boy" of "The Enchanted Bluff" has now reached "his" goal.

> A great cloud-mesa hung over it. It looked lonely and mysterious and remote, as if it were far distant in time—thousands of years away. (*Lewis* 144–46)

Thousands of years. Or perhaps even antediluvian, the word attached to the Acomas in Latour's miserable thoughts, in *Archbishop*.

It seems likely that the Laguna hotel where Cather and Lewis stayed and the cafe where they ate, in this culturally colonizing excursion of Anglo females into Native space, belonged to Leslie Marmon Silko's great-grandfather.

Silko's multi-genre book *Storyteller,* with its rich interplay between text and picture, mingles retellings of traditional stories, family lore, poems, excerpts from letters, and photographs of the Laguna area and people, most of them taken by family members. Notes or captions to the twenty-six photographs that appear in the book are grouped at the end, a fact that affects the reading field of the work by, in effect, mystifying it. Photograph #17, for example, a casual snapshot of the interior of the small eatery showing (presumably) the youthful ancestor himself behind a counter with four stools, appears on a facing page to a photograph of Silko's own father at work, many years later, as a photographer. No explanation of the curious juxtaposition is offered unless one turns to the back of the book, where the caption for #17 reads, "For a while in the late 1920's my great-grandpa Stagner ran a cafe at Laguna. There was also a camp ground there and a few motel cabins but after cars started going faster and U. S. Route 66 was paved, tourists and travellers no longer needed to stop at Laguna" (272). Silko's and Lewis's descriptions of the hotel do not sound quite the same, but after all, the memory on which Lewis was drawing was twenty-seven years old while those on which Silko was drawing were not even her own but family memories reaching back over fifty years.

I would guess that the two little girls who met Cather and Lewis at the train were Silko's great-aunts. The "Indian trader's" at which Lewis and Cather bought crackers and cheese would likely have been Abie Abraham's store; the phrase "Indian trader" customarily refers to a white man who trades with Indians, not to an Indian who trades. Silko's grandfather Henry C. Marmon was employed at Abraham's store when he returned from the

Sherman Institute in Riverside, California—an Indian School that stifled his wish to be an engineer and trained him to be a store clerk instead. Her dating is not precise, but he seems to have returned between 1913 and 1919. A snapshot (268) shows a young Grandpa Hank standing in front of the store. He was "eventually," Silko explains, able to open his own store, whether by buying out Abraham or by starting a competitive enterprise she does not say (192), but apparently was still a clerk, not the owner, when Cather and Lewis bought cheese and crackers in 1925, because Silko says that Grandma Lillie "worked all day at Abie's store" the day she gave birth to Lee Marmon, Henry's son and Silko's own father. This happened on September 20 of either 1925 or 1926 (182). Cather and Lewis, then, were either two months too early or a year and two months too early to be there at the time of the birth. Grandpa Hank sometimes drove tourists to Acoma, but he apparently did not drive Cather and Lewis there; Lewis clearly says their driver was a Carlisle graduate named Sarascino. (Cather agrees, with different spelling, in her second letter to Mabel.) Their pause to look at the Enchanted Bluff would have been standard practice. And a picture of the bluff taken by Lee Marmon appears in *Storyteller.*

Silko makes two comments on the importance of the pictures reproduced in *Storyteller.* In the "Acknowledgment" she writes,

> Special thanks and my love to Denny
> for helping me bring together
> the stories and the photographs
> which are themselves part of the stories.

At the beginning of the text proper, Silko explains that she selected the photographs from family pictures stored in a "tall Hopi basket" decorated with a traditional figure. She then singles out two of the photographers whose pictures appear: her grandpa Hank, who "first had a camera when he returned from Indian School," and her father, who "learned photography in the Army" during World War II (1). Both are important and recurring characters in the text itself. She thus extends the idea that we have noted in Austin's and Cather's southwestern novels, of a peaceful art made in full awareness of war and its effects. In this case, one of those effects was Lee Marmon's expertise in taking pictures. Insisting that "a photograph is serious business" and that "photographs have always had special significance" for the Laguna people, Silko reemphasizes:

> [T]he photographs in the Hopi basket
> have a special relationship to the stories as I remember them.
> The photographs are here because they are part of many of the stories
> and because many of the stories can be traced in the photographs.

We recall Cather's statement that the Benda illustrations to *My Ántonia* were in effect part of the story.[6]

While many of the twenty-six photographs in *Storyteller* are outdoor shots, only six are what we would call landscapes. Silko and her characters rarely look *at* landscape. Indeed, "landscape"—a word that "describes the natural world as an aesthetic phenomenon" or a "static backdrop" (Solnit 45)—is scarcely the right term for place as Silko writes of it. Seen, in most of the pictures, in connection with individuals or the pueblo as a whole, place is not only much more specific than the phrase "natural world" implies, it is more active, the ground of being and of meaning, a composite of the earth itself and what has happened there. Such pictures show a people *in place.* Likewise, it is implicit in Silko's poems, stories, and expository paragraphs that there can be no life, as she knows and values it, that is not rooted in place. Like Austin, she thinks of the Southwest—her own Southwest, the area around Laguna—not merely as an arrangement of visual forms but as a place for living.[7] The beauty of the land is acknowledged, but human events and traditional narratives give the land significance, even as they draw their significance *from* the land.

We can see this oneness of place and story in a motif of black lava running through the text (one of several such motifs). Photograph #13, of the black peaks in the valley near Laguna (figure 7.01), documents that the peaks are really there, while at the same time the note to the photograph associates them with Navajo sacred stories (Silko 271). The ridges or humps of hardened lava seen in the photograph are also, according to tradition, the relics of an event that is explained in "Up North," one of numerous titled narratives in *Storyteller.* The Sun Father battles with Kaup'a'ta, the Gambler, in the

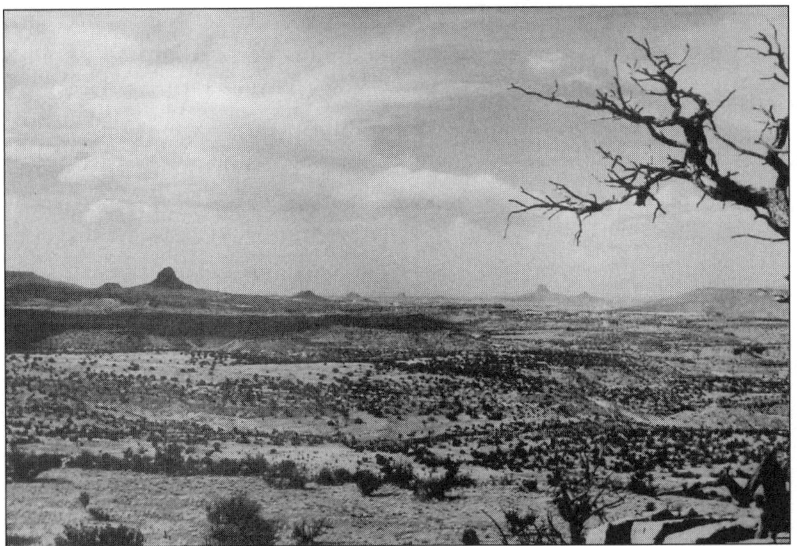

7.01 Lee H. Marmon, photograph #13 from Leslie Marmon Silko, *Storyteller* (p. 139) ("The Navajos say the black peaks in this valley are drops of blood that fell from a dying monster which the Twin Brothers fought and fatally wounded.")

Zuni mountains; their fight does not end with a killing, because Kaup'a'ta cannot be killed, but with a mutilation that might well be thought to have dripped blood over the valley:

> So Sun Man knew what to do:
> He took the flint blade
> and he cut out the Gambler's eyes
> He threw them into the south sky
> and they became the horizon stars of autumn (169)

The black lava reappears in "Lullaby," in which a mother sits on a lava boulder with her children in order to be able to see whites coming to take them away to school (46). In "Tony's Story," when blood gets soaked into the ground as it does in the legend of Kaup'a'ta (124), there is no hint of its forming mounds of lava because this is blood from one of the people, not from the violent oppressor, the "state cop." But at the end of "Tony's Story," after "dark, heavy blood" again soaks into the ground, this time the cop's (129), when Tony sets the patrol car on fire the sky is filled with "spirals of thick black smoke"—a visual reminder of the lava.

The motif of lava and badlands continues in the partly comical but all too serious poem "Long time ago" (which also appears in Silko's *Ceremony*) in connection with a "witches' conference" held "way up in the lava rock hills/north of Cañoncito" (131). In "A Geronimo Story," Laguna riders hired by terrified whites to find Geronimo ride through the malpais (badlands) as they approach the Zuni mountains. Although the lava malpais is a threatening presence—a spoiled land since soil is either absent or thin over the rocks, and a peril to horses and mounted riders, as well as a place for witches—it is also, in keeping with Native theologies, a place of good. If it is cursed in the belief system of the Navajos, it is after all the place where the Twin Brothers killed "a dangerous giant" (217). Where soil *is* present it is warm, so plants grow earlier in the spring, and although it is "easy to lose sight of landmarks and trails" in the malpais, it provides a place where the narrator can sit and talk with his uncle (217). Moreover, for the very reason that the Navajo consider it a place cursed by the blood of a monster, it has provided a place to hide when the Lagunas were pursued, where they kept stashes of food and water. And we see the badlands used in that very way in "The Storyteller's Escape"—the people "leave the village/and hurry into the lava flows/where they waited until the enemy had gone" (248). Sure enough, the enemies abandon their pursuit rather than enter the malpais, and the storyteller herself is back home "sitting in front of her house/waiting for them" when the others come back "from their hide-outs in the lava flow" four days later (253).

These references to the malpais demonstrate how *Storyteller* works, structurally. Motifs run from story to story (whether traditional or realistic) and into poems and family lore, showing how all parts of the whole—myth, daily life, and the land itself—are connected. Black mesas, black mountains, and black dirt add to the motif of the black lava, and black is one of the sacred directional colors of the Laguna people. The stories are recognized as important because they take place in an immemorially sacred place, and each iteration accrues meaning to the whole.

Another pervasive motif in *Storyteller* is water and the need for water. As with the motif of black lava, the repeated instances of this motif accrue meaning through multidimensional and multigeneric resonance, often by juxtaposition. In "Up North," the story with which we began our survey of the lava motif, the reason the Sun Father must gamble with Kaup'a'ta is that the monster has captured the storm clouds. It is a violent story; Kaup'a'ta drains his victims' blood into the blue corn meal he feeds his next victims, thus bewitching them, and Sun Man cuts out Kaup'a'ta's eyes. But the violence is subsumed into the sustaining of life after the Gambler is defeated:

> Then he opened the doors of the four rooms
> and he called to the stormclouds:
> "My children," he said
> I have found you!
> Come on out. Come home again.
> Your Mother, the Earth is crying for you.
> Come home, children, come home." (Silko 169)

This is the culmination, the iteration that most fully captures the accrued meaning of water. But it rests on all the previous iterations.

The water motif begins very near the start of the book in the brief family narrative "Grandma Lillie was born in Los Lunas," with such light hints as references to her baptism, the fact that Great-Grandfather Stagner had run away from a farm in Sweetwater, Texas, and his becoming a driller of water wells, among other enterprises (52). In the story that immediately follows, "Yellow Woman," the first-person narrator meets a mythico-real man from the north, Silva, beside a river. He kidnaps or seduces her—the first of many such abductions unless one counts as an abduction Grandma Lillie's having been taken away to Laguna from Los Lunas, on the Rio Grande. In the story, the avatar of Yellow Woman returns home after her time with Silva by "the path up from the river" (62), never knowing whether she has moved into the myth or myth has moved into her.

In the poem that immediately follows, "Cottonwood Tree Part One: Story of Sun House," Yellow Woman, or Kochininako, reappears in a more purely mythic form. An initially unnamed woman is lured from her village to a "sandy wash" to meet the Sun, who is "only pretending to be/a human being" (63). Then in "Cottonwood Part Two: Buffalo Story" Kochininako meets the "very beautiful" Buffalo Man at a mysterious roiled pool when she is out looking for water for her family during a drought (68). It is a strong and of course entirely natural linkage between water and sex; both bring renewal of life. In this story of magical transformations and redemptive scapegoating, when Kochininako is rescued by Estoy-eh-muut, Arrow Boy, only to be killed for going off with the alluring Buffalo Man, a great many buffalo are found and killed and their dried meat taken home so that "nobody would be hungry then" (76). After a sequence of short segments about hunting and harmony with nature (including the supernatural), reinforced visually with a snapshot of the young Silko and her uncle with five newly killed deer, Aunt Alice tells a story in which Kochininako, as a child, goes hunting and is captured by the giant Estrucuyu, who eats all her rabbits before demanding her clothes and trying to grab her. She is rescued by the Hero Twins, but has had a warning about sexual peril, and the giant's heart, pulled out of his dead body by Ma'see'wi and Ou'yu'ye'wi and thrown "as far as they could throw," lands "right over here/near the river/between Laguna and Paguate" (87). Once again a traditional story is attached to a real place—as it was, perhaps, although with only the lightest touch, in "Grandma Lillie was born in Los Lunas."

After a comical story about a hapless character named Old Man George and his philanderings, Grandma A'mooh tells a story about a philandering woman "long ago" who goes to get water and meets an alluring man, not quite a stranger, "in the tamarack and willow/beside the river." These are again Kochininako and Buffalo Man, in different guises. Leaving her water jar on the river bank, she goes off with him. This time the story takes a comic turn when she returns home:

> "You better have a damn good story,"
> her husband said,
> "about where you been for the past
> ten months and how you explain these
> twin baby boys."
> "No! That gossip isn't true. She didn't elope
> She was *kidnapped* by
> that Mexican
> at Seama feast.

> You know
> my daughter
> isn't
> *that* kind of girl." (95–96)

Myth has again invaded life, if only as an excuse—but then, as we have been told several tales back, Yellow Woman herself returned with twins when she was carried off by the ka'tsina from the north (55).

Another comic twist quickly follows. Right after the line "*that* kind of girl," without page break or title, another quick story begins in which (so it seems) three Laguna women are kidnapped or seduced by four Navajo men. After being tracked along the Rio Puerco by the F.B.I., who follow a "trail/of wine bottles and/size 42 panties/hanging in bushes and trees/all along the road" (oh no—the villainous Navajos are stripping off their clothes and raping them as the giant was about to do to poor little Kochininako!), the victims are rescued:

> "We couldn't escape them," he told police later.
> "We tried, but there were four of them and
> only three of us." (96)

Our assumption as to which were male and which female in this encounter, based as it is on abundant familiarity with who usually gets carried off and raped, is abruptly and comically inverted: three men, four women. The western setting has become what Comer calls a "landscape of female desire" (164). But the irrepressible Silko isn't through yet. Immediately on the heels of our gasp of surprised laughter she produces yet another comic version of the story, this time in the voice of a woman to whom "it's always happening." This time it was

> that Navajo
> from Alamo,
> you know,
> the tall

good-looking
one.
He told me
he'd kill me
if I didn't
go with him
And then it
rained so much
and the roads got muddy.

When she gets home she tries to explain by telling "the story," but her husband, apparently unconvinced, moves back to his mother's house.

I don't blame him either.
I could have told
the story
better than I did.
(Silko 98)

This last throwaway statement quietly underscores the importance of storytelling—one of Silko's major themes.

After this point the motif of life-giving water—often but not always associated with sexual ravishment—continues in, for the most part, a more serious vein, leading up to the culminating story of the Gambler and the Sun Father with which we began. "Old Woman Ck'o'yo's son" from "up north" (the direction of the Ka'tsina who lured away Yellow Woman) entices Ma'see'wi and Ou'yu'ye'wi into such a fascination with magic that the Corn Mother goes away to a lower world taking the rain clouds with her. The earth turns to dust, and the people are starving. It takes extraordinary effort by Hummingbird and Fly, as messengers, to persuade her to return and bring back the rain (111–21). A time without rain is a disaster. Similarly, the abusive Big Cop arrives, in "Tony's Story," when "the sky was wide and hot and the summer rains did not come" (234). When the Big Cop is killed, rain clouds are "gathering" (129). Part of the terrifying evil brought by white people as foretold by the witch who scares all the other witches gathered in a "conference" in the lava rock hills is that they will "poison the water/they will spin the water away/and there will be drought" (134). In the summer when Estoy-eh-muut, Arrow Boy, begins to suspect that Kochininako is meeting with witches, there is a drought and a spring goes dry (140). When Corn Woman gets angry because Reed Woman spends her days splashing in the river rather than working—somewhat like Martha in the Bible when Mary sits listening to Jesus rather than helping in the kitchen—Reed Woman goes below to "the original place" and "there was no more rain then" (159). The solution is not given, but immediately, in the segment just preceding the story of the Gambler and Sun Father's rescue of the storm clouds, we are told of another kind of renewal of life:

certain kinds of clouds—
some white and scattered like river rock
and others
mountains rolling into themselves
swollen lavender before rainstorms

were necessary for Silko's father's art (161). As if in confirmation, a photograph of Lee Marmon at work with his camera shows that there are clouds. The last words of this piece of family lore comprise Lee Marmon's redemptive message that Silko might become a writer and live in the hills near Laguna. Correspondingly, the last words of the Gambler story are the Sun Father's call, "Come home, children, come home" (169). And in the next long story after this, "The Man to Send Rain Clouds," old Teofilo's grandsons appropriate the Catholic priest's sprinkling with water into their own burial rites of tying a feather into his hair and sprinkling the bundled body with cornmeal, in order to ensure that "the old man could send them big thunderclouds for sure" (186).

I have tried to demonstrate, in my summaries, that the various components of this lengthy and varied motif of running water, the need for water, and restoration of life through water (and sex) that runs through *Storyteller* often gains in significance by the way in which segments are juxtaposed. The motif itself may well remind us of Austin's recurrent watercourses in *The Land of Little Rain* and the penalties exacted by a harsh land on those who stray from water, in *Little Rain, Cactus Thorn,* and others. We may be reminded, too, of Cather's stream flowing in the bottom of Panther Canyon, among cottonwood seedlings, in *The Song of the Lark,* or of the life-giving Agua Secreta in *Death Comes for the Archbishop.* Or we might think of the image of "streams in the desert" in the popular devotional book, bringing to bear on the spiritual aspirations of Mrs. Charles E. Cowman's twentieth-century readers (including my own mother, around mid-century) the traditional biblical imagery of desert purification and renewal by water. Biblical precedent, together with imagery from Greek mythology, was almost certainly present in Cather's mind when she wrote the Agua Secreta episode and the episode of the traveling priests who find avatars of the Holy Family while wandering in the desert and are given refreshment (*DCA* 292–96). Cather brought a structure of treasured mythology to her writing about the arid Southwest, which provided a receptive habitation. In Silko's *Storyteller* the realities of an arid place (Laguna and its environs) produce imagery of desert and water and mythologies that reach through her various retellings as well as inventions that echo traditional stories. All are rooted in the land itself and spring from it; they are not brought *to* it from another mythology imposed from the outside. Silko's imagery of drought and water springs directly from her Native identity and her rooting in a specific place, and from her refusal to be co-opted by white hegemony.[8]

Silko's writing is connected with Austin's and Cather's, even so, not only through its siting but through its shifty regendering. She does not in any overt way begin with Anglo visions of an adventurous, masculine West, and proceed to challenge them, but through their very existence her stories told from a perspective of the female and the ethnically other (mixed Native, Mexican, and Anglo) implicitly pose an alternative version. The teller and the teller's identity make a difference in the tale. It *mattered* that two white women, one from Illinois and one from Virginia, found the West and Southwest a fruitful site for their writing. They produced an alternative vision that grew out of their own personhood and experience. Likewise, it *matters* that Leslie Silko, this woman with an outward flamboyance much like Austin's, is a brown-skinned Lagunan. Out of the particulars of her own identity, she writes a different but, like theirs, regendered version of the Southwest. And because of her identity and her immersion in family storytelling, she is able to tell us, as Austin and Cather either cannot or at any rate do not, about the prejudice experienced by Indians in the Southwest, especially those in whose families (like her own) intermarriage has occurred.

The importance of the storyteller's role is emphasized in both direct and embedded ways. The woman who stayed away with the Navajo from Alamo might have kept her husband if she had been a better storyteller. Listen up, Silko tells us, and take storytelling seriously. In "Saturday morning I was walking past Nora's house," her neighbor's grandchildren have found one of her poems in a book, a poem that originally came from one of her grandfather's stories. Grandfather would never tell his story until the listeners gave him something good to eat. Similarly, Silko tells her neighbor, who is in the process of baking bread, that "you're supposed to feed the storyteller good things" (110). The laborer is worthy of her hire. The point is tersely underscored toward the end of the book in "Helen's Warning at New Oraibi," surely referring to Helen Sekaquaptewa, a noted Hopi storyteller often recorded and filmed:

> "You must be very quiet and listen respectfully.
> Otherwise the storyteller might get upset and pout
> and not say another word all night." (254)

We must suppose that the famous storyteller would have heartily approved the modern-day coyote story with which *Storyteller* ends, which involves a Hopi woman called Mrs. Sekakaku. "Helen's Warning" is followed by an at least partially factual story about storytelling. When Franz Boas came through Laguna in 1918, his student Elsie Clews Parsons stayed to collect stories intended to help Boas construct a grammar of Keresan, the language (and mythological system) of Laguna. But Boas, being quite literally tone deaf, was unable to work with inflected languages. The result was Clews Parsons's volume of stories, one of them told to her by Silko's great-grandfather Marmon. In his story, a she-coyote is bringing water in her mouth to her pups when a meadowlark keeps mocking her appearance, and each time—four times, the magic number—the coyote opens her mouth to protest and spills the water. The pups die of thirst. An explicit lesson is drawn:

> A good deal of controversy surrounded
> and still surrounds my great-grandfather and his brother
> who both married Laguna women.
> . . .
> Maybe he chose that particular coyote story
> to tell Parsons
> because for him at Laguna
> that was the one thing he had to remember:
>   No matter what is said to you by anyone
>   you must take care of those most dear to you.
>   (255–56)

A great deal else is also going on in this little story about storytelling. Besides prejudice, water, and numerology, it brings together motifs of translation, transmission, Anglo intrusion, and most emphatically gender. A Native female writer tells about an Anglo female story-gatherer collaborating with a famous but disabled male; her retold story came from an Anglo but long acculturated male (himself performing as coyote, the trickster) who comments on one of his own life lessons by casting himself as a female coyote. Let us take one last walk through *Storyteller,* then, this time singling out in a more intentional way the pervasive motifs of gender. It is obviously not feasible to note all of the book's sixty-six sections, but I will begin at the beginning and proceed in a generally sequential way in order to emphasize, once again, textual and pictorial juxtapositions.

In much the same way as Austin and Cather, Silko regenders the West not simply by feminizing it but by insisting on a strong female presence free from limitation by preconceptions of role or propriety. Like them, she renders a previously masculinized space androgynous. Unlike Austin and Cather, however, Silko shows that one of the primary ways this is accomplished is through complementarity and collaboration between the sexes. This idea is launched with the acknowledgments at the front of *Storyteller:* to Mei-Mei for suggestions, to Jim for letters, to Beth for design, to Jeanette for "patience and faith," to Denny for helping "bring together the stories and photographs." With the first narrative segment, on the very first page, family members emerge as sources of photographs; especially singled out are Grandpa Hank and "my father." Then the first of a sequence of strong women appears: Aunt Susie, born to the Reyes family in Paguate and married to Silko's Anglo great-uncle Walter K. Marmon. Aunt Susie completed Indian school and attended college in Carlisle, Pennsylvania, and after returning home proved herself omni-competent, so that we may well want to regard her as an avatar of one of the Holy People. She "continued her studies, particularly of history," bore children, helped operate a cattle ranch, cooked, taught school, wrote, told stories, and, as Silko's caption to a picture of her chubby young self alongside Aunt Susie tells us, "spent a good deal of time at the Marmon Ranch" (269). The picture (figure 7.02) shows us Aunt Susie's strong connection with the land in the way her dress is blowing and the matter-of-factness with which she rests her hand on a firmly set fence post. Along with the textual tribute, it tells us that Aunt Susie served as an example and model of strength. The section that follows retells Aunt Susie's version of the little girl who ran away from Acoma and drowned in a lake, whose clothes were scattered to the winds by her mother, becoming butterflies. Then another strong female figure is introduced, Great-Grandmother Marie Anaya, who dared to travel by train to Ohio, her husband Robert Marmon's home of origin (perhaps verifying Edith Lewis's observation that the Lagunas had a proclivity for travel), while he stayed at the pueblo and nursed his bitterness at people's calling him "squaw man" and turning his sons away from public facilities (17).

With the importance of family storytellers established, next comes the powerful "Storyteller," with its female Inuit seer who takes both Anglo and Inuit men into her bed, exacts revenge on the white storekeeper who sold poisoned liquor to men of the village, and persists in telling her story to the attorney who would silence her. We then meet Grandma A'mooh, a powerful storyteller, important in Silko's life, who seemingly willed her own death when she was displaced to Albuquerque and had no one to talk to. Then, after a lyric poem about survival through mobility and staying close to water and the earth, comes another story about a little girl from Acoma, who takes her baby sister to the lake where there are many butterflies and then saves her from a flood by carrying her up onto a mesa. Although their own mother has not tried to save them, they join other mothers there who have carried their children to safety. In this state of generational displacement the older sister turns to stone.

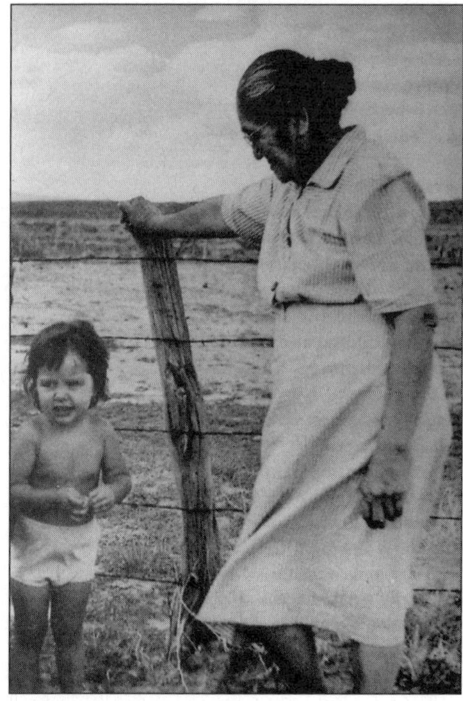

7.02 Lee H. Marmon, photograph #2 from Leslie Marmon Silko, *Storyteller* (p. 2) ("When I was a little girl Aunt Susie spent a good deal of time at the Marmon Ranch . . .")

> The story ends there.
> Some of the stories
> Aunt Susie told
> have this kind of ending.
> There are no explanations. (42)

Aunt Susie is a western storyteller who confronts absolute and unthinkable mystery.

The next story, "Lullaby," also confronts the absolute—death—and the unthinkable mystery of Anglo mistreatment of Native Americans. An old woman named Ayah remembers the pain of poverty, mistreatment, and having her children wrenched away from her to be alienated in Indian schools. At the end she leads her drunken old husband out to a place sheltered by rocks where both she and he will freeze to death, she the more courageously of the two because in his stupor he "would not feel it" (51). This, we must believe, is a far more authentic story of the West than any number of tales of fighting and bronco busting. The last words are Ayah's song affirming human love and the partnership of Mother Earth's nurturance and Father Sky's protection, even in the face of all evidence to the contrary:

> *The earth is your mother,*
> *she holds you.*
> *The sky is your father,*
> *he protects you.*
> *Sleep,*
> *sleep.*
> *Rainbow is your sister,*
> *she loves you.*
> *The winds are your brothers,*
> *they sing to you.*
> *Sleep,*
> *sleep.*
> *We are together always*
> *We are together always*
> *There never was a time*
> *when this*
> *was not so.* (51)

We have already noted that in "Yellow Woman," woman and her sexuality are elevated to mythic status; like the hero of Silko's noted *Ceremony,* she "lives the stories" (P. Allen 128). Here and in the two "Cottonwood" narratives, women attract the notice of divinities as they do in Greek myth, but not so passively or haplessly. Then Silko speaks in her own voice, realistically but with overtones of myth, about hunting expeditions when, carrying her own gun, she encountered a huge brown bear, followed by Aunt Alice's story of the child Kochininako's hunting expedition—these segments, through their sequencing, commenting on each other and proposing a continuity not only between past and present, but between mythical and matter-of-fact time. Then we meet another survivor, Juana, who was captured by slave hunters as a child but survived to work in Grandpa Stagner's household into old age (88–89). In "One time" it is a powerful female figure, Our Mother Nau'ts'ity'i, who gets angry because of the diversion of values due to "Ck'o'yo magic" and must be appeased if life is to go on (115). The mother earth figure in Keresan myth is by no means a passive earth image.

Among these powerful female divinities is Spider Woman, who looks after living beings and gives them advice. Her function, then, is primarily mental, though as a weaver she is also able to put together powerful magic. Spider Woman appears in *Storyteller* in "Estoy-eh-muut and the Kunideeyahs" advising Arrow Boy how to defeat his wife Kochininako after she becomes a witch. Here, the female power that is allied with animals and is always good helps a male to win out over a corrupted female. That is, Silko's stories do not routinely and invariably pit women against men any more than Austin's or Cather's do. Behind Spider Woman, in Keresan cosmology, looms Thinking Woman, the ultimate creator, but she does not appear in Silko's book. The most serious creation stories are not to be revealed to outsiders or spoken of lightly. But the very sacred Spider Woman appears again in "Up North," the story of the Gambler's capture of the storm clouds, where she advises so great a personage as the Sun Father (who addresses her as Grandma).

Immediately after the Sun Father's restoration of the rain clouds in "Up North" comes an excerpt of a letter from Silko to a friend in which she imagines herself as a grandmother, years hence, telling stories of "this rainy lush September" in which plants are blooming that she has never seen bloom before (170). Both from her memories of her own grandmothers and from traditional stories, and now as she looks into the future, we see what powerful figures grandmothers are. After a brief interlude paying tribute to the Acoma poet Simon Ortiz, with whom she has in a sense collaborated by having "a long discussion of goats,"[9] we have the story "Uncle Tony's Goats." Once again the child Leslie Marmon, like the young Kochininako, goes hunting. More precisely, she and a group of other children make inexpertly fashioned bows and arrows and go about trying to shoot things, including Uncle Tony's goats. A greatly prized billy goat with wicked yellow eyes watches them shoot their arrows and stores up Leslie's image for future vengeance. Like the giant who persecuted little Kochininako, the goat is a figure of powerful sexual presence; not an "ordinary goat," when he mounts the nannies he is "powerful and erect with the great black testicles swinging in rhythm between his hind legs" (173). Soon, at her seventh birthday, Leslie is expected to take on more chores, one of which is to turn the goats out of their pen in the morning. But the yellow-eyed goat, still bearing a grudge, knocks her down and runs away, leaving her with a bloody forehead. The truth comes out, and she at once realizes that Uncle Tony—her mother's brother and therefore the primary disciplinarian in her life—is angry. She remembers "what he'd always told us about animals; they won't bother you unless you bother them first" (174). We assume that he, too, remembers the bow-and-arrows incident. He leaves to go track the goat. But when he returns after three days, not having caught him, he essentially says good riddance. "He smiled at me and his voice was strong and happy when he said this" (176). Uncle Tony has decided that the female child is more important than even a very productive male animal, and thereby, perhaps, has feminized his role in the family structure.

"The Man to Send Rain Clouds," noted earlier in connection with the water motif, is also important in relation to gender. In the carrying out of traditional funerary observances here, we see the complementarity of traditional gender roles based on an understanding of mutual respect. Similarly, in the brief "Grandma A'mooh used to tell me stories" we see how both males and females share values of generosity toward those in need. And from the adjacent page Grandma A'mooh herself gazes steadily out at us from a photograph (figure 7.03) taken by Silko's father, Lee Marmon (211). Sharp-eyed and calm, she is clearly a respected authority as well as (so we see from the hook and thread in her hand and the piece of lacy work trailing down into her lap) a whiz at crochet. Both her wisdom-stories and figurative web-spinning invite us to view her as an avatar of Spider Woman.

Grandma Lillie, too, is given tribute; both grandmothers are shown as strong and respected, and both were storytellers. An excerpt of a letter from Silko to a friend measures Silko's experience with a rooster against two versions of a rooster story told by Grandma Lillie. At the same time, Grandma Lillie's story validates what Uncle Tony said about animals' not bothering you unless you bother them first. The letter and its attached segments about roosters, then, continue the idea of complementarity of genders: wisdom comes from both. These segments also underscore the complementarity between animals and humans, tradition and innovation, life and death, that

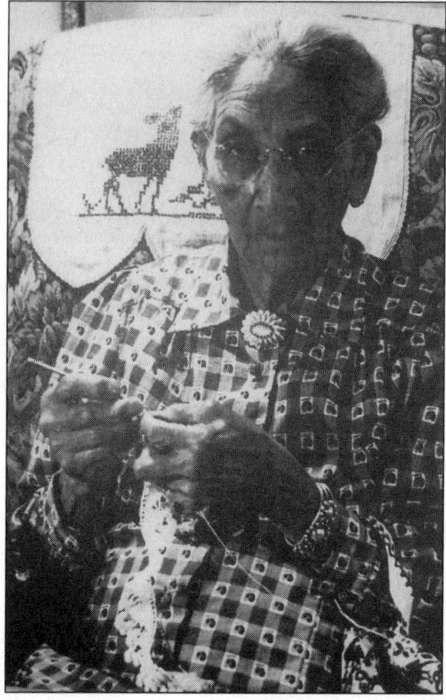

7.03 Lee H. Marmon, photograph #21 from Leslie Marmon Silko, *Storyteller* (p. 211) ("Grandma A'mooh")

has been evident throughout, which quickly shows up yet again in "Skeleton Fixer." Here, Old Man Badger puts bones back together until he completes a skeleton, repeats a spell over it four times, and Old Coyote Woman "jumped up/and took off running" without even a thank-you. The complementarity of genders is enriched by a note acknowledging collaboration, again, with Simon Ortiz (245).

In "The Storyteller's Escape," where the people run into the malpais, it is an old woman who not only keeps the stories alive but outfaces an enemy by waiting to give herself up in death. Not the traditionally masculine activity of pursuing an enemy but her quiet resolution to accept their violence is the act of courage in this story, which ends with her last laugh on enemy and community. And then, again, the anecdote of cooperation between Franz Boas and Elsie Clews Parsons and between Great Grandpa Marmon and his Laguna relatives by marriage. The last story is "Coyote Holds a Full House in His Hand," with a curiously peaceful contention between a male coyote figure and that storyteller of storytellers, Helen Sekaquaptewa, in the comical guise of Mrs. Sekakaku, in which this coyote finds a way to grope a whole clan of Hopi women with impunity. Coyote wins out in this instance, coming home with both pumpkin and cherry pies, but in a very low-key way (as is appropriate for Coyote) and only because he abandoned the field of intended contest.

Silko's Southwest, like Austin's and Cather's, is a place for stories other than the masculine ones of conquest, violence, and ruggedness. She is interested in stories about justice and injustice, preservation of a valued tradition even as that tradition changes, and sexual liberality. Certainly her stories differ from those told by Cather and Austin even at their most revisionist, with their persistent Anglo perspective. Partly as a matter of changing times and standards, Silko's differ in their overt and ebullient sexuality. Yet for all the obvious differences, Silko continues strands of the tradition we have traced in Austin and Cather. Certainly her emphasis on the book-as-object as being importantly a visual presence continues Austin's and Cather's interest in a pictured West. In *Storyteller*, that visual presence contributes to her revisionist gendering of the West and the Western.[10]

Like Austin and Cather, Silko writes stories of the Southwest peopled more regularly and more memorably by strong females than by rugged males. The few rugged and aggressive males who appear are either sinister (the Big Cop in his reflective sunglasses, the yellow-eyed billy goat) or comical (Silko's rooster and the vicious rooster of family lore). She also, like them, revisions gender in a way that is by no means a simple feminizing, as traditional conceptions define the feminine. No more than Cather or Austin does she continue Mary Hallock Foote's insistence on a West of gentle domesticity. Nor does she, any more than Cather or Austin, merely propose that women are as capable as men of rugged adventuring—though that is part of it. Rather, all three envision an androgynous West in which traditional gender roles are shown to be grossly exaggerated extrapolations from sex-linked tendencies. The traditionally gendered view of the West is shown to be based on an unwarranted selective emphasis that results in taking a part for the whole, and a great deal more room is made for individual difference and cooperation among equals. Austin, Cather, and Silko agree in seeing the West as both an opening for escape from stifling conventionality and a place for living.

* * *

I now return to Cather's and Lewis's brief accounts of their 1925 visit to Laguna, in order to read alongside this loosely collaborative account an example of a true collaboration between women in the Southwest, Margaret Randall's book of poems *Into Another Time: Grand Canyon Reflections* (2004), with line drawings by her longtime partner Barbara Byers (both residents of Albuquerque, very near Silko's Laguna). Where Cather's and Lewis's mutually supplementary account is fragmented and dissimilar in voice and style, lacking any intent of real collaboration in the normal sense of the word, Randall's and Byers's is fully integrated, a total work of literature and art. Where Cather's and Lewis's is cautious, reflecting their sense of outsiderness, Randall's and Byers's reflects the confidence of insiders, assured of being welcomed and cradled by place itself. Where Cather's and Lewis's is reticent, disclosing almost nothing about their personal relationship, theirs is open, neither hiding nor flaunting their loving partnership but letting it emerge in our understanding as naturally as a part of the terrain. Because their relationship is fully uncloseted in the text, their collaboration can convey far more clearly than Cather's and Lewis's a picture of the West as a comfortable place of habitation for lesbian women. It can thus be seen as a culminating regendering of the Western's assumptions.[11]

Barbara Byers's line drawings in *Into Another Time* are considerably more intricate, and less straightforward or realistic, than E. Boyd Smith's in *The Land of Little Rain* or W. T. Benda's in *My Ántonia.* In much the same way as Smith's and Benda's, however, they gain their effectiveness largely through the contrast between clean black line and unshaded white paper. Usually a color painter, Byers undertook these drawings as an experiment during a rafting trip with Randall in the Grand Canyon and was surprised at how well drawings that are, in her words, "like cartoons" could capture the presence of landforms. Neither she nor Randall conceives of the drawings as illustrations for the book of poems but as a second "voice" speaking independently in harmony with the voice of the poems. In a sense, both poems and drawings began in notebooks of the trip—Byers's notebook in which she sketched, Randall's which, as she reveals in one of the poems (25), she took along but did not use. Both notebooks seem to me to be real presences in the volume, as if the poems were memory's retrospective entries.[12]

Randall and Byers can be seen as furtherers of Cather's and Austin's tradition both in their revisions of gender and in the fact that these revisions are linked to an insistent picturing of the West. They continue the practice of building from literal, physical sight to vision in the abstract sense, and continue the craft of combining verbal with visual art in the concrete presence of the book. According to cover text of *Into Another Time,* Randall first went to the Grand Canyon—the place that, as we recall, served as one of the chief wellsprings of early southwestern tourism—in 1947 and has been back numerous times. She is by now far more than a tourist. Maintaining her focus on place itself, in its materiality, as her primary interest in the poems collected here, she also makes the canyon a place of the mind.[13] And her writing about the Grand Canyon as a metonym for the Southwest generally proposes implicitly that rugged as it is, just as the aggrandizing nineteenth-century painters showed it, it is nevertheless a place for women.

Much as Mary Austin did, Randall sees the arid West as a harsh and frightening terrain but at the same time a place of habitation and community, a place of embrace. This multifacetedness—not merely a duality but a rich range of perceived qualities and meanings—is enunciated in many of her Grand Canyon poems, but nowhere more powerfully than in "There is a river." Here, thinking of her vigorous but not unafraid rafting and hiking along with a "you" that I take to be Byers, she draws an analogy with Johann Sebastian Bach's *Sheep May Safely Graze,* but quickly corrects herself to recognize that the sheep she saw were real and vulnerable:

> . . . This Canyon's
> bighorn sheep gain narrow ledges, graze
> without concern for safety, sometimes fall.
> A tumble of whitened bone reveals its story
> of harsh terrain. (7)

Harsh as it is, its rocks always ready to smash one who falls, the canyon is also a place of beauty. Randall postulates this fairly predictable duality most explicitly, perhaps, in "Deer Creek II" when, standing on a "narrow ledge above the gorge," her "heart pounds in unrelenting fear/but my eyes sing" (42). More surprising, and more significant in the context of the volume as a whole, is the claim that it is also a place of loving welcome and reassurance:

> Days follow water and sun. Nights offer their display
> of stars. Translucent walls mass ochre, red, pale
> gold, slashed through by unforgiving shadow.
> Then comfort spreads her arms. You place one foot
> before the other. (7)

The pronoun "her" ("comfort spreads her arms") is the poem's first gendering of place, even by implication. At the moment when this assurance comes to the hiker, as if from the earth itself, the frightening ledges become a version of Mother Earth and the hiker, like a more aware but equally surefooted (yet equally vulnerable) sheep, "place[s] one foot/before the other."

Bach's sheep that "may safely graze" are, of course, the metaphorical ones familiar to us from the Bible. Randall's sheep are quite literal. But in the analogy between human and animal placement of feet on these steeps and ledges, she also maintains and preserves the metaphoric identification—as she does with a similar merger of human and animal that draws on an entirely different mythology, the Deer Dance of Pueblo ceremonial. In that instance, also in "There is a river," the "you," Byers, now becomes also Deer Dancer, as she uses "dual walking sticks to steady/unfaithful legs" (unfaithful because of illness) just as the Deer Dancer uses dual walking sticks to simulate the animal's front legs. The fusion of human and animal, ceremonial figure and companion, achieved through Randall's invocation of this regionally apt visual image facilitates her own and her (rafting and hiking) partner's move into the landscape and at the same time, through an image of "millennia of rock," into the temporal spaciousness of Native life in the Southwest.

"There is a river" is one of a group of six poems placed as a kind of introduction or overture to *Into Another Time,* greeting readers as they enter. We open the book, we read the six poems, and we then see the first six line drawings. Much as Randall's opening six poems enunciate a vision of a harsh and dangerous land that occasionally spreads its (her) arms in welcome, so Byers's first six drawings show a world of hardness, sharpness, and steep drop-offs, but imply welcoming depths and hollows. The narrowness of ledges is particularly evident in the fifth of the opening group of six drawings (figure 7.04). The river—sometimes a relief from the parched land, sometimes a peril all its own—is not seen; it is cut out of the field of vision by the partial and rather playful inner frame at the bottom.

Sometimes closing off her pictures with emphatic lines forming a square or rectangle, sometimes making one or more of the border lines jagged like the country itself or broken by open space, or sometimes leaving a whole side or more entirely open, Byers plays with closedness and openness throughout the volume. In the drawing immediately preceding the one shown in figure 7.04, an open top implies unlimited sky much as it does in Smith's line drawings in *The Land of Little Rain.* In this drawing, the frame within a frame becomes sometimes a conventional arbitrary enclosure, sometimes part of the landscape. At four places it veers into the drawing as if (vaginally?) inviting us in. Still, the form and medium of Byers's work here, line drawings with an abundance of white space, unsoftened by either color or shading, insist primarily on austerity, vastness, and harshness.[14] Despite their multiple indications of rock facets, they avow—through their refusal to soften the contrast of black and white and their insistent incompleteness, especially at points of interruption of borders—a minimalist aesthetic much like the one traced in Smith's and Benda's drawings, O'Keeffe's paintings, and Gilpin's photographs.

The theme of harshness combined with welcome returns in the poem "Around the Bend," with its obliterating "thunder" of rapids "explod[ing]" at the gunwale and, at the same time, its "unknown landscape/offering its hand,/pulling us safely across" (28–29). Placed between "Around the Bend" and the following poem, "Feeling and Knowledge," dedicated to her mother, in which Randall again explores the idea of a complex of seemingly inconsistent qualities in the landscape, is the rather reassuring drawing of the river at the canyon's floor reproduced in figure 7.05. Although the river through the Grand Canyon can be harrowing in its own right, here it offers the restorative quality we have seen associated with water in Austin's, Cather's, and Silko's writing.

"Feeling and Knowledge" posits the canyon as a place for family by recalling a sequence of visits: a vacation trip when Randall was a child, when her father took her down the trail by mule (the standard way, Bright Angel going down, South Kaibab coming back up); later visits with husbands and lovers and children; and a return visit when her parents were elderly. In old age, they seemed to merge in gender, the father no longer the strong leader, the mother losing a prosthetic breast somewhere along the trail, which Barbara ran back to find. Randall recalls, on this same trail, a moment of reconciliation with one of her daughters, recalls riding it with her son, and then

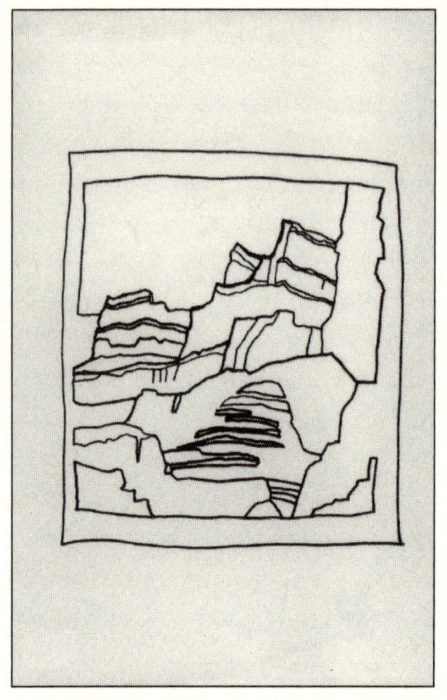

7.04 Barbara Byers, untitled line drawing from Margaret Randall, *Into Another Time* (p. 14)

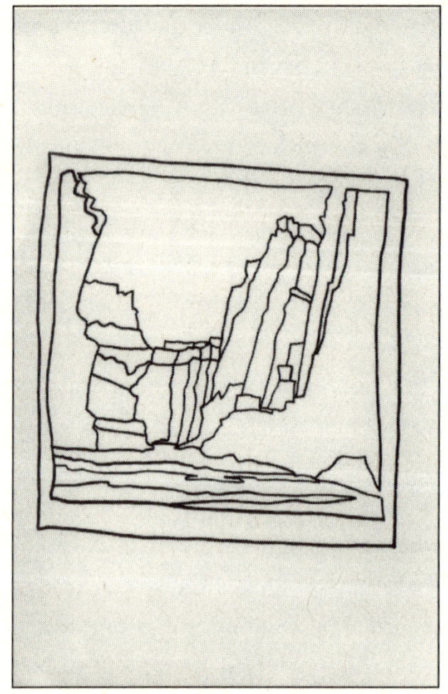

7.05 Barbara Byers, untitled line drawing from Margaret Randall, *Into Another Time* (p. 27)

with grandchildren who have become the confident ones (24–25). She remembers a dream in which Mary Elizabeth Jane Colter (the architect and interior designer for the Fred Harvey Company who built Hopi House, the gift shop at the Canyon, in 1905) came to her and told her that she and Barbara would find the matching rings they wanted at the Canyon gift shop. And they did (25). A fuller version of the story of the rings has been given earlier in one of the six introductory poems, "Our anniversary," where Colter's identity is provided in a note. Together, the two poems that give the ring episode regender the rugged canyon in multiple ways, especially when we note how the figure of the mother who "always wants to go back" to the Grand Canyon pervades "Feeling and Knowledge," from its epigraph to its next-to-last section, where the "you" in the following passage means mother:

> I trusted the mules
> before I learned to trust my feet,
> vertigo and fear of heights
> pulling me back from the trailhead
> until the morning you took my hand
> and we made it past the first turn,
> my breath frozen against fear
> then released to new knowledge
> opening around the next switchback. (26)

But in the sixth and last section of the poem "you" becomes the Canyon itself. The female presence addressed in the familiar second person, then, shifts from lover to mother to the land, but does so in a way utterly unlike the domineering or "plowing" tone of earth-as-woman tropes from a male perspective as discussed by Kolodny in *The Lay of the Land.* Randall's rewriting of masculinist convention is similarly evident in "I Walk Outside," from the volume *Dancing with the Doe,* when her phrase "my mountain" conveys no trace of imperialist claiming of the land, but only affection (24).

The female gendering of Grand Canyon evident in "Feeling and Knowledge" and "Our anniversary" becomes explicit in "North Canyon," where the verges become "lips of stone" (we recall the "stone lips" of *Death Comes for the Archbishop*) or the "open lips/of a great vulva" (32). In this vaginal place Randall thinks of her childbirths and of her grandchildren moving "away and out of sight." Byers's drawing immediately following "North Canyon" (figure 7.06) abandons framing altogether in favor of openness and hollows, with a sense of incompleteness perhaps conveying the disappearance of younger generations into the future story.

In "Nankoweap" (the title refers to the name of a side canyon) Randall's acknowledgment of the harshness of the land yields to an interest in its geology. Her eye sweeps over broad formations of "delta, once fertile farmland" or "splay of boulders/fanning into the river,/evidence of repeated floods" (35), much as Austin's wide-ranging vision does in *The Land of Journeys' Ending.* Sweeping vertically even as it is swept along horizontally by the river, her gaze recognizes geological strata:

> Bright Angel Shale
> is about to make its appearance here,
> lifting Muav Limestone and Unclassified Dolomites
> supporting the Redwall that closes about us
> rising from either river bank.
> Kaibab, Toroweap, Coconino, Hermit:
> formations named by students of their phenomena,
> incised and chiseled in pre-human time. (35)

This sense of geologic process invites the poet's awareness to reach back in time, invoking once again the merger of space and time first signaled in the title of the volume, *Into Another Time* (rather than, say, into another country). Up to this point in "Nankoweap," the language has been factual, scientific. Both Randall and her readers have enjoyed feeling the shape of these names of geological formations in the mouth. Nothing living, in an organic sense, has been mentioned. But now, "high in the natural wall," the poet's eye picks out "four windows"—the windows seen in the facing-page drawing (figure 7.06). The movement of ideas follows the poet's gaze—vision leading meaning—complemented by the artist's image. Together they allow the reader's own gaze to move up the canyon wall, guided by the moving and jutting diagonal, to the same windows.

At that moment a shift occurs in tone and emphasis. Picking out in the

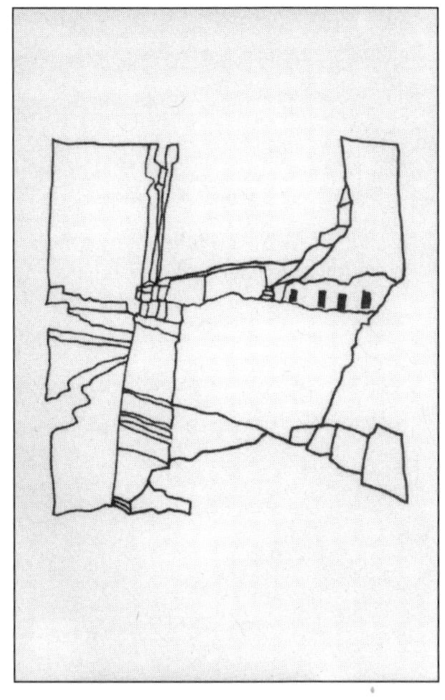

7.06 Barbara Byers, untitled line drawing from Margaret Randall, *Into Another Time* (p. 34)

rocky landscape these "hard to identify until seen" windows, Randall reminds herself that they were "constructed by human hands/at least eight hundred years before,/the Anasazi granaries" (35). With this shift from the geological to the human past, the language of the poem becomes more personal. In a passage reminiscent of Thea's sense of the pull in the thighs and the weight on the backs of women carrying water up to their cliff-side homes from the canyon floor with babies slung on their backs, in *The Song of the Lark,* it is "our steps" that are "threaten[ed]" by "loose scree . . . as we ascend"; "we" climb to "narrow balconies . . . before these openings in the cliff" and think what they meant in human terms. It is "we," the shared first person, who are

> . . . made dumb
> by the effort of ancestors,
> their backs bent beneath the weight
> of what nourished and sustained,
> their feet rising in continuous journey
> from the delta below. (36)

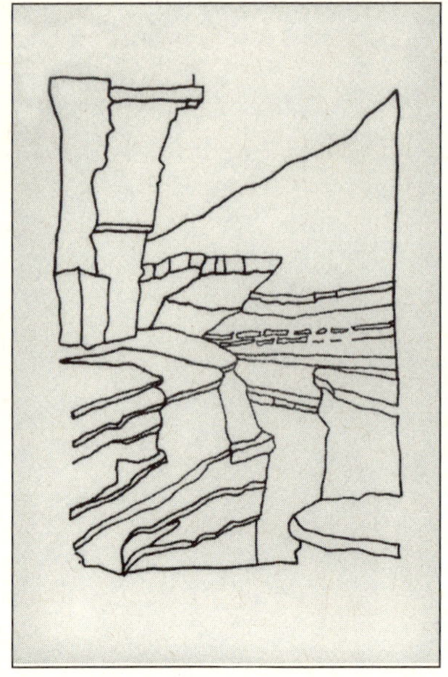

7.07 Barbara Byers, untitled line drawing from Margaret Randall, *Into Another Time* (p. 43)

With this realization comes a sense of a friendliness extending not so much from the land itself, as before, but from these hardworking people reaching out to the poet from centuries past: "their spirits reach out and take my hand/as I begin the long descent."

If we look back at the line drawing facing "Nankoweap" (figure 7.06) and compare it with one of the six introductory drawings (figure 7.04), we can readily see how Byers's playfulness with borders has modulated into greater and greater openness. A similar openness—at the top, implying the sky, but also, more whimsically, at the sides and bottom—appears later in the book in the drawing shown in figure 7.07. Becoming less and less committed to realism, more and more open to abstraction, Byers continues to play with closedness and openness, straightness and tiltedness, and heights that turn into depths (with even an inexplicable straight line standing unsupported in the midst of crags) until, two drawings further on, she reaches her ultimate minimalism in a slope of unsupported scree, poised surrealistically against blankness, with a partial border proclaiming its status as work of art, rather than reproduction of nature (figure 7.08). In the stylization of the drawing reproduced in figure 7.08 and in the playfulness of the artist's

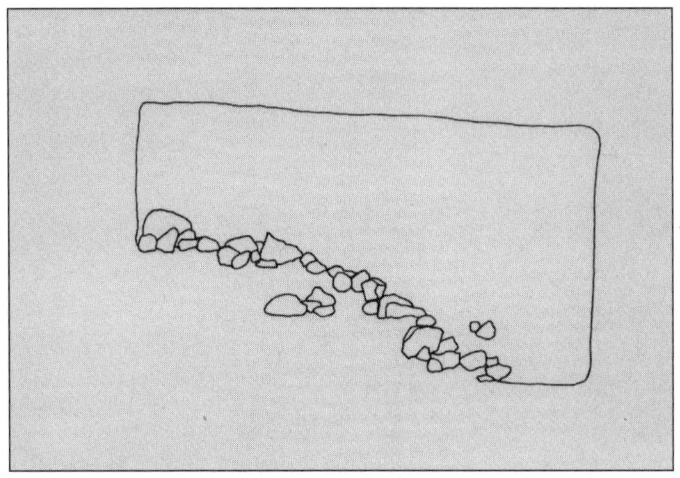

7.08 Barbara Byers, untitled line drawing from Margaret Randall, *Into Another Time* (p. 51)

sequential questioning of closure, perspective, and "realistic" modeling, we see how fully she belongs within the minimalist tradition more familiarly represented by O'Keeffe and Gilpin. At the same time, her playful transformations call to mind the playfulness and multidimensional transformations that characterize the work of a noted precursor in the cartoon art of the Southwest (to adopt Byers's own term for her drawings here), George Harriman, the author-artist of *Krazy Kat,* which ran in newspapers from 1913 to 1944. The minimalism of Harriman's rendering of Krazy's adventures in Coconino County (Grand Canyon country) is evident, for example, in the strip from April 16, 1922 (figure 7.09).

Other examples of Harriman's play with conventions of closedness and openness, as well as arid heights and canyon rivers, are provided by Eric Gary Anderson in *American Indian Literature and the Southwest.* As Anderson compellingly argues, *Krazy Kat* was also an example of radical regendering in a southwestern setting, in work entailing pictorial and verbal interplay.[15]

From the bare minimalism of her drawing of scree, Byers moves to an interpretive rendering of a curiously gynecological, partially open concentric-circle petroglyph, then to a sequence of near-abstractions related to the land-

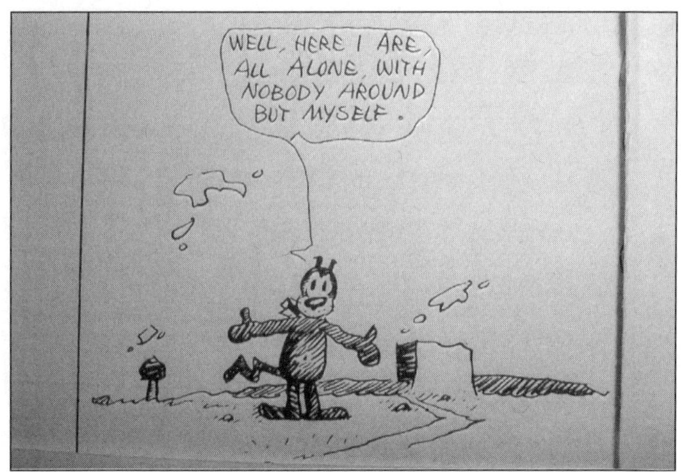

7.09 George Harriman, from *Krazy Kat,* April 16, 1922, syndicated 1876.

scape only by their resonance of the earlier, more representational drawings. In the next to last of this sequence (figure 7.10), she reaches perhaps her fullest merger of visual image and abstract idea—the idea, perhaps, of origin.

At the same time, Randall also moves out from literal, visual landscape—"the lens frames this image/then lets it go/as I slowly sweep walls" with "my camera" (47)—to historic sweep and ideas of death and recurrence. If Randall shares with other writers of the southwestern landscape the sense that she is confronting the "absolutely real" (Tompkins 3), in its hardness and impersonality, she also shows that love, human connection across time as well as space, and the sad sweep of human justice and injustice are as much a part of that reality as the harsh rocks and declivities. In the poem "Indian Discovery," especially, she confronts the "arrogant history" of Anglo conquest. "Hopi ghosts touch my shoulder," she acknowledges, realizing that by taking the role of tourist in country where living Hopi men "still come" for sacred purposes (85) she is also taking part in this imperialist history.

What are we to make of this muddled, cruel, majestic place and history? Probably we can no more be certain of these enigmas than we can of the meaning of Byers's glyph of partly closed, partly open circles (figure 7.11).

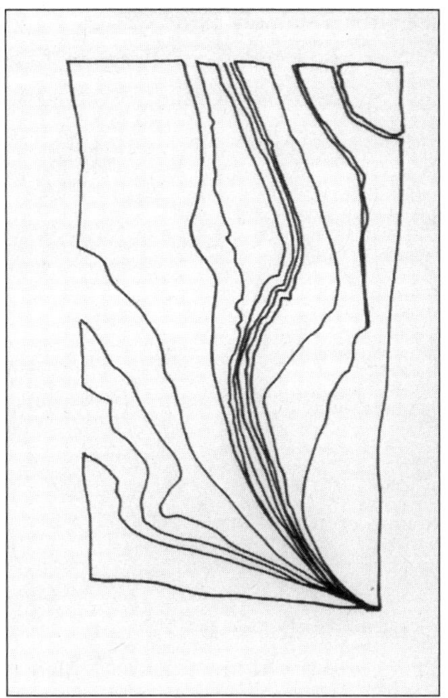

7.10 Barbara Byers, untitled line drawing from Margaret Randall, *Into Another Time* (p. 74)

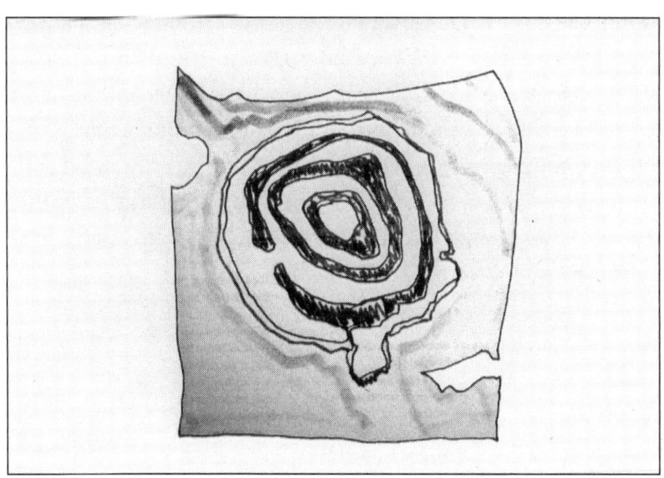

7.11 Barbara Byers, untitled line drawing from Margaret Randall, *Into Another Time* (p. 61)

An image at once female and male, it is a suitably androgynous one for the space regendered in androgynous terms by Randall and Byers, by O'Keeffe and Gilpin, and, most emphatically, by Austin and Cather.

> Someone seven
> centuries ago
> or more or less
> held a stone in his hand
> (her hand?)
> and left this image
> that greets us now, oblivious
> that others
> hundreds of years distant
> would try to imagine what it means. (60)

Randall resolves to take her refuge in that most modernist of fullnesses, silence: "Full silence/is where I want to spend my time" (65). Silence was a refuge chosen variously by Willa Cather, by the modernist musician and theorist John Cage, and figuratively by Georgia O'Keeffe, as she retreated from narrative painting of the West. And indeed the third-from-last poem of *Into Another Time* is entitled "Silence." Here, as at other moments in both Randall's and Byers's work, their collaborative volume amply fulfills theorists' standards of the complementarity of black lines of type or drawing and white space. But the very last poem of the volume, "Edge," returns us to the landscape itself, now fully humanized and harmonized with its history of natural process in vast time:

> You face your wholeness,
> I mine.
> The edge between us
> is stunning and complex:
> product of our geology's desire. (93)

For Willa Cather and for Mary Austin, as well, the Southwest was finally the place where their own desire could be realized and measured against geology's—and history's—desire in a way that included the wholeness of mutuality rather than aggression. It was a place where they could visualize health and freedom for women of all expressions of gender as well as for men of equal freedom and goodwill.

We would be as foolish to imagine that the Western and western art no longer carry on the conventions of aggressive masculinity that Austin and Cather challenged and revised throughout their careers as we would to imagine that hostility no longer ever colors the relations among Anglos, Spanish or Mexican, and Native peoples in the Southwest. Even so, those are no longer the sole or even the prevalent modes in which the West is imagined and pictured. A tradition of women's own—more irenic, more nurturant, freer from preconceived modes of acting out gender identity—is now firmly established alongside the white male tradition that once held sway, in partnership with a variety of firmly established and vital ethnic traditions in and of the West. For many reasons, not least a willingness in the academy to examine and discuss questions of human difference, the voices and images of the West that enrich our time are far more various and more nearly equal in their public reception than Cather and Austin could have imagined.

NOTES

Chapter 1

1. Clearly customary terminology for these regions as the West or the Southwest reflects a subject perspective of easternness—the perspective, that is, of the "Anglo" people, northern and western European in origin, who invaded this continent through New England and Virginia and then looked (and moved) westward from a vantage grounded on the Atlantic seaboard. It was they and their descendants, plus subsequent immigrants from Europe, who, to borrow Richard Drinnon's title phrases, "fac[ed] west" in their "Indian-hating and empire building." That is, the geographical terminology that we use in designating this region of dry plains, mountains, and deserts is inherently ethnicized, racialized, and certainly politicized.
2. The 1889 and 1894 volumes of *Century,* with individual issues bound together, are among print materials in the Cather family library, available at Red Cloud, Nebraska. I am indebted for this information to Kari Ronning, of the Cather Project at the University of Nebraska, who adds that these would not have been the only issues the family had access to, since they belonged to a kind of round-robin group that shared magazines. Travel writings about California by Helen Hunt Jackson, who was in fact an acquaintance of Mary Hallock Foote, also appeared in *Century.* For this reason as well as because of her widely read *Ramona* (1884), we can assume that Cather was aware of Jackson, too, as a writer of the West, but so far as I am aware she never commented on either.
3. Unpublished letter from Charles Cather to Jennie Cather, October 30, 1870, in Cather Family Papers, Nebraska Historical Society; duplicate at Love Library, University of Nebraska.
4. Unpublished letter, George P. Cather to Jennie Cather Ayre, March 17, 1876, Nebraska Historical Society.
5. It is not true, however, as Joni L. Kinsey proclaims, that the "*earliest* artistic

encounters with the central grasslands occurred in the context of expeditions . . . that explored, perused, and surveyed the American West throughout much of the nineteenth century" (6, emphasis mine). The Native peoples who lived on the plains (as well as in the Rio Grande pueblos and elsewhere in the western half of the continent) had been producing decorative and domestic art for centuries before either the Spanish or the Anglo explorers arrived. Although my subject here is limited to Anglo art beginning (as Kinsey says) in the mid-nineteenth century, I hope that limitation does not reflect the kind of unconscious exclusivity I have singled out in her otherwise exemplary study *Plain Pictures.* It is a necessary limitation for two reasons: because of my own lack of qualification to discuss Native and Spanish/Mexican conceptions of El Norte and because my interest is in the exclusionary, masculinist, and racially triumphalist tenor of the Anglo art and literature of the West against which, to varying degrees, Austin and Cather wrote.

6. Another such report was the *Reports of Explorations and Surveys to Ascertain the Most Practicable and Economic Route for a Railroad from the Mississippi River to the Pacific Ocean,* published by the federal government between 1855 and 1861, a twelve-volume series Robert Taft calls "probably the most important single contemporary source of knowledge on Western geography and history" with its "many beautiful plates in color of scenery, native inhabitants, fauna and flora of the Western country" (5).
7. Although "the West" has been a movable concept throughout American history, as usually understood today and for purposes of this study the West consists of the Great Plains (the Dakotas, Nebraska, Kansas, most of Oklahoma, central and western Texas), the Mountain West (Montana, Wyoming, Colorado, New Mexico, Arizona, Nevada, Utah) and on westward to the Pacific, although northern California, Oregon, and Washington are often thought of as a separate region unto themselves. The geographic scope of my discussion is the Great Plains and the Southwest (primarily New Mexico, Arizona, and southern California).
8. More precisely, the term "the Great Desert" was fixed on it by the botanist and geologist Edwin James who accompanied Long and whose report of a "wide and sandy desert" was quickly picked up by major newspapers back east, but was associated with Long's name (John L. Allen 211; see also Thacker 38). Long himself reported to the powerful southern senator John C. Calhoun that the prairie was "a great wasteland" unsuitable to habitation by agricultural people (quoted in Kinsey 37).

9. Surprisingly, Catlin was unable to find a publisher for his elaborately illustrated book *Letters and Notes on the Manners, Customs, and Conditions of the North American Indians,* and had to have it printed himself in 1841—with great success (Thacker 56).
10. Pratt and Boime interpret the painterly convention of small figures in a vast natural vista—when those figures are shown on an elevation overlooking miles of wilderness—in a way directly opposite to that of Donald A. Ringe, who argues that both painters and writers of the early nineteenth century invoked such scenes to convey an ultimately religious sense of a vast universe in which "man is small" (29). On "racialism" in the idea of Manifest Destiny, see C. Wilson, 48–52.
11. Both the monumental size of Bierstadt's paintings and their sharp decline in value after their early capturing of the interest and imaginations of American viewers play a role in *Silver Light* (1990), David Thomson's novel about the West, Westerns, and photography. Thomson's hero, Matthew Garth, based on a character in the Howard Hawks movie *Red River,* sees a painting by Bierstadt (perhaps intended as his famous *Long's Peak)* when he arrives at a ranch in Montana to deliver a herd of cattle in 1865 (159–60). When the intended purchaser of the herd turns out not to have the agreed-on price, Garth takes the painting instead (175). It is then valued at $20,000. He sells it in 1881 for $10,000 (185). Interestingly, Willa Cather also makes a cameo appearance in Thomson's novel, which thereby shows its astuteness as to her linkage with the aesthetics and history of the West.
12. See Naef and Wood, 36–37, and plates 68 to 87.
13. Marta Weigle and Kyle Fiore, in *Santa Fe and Taos,* make the related point that although Anglo-American "government and military personnel, journalists, illustrators, novelists, scholars, health seekers and tourists" came to New Mexico throughout the Territorial period (1850–1912), New Mexico remained for some years an "'almost unknown region'" though "'interesting to the public'" (3, quoting William W. H. Davis, U.S. District Attorney for the Territory of New Mexico in the early to mid-1850s).
14. Anderson writes accurately that Austin's "interventions" in American Indian cultures were "problematic" (113). Such interventions were especially problematic in her first novel, *Isidro,* and in some of her earliest periodical publications. In "The Wooing of the Señorita" (1897), the señorita's "greasy" clothing comes very near to invoking the derogatory term "greaser," and in "The Conversion of Ah Lew Sing" Asians in California are regarded with faint amusement. The illustra-

tions of both stories in the *Overland Monthly* adopted stereotypes of western fiction.

15. Garland's statement was made in 1903, a time of heated debate over American imperialism.
16. Teague observes that in some of Remington's late works, but only the late ones, western landscapes become "subjects in their own right," sometimes with no human figures shown at all (65).
17. Raphael James Cristy regards Russell's paintings as "transferred [versions of] his narrative skills" (1).
18. Cristy explains that one of Russell's acquaintances in Montana, Johnny Skelton, a man with a "wild reputation" and "many unsavory associates," together with three such associates, "rode their horses into a Stanford saloon in 1881 and then told Charlie Russell all about it the next day." He continues that although Russell knew personally a number of cattle men and ranch hands who "continued the cowboy life and vocation into the 1920s," he "preferred the earlier, nomadic variety" who, in Russell's own words, "'left tracks in History that the farmer can't plow under'" (Cristy 154–55).
19. Anderson astutely refers to Cushing's anthropological work, as well as Adolf Bandelier's, as "aesthetically minded" (88).
20. Although Patricia Janis Broder judges that Henri's paintings of individual Indians are done in a modernist realistic mode that avoids "sentimentality" or idealization of them as "noble savages or children of nature" (*Modern Vision* 29, 43), the faces in most of his paintings have a glamorized comeliness that to me suggests a prevailing romanticism.
21. The extent to which commercial and artistic purposes interacted in the paintings purchased by the Railway is indicated by a letter from Simpson to Blumenschein on June 8, 1911, expressing a preference for an "Indian subject with Taos Pueblo in background [sic], if such a thing is feasible" (quoted in Schwarz 37). That it was indeed feasible is demonstrated by *Taos Indian Holding Water Jug*, purchased in 1911, as well as by *Evening at Pueblo of Taos.*
22. Inaccuracies do inevitably creep in. Gerard C. Delano's very beautiful Navajo Shepherdess shows its title figure in juxtaposition with a large saguaro cactus (the tall cactus with arms in a "holdup" position—everybody's favorite). The saguaro does not grow on Navajo land, however, but farther south. Either the shepherdess or the cactus has gone astray. Blumenschein's *Taos Indian Holding Water Jug* would seem to go beyond romanticizing to the point of exoticizing the native person even more emphatically than his *Evening at Pueblo of Taos*, partly

by setting the eyes of the up-close and directly frontal figure in deep shadow so that the face becomes almost a mask, a mystery, and partly by shrouding the upper body entirely in a closely wrapped blanket and placing on his head an elaborate feather headdress, the kind often called a war bonnet and usually worn by Plains Indians. Upon inquiring about the accuracy or inaccuracy of the headdress, however, I was informed by Richard Archuleta, of the Office of the Governor of Taos Pueblo, that it can be explained by the well-developed trade relations between the Pueblo and tribes such as the Cheyenne, the Arapaho, and the Kiowa until the late 1800s. Songs and dances, as well as "wear and wares," were exchanged. The wearing of headdresses such as that shown in the painting was not "a traditional custom" but might occur during these "borrowed" dances. Thus, the portrayal of the Taos Indian by Blumenschein, showing "plains attire acquired through trade," should not be considered inaccurate. Private communication from Richard Archuleta, October 20, 2004.

23. See Lois Rudnick's 1987 introduction to Mabel Dodge Luhan's *Edge of Taos Desert* on the hegira of creative postwar thinkers who found in New Mexico "a people that were not implicated in the disaster of war and a place unmarred by the industrialization that blighted the Northeast" (viii). Also, see Helen Delpar, *The Enormous Vogue of Things Mexican.*
24. The impact of the mid-nineteenth-century spread of railroads and the increase in rail travel on what he calls "formulations of American landscape and history" is discussed by Stephen Daniels, 168–96. See also (as Daniels indicates) Leo Marx, *The Machine in the Garden: Technology and the Pastoral Ideal in America* (1964), Susan Danly Walther, ed., *The Railroad in the American Landscape 1850–1950* (1981), and Susan Danly and Leo Marx, eds., *The Railroad in American Art* (1988). Daniels points out that as early as 1852, in "triumphalist" comments on the Erie Railroad, Bayard Taylor extolled the panoramic possibilities of the viewing of landscape from a train window (168).
25. Jane Tompkins sees as two of the primary definitions of Westerns their satisfaction of "a hunger to be in touch with something absolutely real" and their dramatization of the West's "functio[n] as a symbol of freedom, and of the opportunity for conquest" (3–4).
26. Daniels points out that much of the Currier and Ives production was given to a visual rhetoric of "continental conquest" and that some of their lesser series included "comic" pictures that were degrading to both women and African Americans (179–80). Thus Fanny Palmer participated in a masculinist aesthetic in multiple ways.

27. See Trenton, "'Islands on the Land,'" 20. Marianne Stoller points out that Hispano and Native women artists in the Southwest were also late in taking up plein-air and representational landscape painting, but for very different reasons. The primary art forms in which these women worked, both early on and after the revival of traditional folk arts in the 1930s, did not include easel painting. Painting on pottery or on walls of houses, or similarly woven or embroidered patterns, included landscape as abstract motifs, rather than representational depiction. The land itself, Stoller emphasizes, was present in these artisans' works in patterns of line and in the material into which women potters plunged their hands. "Only the most cursory attention," Stoller adds, "has been paid to Hispanic women artists" (127).
28. Information provided by Audrey S. Kauders, director of the Museum of Nebraska Art, Kearney, Nebraska.
29. I am distinguishing the women anthropologists, painters, and photographers I discuss here from the women settlers whose diaries and letters are so valuable to our understanding of women's responses to the West, which have been carefully and importantly studied by such scholars as Annette Kolodny, Vera Norwood, and Julie Roy Jeffrey.
30. In a 1920 letter Boas wrote, "I have had a curious experience in graduate work during the last few years. All my best students are women" (quoted in Deacon 255).
31. Surprisingly, despite her apparent friendship with Clara True, Parsons later owned land that she obtained by foreclosing a mortgage for nonpayment of a loan she had made True (ECP letter to Mabel Dodge Luhan, December 4, 1922, American Philosophical Society, Philadelphia). Another irony of their acquaintance is that prior to 1910 True had taught at Indian schools, where she supported an assimilationist, as opposed to Parsons's culturally affirming, stance; crusaded against "sexual immorality" among Indians, which she contrasted with the supposed moral purity of white women; and "utterly failed to see the significance of Indian religion" (Jacobs 30–32, 57). Parsons's work was largely focused on understanding the Native religious practices True deplored, and in both her sociological scholarship and her own life she affirmed sexual freedom for women.
32. Letters from a long correspondence between Mabel Dodge Luhan and Elsie Clews Parsons, in the Parsons Papers at the American Philosophical Society, make no reference to Cather.
33. Scharff adds inaccurately that it was from the Taos art colony that "women as various as Mary Austin, Willa Cather, Dorothy Brett, and Georgia O'Keeffe

emerged ready to seek their own Western visions" (5). Austin and Cather had established their "Western visions" earlier, independent of Mabel's art colony, as had Georgia O'Keeffe, who produced paintings of the plains while she was in Texas in the 1912–1918 period.

34. Patricia Limerick calls this sense of the real into question by pointing out that ideas of the desert as "interesting and even beautiful" arose as Americans were able to feel "insulated and protected" from it (*Desert* 91–92). This would not seem to be true of the early Austin. We might compare, however, the romanticizing of Native Americans once they were perceived as disappearing.

Chapter 2

1. Illustrated novels were very popular from around the 1890s through the first two decades of the twentieth century, but after World War I rising production costs forced a decline. The practice of illustration continued mainly in art-press publications, children's books, some nonfiction (depending on subject matter), advertising, and (mainly in the form of photographs) in periodicals. My thanks to Samantha Rippner, of the Metropolitan Museum of Art, and to Virginia O'Hara, Brandywine River Museum, for assistance in understanding this matter.
2. The Society of Illustrators was formed in 1901. Despite the notable successes of women such as Mary Hallock Foote, women were not admitted until after 1921 (Larson 31).
3. Austin made this point herself rather "condescendingly" in a letter to Ansel Adams about their collaborative book *Taos Pueblo* (August 30, 1929, quoted in Lanigan Stineman 194).
4. According to Lanigan Stineman (67), Austin disliked at least one of Smith's drawings, the one of the girls of Las Uvas (on p. 167 in the paperback edition published by the University of New Mexico Press in 1974). The two sizes in which *The Land of Little Rain* was issued were 21-1/2 cm x 16 cm, with a small block of print and very wide margins, and 17-1/2 cm x 11-1/2 cm. Many drawings that occupy a full page in the smaller book are placed in the margin of the larger. Lummis made a positive, albeit indirect, reference to the illustrations of the book in his review in the December 1903 issue of *Out West.* Calling it a book of "truth-telling" and "one of the relatively few books that really count," he added that the physical volume was "a delight to the eye" (679).
5. See Lanigan Stineman, 194. Virginia O'Hara, at the Brandywine River

Museum, a center of knowledge about the practice of illustration, especially among the students of Howard Pyle, has kindly shared with me her knowledge of customary professional practice.

6. The illustrator, Henry Sandman, "retraced" Jackson's travels of southern California along with her and "later complained she was always at his elbow" while he sketched (May 86). Sandman would later provide illustrations for *Ramona*.
7. See Esther Lanigan Stineman's biography of Austin, 25–31; also Augusta Fink's biography, 35–39.
8. Lanigan Stineman and others have emphasized the importance of Emerson to Austin's "photographic imagination" (12, 74). Austin herself recalled, in *Earth Horizon,* that her father had been "particularly" interested in Emerson and that Emerson was the only writer she read in college who "affected her style" (34, 165).
9. Beale is noted for having tried out camel transport in the Southwest, with the result (so it is sometimes said) that there are groups of wild camels in the region even yet.
10. We should note, however, that Austin had majored in natural science at Blackburn College; thus her training in observation of natural phenomena did not begin when she went to California.
11. I have been unable to locate correspondence or office records that would tell us how involved Austin was. Letters between Smith and Houghton Mifflin archived at the Houghton Library, Harvard University, unfortunately do not include these years, although it is possible that additional materials may remain uncatalogued. It is difficult, too, to assess Smith's standing. Certainly his employment by Houghton Mifflin bespeaks professional standing. Lee Kingman, in the introduction to *The Illustrator's Notebook,* refers to him in passing as a "seminal" figure among American illustrators. Yet he is not one of the artists singled out for more extended notice either in that volume or in several others that I have consulted.
12. It is difficult to say precisely when the halftone process was developed because several different processes for making halftone plates (variously known as Meisenbach process, chemical etching, phototype, photoengraving, and zinc halftone) were patented between about 1865 and 1885. The type of screen now in general use was patented by Frederick E. Ives of Philadelphia in 1885–1886. It uses two sheets of glass with opaque lines ruled on them at right angles to each other, so that when the image is photographed the light passing through the

double screen is broken up into small dots. The fineness of the lines varies from 60 per inch for newspapers to 120 per inch in general use, to even as many as 400 per inch. Varying densities of dots produce shading. Black dots can be "photomechanically" eliminated in highlights, thereby making use of the whiteness of the paper. See www.haleysteele.com/hs_root/learning/technical/half_tone.html, consulted December 3, 2004.

13. In the large-format editions, however, such as the 1904 "Third Impression," the reading field is confused and the precise stylistic correspondence of image and text spoiled by the addition of four halftone plates, also by Smith, whose style and content—dramatically heightened vignettes—clash with those of the spare line drawings. The overly wide margins are cluttered with drawings that, in the small editions, appear as full-page illustrations. That Austin herself was not pleased can be inferred from her apologetic statement to Eve Lummis (to whom the book was dedicated) that she seemed to have tacked Lummis's name onto a book that had turned out to be "more margin than literature" (quoted in Lanigan Stineman, 66, who dates the letter conjecturally 1904).
14. Smith's drawing is very similar, though not identical, to an emblem frequently used in the magazine *The Land of Sunshine.*
15. Among the most spectacular demonstrations of the importance of an aesthetic of big sky in both vernacular and artistic envisioning of the Great Plains are the paintings of Keith Jacobshagen, some of which are held by the Great Plains Art Collection at the University of Nebraska, Lincoln.
16. Austin had fostered Adams professionally by collaborating with him on *Taos Pueblo* in 1930.
17. But in the large format, both coyote and moon are moved to the wide margin with no interposing landscape of print.
18. See Barney Nelson, *The Wild and the Domestic.* Nelson argues that in *The Flock,* Austin "defends both sheep and shepherds, almost point by point, from Muir's earlier published accusations. . . . Through sheep, Austin, as the true leveler, struggles to understand the complexities of ecological interdependence and equality," contrary to Muir's "elitist" views of "western land value and use" (23). Anne Raine points out that Austin differed from Muir and "other wilderness preservation advocates" who wished to "protect the natural landscape's intrinsic aesthetic and spiritual value from contamination by urban and technological expansion and the hegemony of exchange value." In *The Ford* and in other writings, Raine continues, Austin "recognized that the borders between human economies and natural ecosystems could not be so neatly drawn" (248–49).

19. My dictionary of Latin American Spanish gives *barranca* as a ditch, channel, or gulch, but Austin's adjective "tall" clearly implies a different meaning.
20. See Ruppert, "Discovering America," 250. Karen Langlois discredits Austin's reputation in "Marketing the American Indian," calling her involvement in Native American matters her "stock in trade" (158).
21. Lanigan Stineman proposes, indeed, that Austin should be numbered among "modernist literary and visual experimenters" such as Proust, Joyce, and Picasso (185). It is doubtful that she will ever be grouped with these giants, in part because of her choice of genres and in part because her vision bears the supposed taint of regionalism.
22. The bracketed emendation in this passage is my own. The phrase is printed "from whose top, streams cloud like smoke" in the first edition and in the reprint published by the University of Illinois Press in 2003. I am convinced that the printed version represents an unnoticed typographical error.
23. Austin to Alice Corbin Henderson, April 7, [1915?, 1919?], Harry Ransom Humanities Research Center, University of Texas at Austin.
24. We might note, however, that according to rangers at the Saguaro National Monument this scene is inaccurate; the pulp of cactus in fact produces sickness or death.
25. The tone of Austin's statement in a letter to Amy Lowell (written from Taos on July 20, 1923) that she was going to build a house in Santa Fe implies that her decision was reached after a comparatively short period of consideration. Her familiarity with New Mexico and Arizona had been built up over a period of several years, however, even though intermittently.
26. Lanigan Stineman, 124, 132. A letter to Alice Corbin Henderson written from the Desert Laboratory, Tucson, and dated December 15, [1919], is found in the Austin-Henderson correspondence at the Harry Ransom Humanities Research Center, University of Texas at Austin.

Chapter 3

1. My reference here to Austin's writings of the Southwest refers to her writings about, and in, New Mexico and Arizona. To be sure, southern California can appropriately be included under that term, as the westernmost extension of the Southwest's arid plains and mountains, and was so designated in the pages of *The Land of Sunshine*, Charles Lummis's magazine that Austin knew well. Even so, for both clarity and convenience, I generally distinguish between them,

reserving the term "the Southwest" for Arizona and New Mexico.

2. T. M. Pearce called her "a feminist before all else" (*Literary America* 251). Subsequent scholars have usually agreed.
3. See Staples, especially 195–96.
4. Austin might well have compared the treatment of Native women to that of African American women, but did not.
5. The significance of the adjective "swarthy" is evident in the fact that the biracial (Scottish and Native American) heroine of Helen Hunt Jackson's *Ramona* is said to have "just enough of olive tint in complexion to underlie and enrich her skin without making it swarthy" (38).
6. In dime novels, too, there were exceptions to the pattern in the form of counter-stereotype heroines; see Faith Jaycox, "Regeneration," 7. As Jaycox points out, Henry Nash Smith drew attention to these heroines in his influential 1950 study *Virgin Land.*
7. James Ruppert, expressing misgivings about the extent to which Austin carried her belief in the shaping power of landscape, calls it "an assumption that I must call geographic determinism" (252). Probably many readers would indeed stop short of Austin's belief that the landscape itself somehow produced a characteristic rhythm in American poetry.
8. Eudora Ballintin's wealth, personal drama, and proclivity for gathering scintillating company about herself, together with her coming to New Mexico from the East and spending enormous sums on the construction or renovation of her house, make her almost certainly a portrait of Mabel Dodge Luhan, even though another woman is referred to in the book as "that woman at Taos who married an Indian" (*SA* 264). The throwaway reference to the woman at Taos may have been designed to put readers off the trail.
9. Melody Graulich, however, in her foreword to *Cactus Thorn*, includes it with *The Land of Little Rain, Starry Adventure, and Earth Horizon* as "a series of books which explored her most cherished theme, the influence of the desert landscape on human character, culture, and art" (viii).
10. Austin is by no means the only devoted observer to see the arid West as being predominantly orchid or mauve in undertone. My friend and colleague Mary Ann O'Farrell pointed out to me, years before I moved to New Mexico, the "different palette" there.
11. Mora's poem serves as the epigraph to Vera Norwood and Janice Monk's important collection of essays whose title borrows her phrase, *The Desert Is No Lady.*
12. See, however, Nelson's carefully developed and well-informed analysis of Muir's

career and of the presence of classist and racist as well as misogynist strains in his writing (74–88).

Chapter 4

1. Cather's copy of the Mathews guide is among a small number books from her personal library held by the Harry Ransom Humanities Research Center at the University of Texas at Austin. See also John and Cheryl Swift's article "Willa Cather and American Plant Ecology." The Swifts have presented valuable information on botanical accuracy in Cather's fiction in a series of conference papers.
2. This point is argued more fully in my article "Seeing and Believing: Willa Cather's Realism."
3. Willa Cather (henceforth WC) to Dorothy Canfield Fisher, n.d. (except for the notation "Wednesday" but probably written March 8, 1922), Vermont. Also, interview November 27, 1921, reprinted in Bohlke 39.
4. WC to Carrie Miner Sherwood, February 11, [1919?], Willa Cather Pioneer Memorial (henceforth WCPM), Red Cloud, Nebraska; Stout, *Calendar* #452, but the reference to the Christmas gift is not included in the *Calendar* summary.
5. See WC to Sergeant, April 22, [1913], J. Pierpont Morgan Library, New York; *Calendar* #257. This insight has been confirmed by the responses of many readers, such as Fryer, "Desert, Rock, Shelter, Legend," 32, and Thacker 152.
6. WC to Carrie Miner Sherwood, July 4, [1932], WCPM, Red Cloud; *Calendar* #1115. My summary of this letter, as well as others, paraphrases the original language.
7. See *Calendar of Letters* numbers 1115, 218, 400, 402, 411, 412, 413, 420, 423, and 424.
8. See *Calendar* numbers 127, 143 [original letter, at Columbia University, includes the statement about illustrations], 146, 165, 175, and 271. The letter to the recalcitrant artist has become available at Drew University since the publication of the *Calendar*; WC to Florence Pearl England, September 10, 1896.
9. *Calendar* #144, but see original letter at Texas Woman's University. In November 1909, slightly less than a year after this December 1908 letter to her sister Jessie, *McClure's* would publish a group of pictures by Jessie Willcox Smith called *A Child's World*, all very lush and in rich colors. These may give us a hint as to what it was that Cather found tiresome.
10. On Lummis's work as "quaint and picturesque," see Rudnick, "Re-Naming," 240.

11. The definition of vignette work is quoted from museum notes to W. H. D. Koerner's *The Last Trail,* published in *Saturday Evening Post* in 1930 (Museum of New Mexico, Summer 2005).
12. On the title page of *A Girl of the Limberlost,* Benda's name is shown with his full first name, Wladyslaw. In his listings in *McClure's,* he retained that usage until at least 1914. It is curious, then, that in *My Ántonia,* with its emphasis on an immigrant presence, his name is shown with only the initials, without the strongly ethnic first name.
13. Bintrim argues, on the basis of detailed evidence, that Cather had earlier executed her own illustrations for (among others) "Peter," "On the Divide," "The Dance at Chevalier's," and "The Affair at Grover Station."
14. See WC to Ferris Greenslet, November 24, [1917], and February 15, 1926, Houghton Library, Harvard University; *Calendar* #399 and #824.
15. Benda's illustrations also appeared in *Century, Scribner's,* and *Cosmopolitan*, as well as in books.
16. See Schwind, especially n. 4; also Samuels and Samuels, cited by Schwind. The letters to Ferris Greenslet and Roger L. Scaife on which I am drawing for the production history of *My Ántonia* are at the Houghton Library, Harvard University, bMS Am 1925 [341].
17. The frontispiece to *O Pioneers!* was done by Clarence Underwood.
18. Letter to Miss [Helen] Bishop, Secretary to F. Greenslet, "Saturday" (probably February 2, 1918); *Calendar* #408.
19. WC to R. L. Scaife, April 7, [1917], Houghton Library, Harvard University; *Calendar* #384.
20. In the process of preparing the present chapter, I was surprised to discover, or rediscover, that Jean Schwind cites this distinction in "The Benda Illustrations to *My Ántonia*: Cather's 'Silent' Supplement to Jim Burden's Narrative." Although I had long admired Schwind's article and believed I remembered it well, I had forgotten this detail and therefore unfortunately failed to cite her on this point in "The Observant Eye, the Art of Illustration, and Willa Cather's *My Ántonia.*"
21. WC to Greenslet, October 18, 1917, and November 24, [1917], Houghton Library, Harvard University; *Calendar* #394 and #399.
22. I find Schwind's argument that Benda's art of an "unbucolic Nebraska . . . thoroughly confounds" the pastoral vision asserted in the Knopf logotype on the title page ("a miniature portrait of Arcadian Pan") and that Cather emphasized it for ironizing purposes through her addition of the Virgilian motto *Optima dies . . . prima fugit,* while provocative, finally implausible.
23. WC to Miss [Helen] Bishop, "Saturday" (probably February 2, 1918),

Houghton Library, Harvard University; *Calendar* #408.

24. We know that Cather was keenly aware of Garland and thought his "veritism" grim; see Curtin, 137n, 155. Nevertheless, Woodress conjectures that she may have been imitating Garland in her own equally harsh early stories of life on the plains (78, 106). I am not aware of any evidence that she was acquainted with *The Moccasin Ranch* specifically.
25. Indeed, the file of Cather's correspondence with Houghton Mifflin held by the Houghton Library at Harvard University includes a letter dated December 4, probably 1917, addressed to a Miss Van Tuyll at the company, asking for two of the *Song of the Lark* dust jackets so that Benda could pick out certain details that she wanted him to use in one of the illustrations for *Ántonia.* Since the brief summary of this letter given in *Calendar* #401 does not include this detail, see the original.
26. Archival evidence of Cather's and Austin's personal acquaintance is to be found at the Houghton Library, Harvard University, and at the Huntington Library. T. M. Pearce's edition of selected letters of Austin, *Literary America*, prints a short letter to Austin from Cather. See McNall; Porter; and Stout, "Willa Cather and Mary Austin." Regarding biographical parallels, see Gelfant; also Stout, *Through the Window, Out the Door.*
27. WC to Elizabeth Shepley Sergeant, June 23, [1917?], Alderman Library, University of Virginia; *Calendar* #387.
28. WC to Greenslet, February 15, 1926; *Calendar* #824.
29. For a survey of early visitors and their sense of being overwhelmed by the strangeness and vastness of the prairie, see Thacker's chapter "Beyond the Borders of Culture: Explorers, Traders and Travelers," 13–53.
30. WC to Bynner, June 7, 1905; *Calendar* #105.
31. "Peter" appeared in the university publication *Hesperion*, which Cather edited. "On the Divide" was in *The Overland Monthly,* a nationally distributed magazine published in San Francisco. "The Dance at Chevalier's" appeared in the short-lived Pittsburgh magazine *Library*, of which only two microfilm copies are known to exist. See Bintrim, "Cather as Illustrator."
32. Cather, "Enchanted Bluff," *Harper's,* 774; reprinted in Faulkner, ed., 69, where "scrub-oaks" is rendered as "scrub oaks."

Chapter 5

1. When Cather would have given the interview published as the *Century* article in July 1925 is unclear. Her correspondence demonstrates that she was in Lamy, New Mexico, by at least June 12 and did not return to New York until long after the article appeared. It has been conclusively established that so-called interviews with Cather were sometimes solely her own work. See David Porter, "Cather on Cather." On the other hand, since the published interview is quite vague as to when the writer went to Cather's apartment to talk with her, he could have been drawing on scattered conversations.
2. Charles Lummis's column in the October 1897 issue of *The Land of Sunshine* called the West "the only portion of the United States which has antiquity" (7, no. 5: 207).
3. Audrey Goodman incorrectly places Cather's visit to Mesa Verde in 1912 (*Translating Southwestern Landscapes* 140). She did see cliff dwellings in 1912, but at Walnut Canyon.
4. WC to Greenslet, September 13, [1915], Houghton Library, Harvard University; Stout, *Calendar* #322. Greenslet's reply, dated September 22, 1915, makes it clear that the proposed book would have been an "illustrated Cliff Dweller Country." Greenslet's letters, along with Cather's side of the correspondence, are at the Houghton Library, Harvard University.
5. For the cryptic reference that I take to be to Austin, see the original letter WC to Ferris Greenslet, September 13, [1915], at the Houghton Library, Harvard University.
6. See March, 446; Murphy, Historical Essay, 352; and Lewis, 143.
7. The assumptions of white women such as Luhan and Austin are by no means free of their own kind of conquest, and have been roundly resented by Native thinkers. Even so, I would stress that they offer a constructive, as well as distinctively female, alternative to the models of conquest represented by, say, the U.S. Cavalry and celebrated in masculinist Westerns galore.
8. Papers of the Houghton Mifflin company at the Houghton Library, Harvard University, reveal that staff members at the press had worried about the suitability of Breton's painting from the first.
9. One wonders how Cather would have felt about the cover art of the 1991 Bantam paperback edition, the form in which students of the past decade and more have usually encountered the novel. Rather than the Breton painting, the Bantam cover features Thomas Eakins's *The Pathetic Song*, whose solemn, overdressed, and far from animated singer in a dusky interior setting scarcely conveys

the vigor and independence of Thea Kronborg, let alone the setting of her decisive experiences in Panther Canyon.

10. The article is conveniently reprinted in its entirety in the scholarly edition of *The Professor's House*, 327–34.
11. Susan Rosowski and Bernice Slote also analyze, in "Willa Cather's 1916 Mesa Verde Essay," ways in which "Tom Outland's Story" draws on the earlier article and point out, importantly, that the article indicates "the extent to which Cather drew upon her own experience in creating Tom Outland, previously traced almost exclusively to Richard Wetherill" (86).
12. I do not mean to suggest that Cather borrowed from Luhan in this particular. It is not clear how long Mabel worked on *Edge of Taos Desert,* in which the sentence I have used as an epigraph appears, or how much she and Cather may have discussed their sense of the landscape. We do know, from a 1934 letter to Luhan from Edith Lewis (Beinecke Library), that discussion of Luhan's memoirs occurred while they were in progress. Lewis states that she has read *Taos Seasons* (referring to *Winter in Taos),* finds it beautiful in the way its language conveys the sense of the place, and hopes it will be published. Cather, she says, has not yet read it. But since Cather elsewhere comments on other volumes of the memoir in letters to Luhan, one would suppose that she did so. *Winter in Taos* was published in 1935 and *Edge of Taos Desert* in 1937, ten and twelve years after *The Professor's House*, so it is possible and even likely that Mabel's wording was influenced by Cather's in "Tom Outland's Story."
13. A Territorial Bureau of Immigration was established by Congress in 1880, charged with disseminating information about the "inducements and advantages" New Mexico offered to prospective immigrants. Weigle and Fiore, 8, citing Billy M. Jones, *Health Seekers in the Southwest, 1817–1900* (Norman: University of Oklahoma Press, 1967).
14. The connection between Cather's family history and the popular belief in the restorative powers of the West's dry air is one more demonstration of the value of reading the letters along with the fictional texts. Susan Rosowski observes, "When I read Cather's western fiction against a background of the Cather family letters, I also recognize metaphors of health and disease that I had previously overlooked" (*Birthing a Nation* 56).
15. *Calendar* #383 and #384, but see original, WC to R. L. Scaife, April 7, [1917], Harvard University, bMS Am 1925 [341] folder 5.
16. *Calendar* #398 and #407, but see original, WC to Ferris Greenslet, [February 1, 1918], Harvard University, bMS Am 1925 [341] folder 7.

17. Cather seems not only to have wished to keep Grant Wood out of *Ántonia* but to have disliked his paintings in general. In one of the Depression years, probably 1936, she sent Christmas cards that she had apparently bought for a charity fundraiser, for which she felt it necessary to apologize. A note in her card to Margaret Crofts said that she didn't like pictures in the Grant Wood style on Christmas cards and made a humorous suggestion that Crofts "think of the cowboy-looking shepherds as C.C.C. fellows" and "one of the angels above as President Roosevelt" (*Calendar* #1346). Similar remarks appear in her Christmas notes to Carrie Miner Sherwood and unnamed recipients, possibly Mr. and Mrs. George Whicher.
18. *Calendar* #399, but see original letter dated November 24, 1917, Houghton Library, Harvard University. For the origin of the statement about the second edition's looking as if it had been done on a country press, Mignon cites unpublished notes by Alfred Knopf at the H. C. Ransom Humanities Research Center, University of Texas at Austin.
19. We recall that among the Benda drawings for *Ántonia* there is one of Lena Lingard that shows her face as well as figure very explicitly. Although I cannot speak for other readers, that image has never interfered with my imagining of Lena. The other Benda illustrations are far less delimiting in their depictions of Jim and Ántonia and thus can hardly interfere with one's "seeing" of them for oneself. Two of the drawings show Ántonia, but there is no close-up of her face, rather her whole body and expressive kinesthetics. Only one drawing seems to depict Jim, and even then we see only the back of his head and shoulders. Lacking close-up depiction of their faces, then, the drawings cannot intrude on our readerly construction of these two central characters. Whether this reticence in the visual "supplement" to the text was Cather's wish is unknown.
20. See WC to Thomas Masaryk, February 12, [1929], at the University of California at Berkeley. Perhaps her urge to tell Masaryk this reflects a certain uneasiness.
21. In height, the sizes of the sixteen footers are as follows (all being approximate measurements): one inch—4, one and a quarter inch—1, two inch—1, one-third page—5, one-half page—4, and two-thirds page—1. In width, all sixteen footers are the same as the block of type.
22. See *Out West* 29, no. 1 (July 1908): 2–3.
23. Here my view differs from that of Mignon, who judges the pictures to be "appropriate to Cather's own style of legend" (Textual Essay 555).
24. Robert and Doris Kurth Cather Collection, University of Nebraska-Lincoln

Archives/Special Collection, SPEC PS 3505 A87D4 1930. See Charles Mignon, "Cather's Copy" and "Willa Cather's Archbishop." It has been suggested that perhaps it was Edith Lewis who pasted the snapshot into the book, but I believe that is unlikely.

Chapter 6

1. As Fink points out, Austin's husband also liked to hike and camp in the mountains near their home and liked Mary to go along, but only so long as he could set the pace and manner of their excursions, an assumption that reminded her of the "narrowness of her existence" with him (121). See also Lanigan Stineman, 74.
2. For a fuller argument of this point, with visual evidence such as John Singer Sargent's painting *Repose* (1911), see Stout, *Willa Cather: The Writer and Her World,* 138–40.
3. On the performativity of gender, see Judith Butler.
4. See Fink 156; Langlois, "Mary Austin and Lincoln Steffens," 364; Lanigan Stineman, 146, 169–70; and Graulich, Afterword to *Cactus Thorn,* 113–14.
5. John Murphy, in the explanatory notes accompanying the scholarly edition of *Death Comes for the Archbishop*, attributes Cather's "narrative's presentation of New Mexican history," presumably including her characterization of Kit Carson, primarily to her reading of Ralph Emerson Twitchell's *Leading Facts of New Mexican History* (382). I wonder if she also modeled her idealizing conception of Carson on the picture of him given in an interview article with Jessie Benton Frémont (presumably written by Charles Lummis) in the February 1897 *Land of Sunshine.* The comments attributed to Mrs. Frémont (the widow of John C. Frémont) emphasize Carson's "Saxon" blondness (Cather refers to his blond mustache), his "true courtesy," and his gentleness—all attributes that characterize the Kit Carson of *Archbishop.*
6. This does not, by any means, indicate that Austin wrote in promotion of so-called development in the Southwest, as her sometime mentor Charles Lummis did. If she saw southern California as a land of opportunity, it was a very different kind of opportunity. At the center of her difference with Lummis was the city of Los Angeles, whose growth he celebrated and furthered, but which she saw as a blight on the land, stealing water from the central valley.
7. Austin writes in *Earth Horizon* that she and her mother "missed each other" (221)—missed, that is, in the sense of failing to connect.
8. See my articles "'Poor Caliban'": Willa Cather and the Song of the Racial Other"

and "Brown and White at the Dance: Another Word on Cather and Race."

9. Interestingly, Caffey makes the point that Oliver La Farge's 1929 novel *Laughing Boy,* which Cather greatly admired, was so "lyrical" in its approach that La Farge later came to believe readers had missed his intended critique of the cultural dispossession of southwestern Native peoples. La Farge produced a short story in 1934 and a novel (*The Enemy Gods)* in 1937 that more inescapably conveyed his "bitterness over the imposition of American values and Christian religion on the native peoples" (40–41). So far as I am aware, Cather did not comment on La Farge's works after *Laughing Boy.*
10. Austin's use of the word "swarthy" in "Bitterness of Women" is not so directly derogatory.
11. The cave is sacred to the defunct Pecos tribe, not the Navajos, as Judith Fryer says in "Desert, Rock, Shelter, Legend."

Chapter 7

1. Donald Ringe examines the pictorial mode as used by William Cullen Bryant and James Fenimore Cooper in *The Pictorial Mode* (1971). For these writers, as for Austin and Cather, visual art was an important medium and one with which, as Ringe argues, their writing had notable continuities.
2. The readiest example of such a plot is Stephen Crane's "The Bride Comes to Yellow Sky," but it is omnipresent, extending, for example, to Larry McMurtry's complaint that the "masculine" frontier has been "engulfed" by an urbanism he genders feminine (17). Stegner is quoted by Comer (40), who insists, however, that he "exceeds by every measure any other male rendering of the literary past" (46).
3. Rebecca Solnit writes surprisingly that landscape was "not significant in modern art," although it has become "increasingly significant in the recent strains of art that aren't part of modernism" (*As Eve Said* 45). Certainly landscape was important to Paul Cezanne, often regarded as the father not only of modernism in visual art but of the modernist consciousness. Although O'Keeffe persistently eludes definition as belonging wholly to any one type or school, we would surely think of her as a modernist, whatever other terms (such as symbolist) also come to mind. And landscape was of great importance to her.
4. A thread of connection, albeit a tenuous one, also extends between Newhall and Cather. In a separate collaboration published in *Arizona Highways*, later issued as a small book, Newhall and Adams did an article about the mission church near Tucson, San Xavier del Bac. This same old church appears in *Death Comes*

for the Archbishop, where Father Vaillant admires it and seeks to have it restored.

5. For an informative, concise discussion of the linked roles of environmental concern and gender in the "distinct cultural region" of the Southwest, see Vera Norwood and Janice Monk, Introduction, *The Desert Is No Lady.*
6. Stout, *Calendar* #824, but see the original letter at the Houghton Library, Harvard University, bMS Am 1925 [341], folder 16 of 45. Neither my paraphrase here nor the necessarily brief paraphrase in *Calendar* gives an adequate idea of Cather's statement.
7. In the important story "Storyteller," the area around the Inuit narrator's village functions the same way.
8. As Comer trenchantly writes, "The relationship of American Indian cultural production to western spatiality is one of the most complex examples of spatial politics in western cultural history" (37).
9. Since the language and myth system of Acoma is also Keresan, Ortiz and Silko share a common body of stories.
10. Like Austin, as well, Silko most emphatically revises the Western by not only acknowledging but featuring the "serious presence" of Indians as "individuals with a personal history and point of view" that as Jane Tompkins points out and laments is absent from both novel and movie Westerns (7–10).
11. Cather's and Lewis's relationship is only barely hinted at in recorded accounts of their life together and their joint work on drafts and proofs. Charles Mignon refers to Lewis as Cather's "editing partner" and "copyediting alter ego"; "Willa Cather's Process of Composing," 167, 174. Only one letter from Cather to Lewis is presently available (at the Willa Cather Pioneer Memorial in Red Cloud, Nebraska). Written on October 4, 1936, from Jaffrey, New Hampshire, its tone and the use of an endearment in the opening give a sense of loving devotion. See *Calendar* #1328.
12. For the reference to cartoons as well as for information in this paragraph about the origins of *Into Another Time* in Byers's and Randall's notebooks, I am indebted to Byers in a telephone interview, April 25, 2005.
13. We should note that Randall is by no means a writer exclusively of landscape ecology. The poems in her earlier volume *Dancing with the Doe* (1992) are primarily political in emphasis.

14. My friend Jim Sullenberger, who brought Randall's and Byers's book to my attention, is a frequent and longtime camper in the Grand Canyon. He says that the edges indicated by Byers's clear lines remind him of how, when he first awakes in his sleeping bag, the sight of the canyon walls' clear outlines against the sky or background walls immediately tells him where he is.
15. See especially the *Krazy Kat* strip of September 3, 1922, reproduced in Anderson, 176. On *Krazy Kat* and gender, see (for example) Anderson, 147–48.

ILLUSTRATION CREDITS

Material relating to Austin's *The Land of Little Rain* and Cather's *My Ántonia* is in part reprinted from *Cather Studies 5: Willa Cather's Ecological Imagination*, ed. Susan J. Rosowski, by permission of the University of Nebraska Press; © 2003 by the Board of Regents of the University of Nebraska.

Drawings by Barbara Byers from Margaret Randall's *Into Another Time* are reprinted by permission of the artist.

Illustrations by E. Boyd Smith from *The Lands of the Sun* by Mary Austin (© 1927 by Mary Austin, renewed 1955 by Kenneth M. Chapman and Mary C. Wheelwright) are reprinted by permission of Houghton Mifflin Company; all rights reserved.

Jules Breton, *The Song of the Lark*, and Georgia O'Keeffe, *Black Cross, New Mexico* are reproduced by permission of the Art Institute of Chicago.

Ten paintings and photographs are reproduced by permission of the Amon Carter Museum, Fort Worth, Texas: Stuart Davis, *New Mexican Landscape*; Laura Gilpin, "Big and Little Shiprock, New Mexico"; Laura Gilpin, [Kellywood, Timothy's Mother and Child], otherwise captioned "Timothy's Mother Who Lives in Lucachukai" in Gilpin's book, *The Enduring Navajo, 1968*, p. 75; Laura Gilpin, "The Prairie"; Thomas Moran, *Cliffs of Green River*; Georgia O'Keeffe, *Light Coming on the Plains No. II*; Georgia O'Keeffe, *Ranchos Church, New Mexico*; Frederic Remington, *The Grass Fire*; Frederic Remington, *His First Lesson*; and Charles M. Russell, *Loops and Swift Horses Are Surer than Lead.*

John Gast, *American Progress*, is reproduced by permission of the Autry National Center (Museum of the American West).

Emanuel Leutze, *Westward the Course of Empire Takes Its Way*, and George Catlin,

ILLUSTRATION CREDITS

Nishnabottana Bluffs, Upper Missouri, are reproduced by permission of the Smithsonian American Art Museum.

Illustrations from the second edition of Willa Cather's *Death Comes for the Archbishop* are reprinted by permission of Knopf.

Snapshot of Willa Cather on horseback, pasted into her personal copy of *Death Comes for the Archbishop*, is reproduced by permission of the University of Nebraska Libraries.

Photographs by Lee Marmon, published in Leslie Marmon Silko's *Storyteller*, are reproduced by permission of Lee Marmon.

BIBLIOGRAPHY

Adam, Hans Christian. "Edward S. Curtis and the North American Indians." Introduction to *The North American Indian: The Complete Portfolios,* by Edward S. Curtis, 6–32. Küln: Taschen, 2003.

Adams, Andy. *The Log of a Cowboy.* Illustrated by E. Boyd Smith. 1903. Reprint, New York: Time-Life Books, 1981.

Albertine, Susan, ed. *A Living of Words: American Women in Print Culture.* Knoxville: University of Tennessee Press, 1995.

Alcoff, Linda. "The Problem of Speaking for Others." *Cultural Critique* (Winter 1991): 5–32.

Allen, John L. "The Garden-Desert Continuum: Competing Views of the Great Plains in the Nineteenth Century." *Great Plains Quarterly* 5 (Fall 1985): 207–20.

Allen, Paula Gunn. "The Feminine Landscape of Leslie Marmon Silko's *Ceremony.*" In *Studies in American Indian Literature,* edited by Allen, 127–33.

Allen, Paula Gunn, ed. *Studies in American Indian Literature: Critical Essays and Course Designs.* New York: Modern Language Association of America, 1983.

Ammons, Elizabeth. "Cather and the New Canon: 'The Old Beauty' and the Issue of Empire." In *Cather Studies 3,* edited by Rosowski, 256–66.

Ammons, Elizabeth. *Conflicting Stories: American Women Writers at the Turn into the Twentieth Century.* New York: Oxford University Press, 1992.

Anderson, Eric Gary. *American Indian Literature and the Southwest.* Austin: University of Texas Press, 1999.

Armitage, Shelley. "The Illustrator as Writer: Mary Hallock Foote and the Myth of the West." In *Under the Sun,* edited by Barbara Meldrum, 150–75.

Austin, Mary. *Cactus Thorn.* Reno: University of Nevada Press, 1988.

Austin, Mary. *California: The Land of the Sun.* Painted by Sutton Palmer. Described by Mary Austin. London: Adam and Charles Black, 1914.

BIBLIOGRAPHY

Austin, Mary. *The Children Sing in the Far West.* Illustrated by Gerald Cassidy. Boston: Houghton Mifflin, 1928.

Austin, M[ary]. "The Conversion of Ah Lew Sing." *Overland Monthly* 30 (October 1897): 307–12.

Austin, Mary. *Earth Horizon.* 1932. Reprint, Albuquerque: University of New Mexico Press, 1991.

Austin, Mary. *The Flock.* 1906. Reprint, Reno: University of Nevada Press, 1997.

Austin, Mary. *The Ford.* 1917. Reprint, Berkeley: University of California Press, 1997.

Austin, Mary. *Isidro.* Illustrated by Eric Pape. 1905. Reprint, Upper Saddle River, NJ: Literature House/Gregg Press, 1970.

Austin, Mary. *The Land of Journeys' Ending.* Illustrated by John Edwin Jackson. New York: Century, 1924.

Austin, Mary. *The Land of Little Rain.* Illustrated by E. Boyd Smith. Boston: Houghton Mifflin, 1903. Reprint, Albuquerque: University of New Mexico Press, 1974.

Austin, Mary. *The Land of Little Rain.* With photographs by Ansel Adams. Introduction by Carl Van Doren. Boston: Houghton Mifflin, 1950.

Austin, Mary. *The Lands of the Sun.* Illustrated by E. Boyd Smith. Boston: Houghton Mifflin, 1927.

Austin, Mary. Letter to W. I. Booth. April 27, 1907. Houghton Library, Harvard University, bMS Am 1925 (83).

Austin, Mary. Letters to Alice Corbin Henderson. The Harry Ransom Humanities Research Center, University of Texas at Austin.

Austin, Mary. Letters to Amy Lowell and Ferris Greenslet. The Huntington Library, San Marino, CA.

Austin, Mary. *Lost Borders.* [Illustrated by Denman Fink.] Boston: Houghton Mifflin, 1909.

Austin, Mary. "One Hundred Miles on Horseback." 1889. In *Beyond Borders: The Selected Essays of Mary Austin.* Edited by Reuben J. Ellis, 24–30. Carbondale: Southern Illinois University Press, 1996.

Austin, Mary. *Outland.* 1910. New York: Boni and Liveright, 1919.

Austin, Mary. "Regionalism in American Fiction." In *Beyond Borders: The Selected Essays of Mary Austin.* Edited by Reuben J. Ellis, 129–40. Carbondale: Southern Illinois University Press, 1996.

Austin, Mary. *Santa Lucia.* New York: Harper and Brothers, 1908.

Austin, Mary. *Starry Adventure.* Boston: Houghton Mifflin, 1931.

Austin, Mary. *Stories from the Country of Lost Borders* [including *The Land of Little*

Rain and *Lost Borders*]. Edited by Marjorie Pryse. New Brunswick, NJ: Rutgers University Press, 1987.

Austin, M[ary]. "The Wooing of the Señorita." *Overland Monthly* 29 (March 1897): 258–63.

Babcock, Barbara A., and Nancy J. Parezo. *Daughters of the Desert: Women Anthropologists and the Native American Southwest, 1880–1980.* Albuquerque: University of New Mexico Press, 1988.

Babcock, Barbara A. *Pueblo Mothers and Children: Essays of Elsie Clews Parsons, 1915–1924.* Santa Fe, NM: Ancient City Press, 1991.

Banta, Martha. "The Excluded Seven: Practice of Omission, Aesthetics of Refusal." In *Henry James's New York Edition: The Construction of Authorship,* edited by David McWhirter, 249–60. Stanford, CA: Stanford University Press, 1995.

Beidler, Philip D. *The Good War's Greatest Hits: World War II and American Remembering.* Athens: University of Georgia Press, 1998.

Berger, John, et al. *Ways of Seeing.* London: British Broadcasting System and Penguin Books, 1972.

Berthold, Dennis. "Parasols in the Landscape: Domesticating the American Sublime." Paper delivered at annual meetings of the American Literature Association, 1990.

Best, James J. *American Popular Illustration: A Reference Guide.* Westport, CT: Greenwood, 1984.

Bintrim, Timothy. "Cather as Illustrator." *In Willa Cather: New Facts, New Glimpses, Revisions,* edited by Merrill Skaggs, 61-75, Madison. N.J.: Fairleigh Dickinson University Press, 2007.

Blend, Benay. "Mary Austin and the Western Conservation Movement, 1900–1927." *Journal of the Southwest* 30 (1988): 12–34.

Bohlke, L. Brent, ed. *Willa Cather in Person: Interviews, Speeches, and Letters.* Lincoln: University of Nebraska Press, 1986.

Boime, Albert. *The Magisterial Gaze: Manifest Destiny and American Landscape Painting, c. 1830–1865.* Washington, DC: Smithsonian Institution Press, 1991.

Bolinder, Matthew. "'Appropriated Waters': Austin's Revision of Thoreau in *The Land of Little Rain.*" In *Such News of the Land,* edited by Edwards and DeWolfe, 37–46.

Broder, Patricia Janis. *The American West: The Modern Vision.* Boston: Little Brown, 1984.

Broder, Patricia Janis. *Great Paintings of the Old American West.* Foreword by Fred Myers. New York: Abbeville Press, 1980.

Brodhead, Richard. *Cultures of Letters: Scenes of Reading and Writing in Nineteenth-*

Century America. Chicago: University of Chicago Press, 1993.

Bryant, Keith L., Jr. "The Atchison, Topeka and Santa Fe Railway and the Development of the Taos and Santa Fe Art Colonies." *Western Historical Quarterly* 9 (October 1978): 437–53.

Bryant, William Cullen, ed. *Picturesque America.* See Bunce, Oliver B.

Buell, Lawrence. *The Environmental Imagination: Thoreau, Nature Writing, and the Formation of American Culture.* Cambridge, MA: Harvard University Press, 1995.

Bunce, Oliver B., ed. *Picturesque America; or, The Land We Live In. A Delineation by Pen and Pencil of the Mountains, Rivers, Lakes, Forests, Water-Falls, Shores, Cañons, Valleys, Cities, and Other Picturesque Features of Our Country.* With Illustrations on Steel and Wood, by Eminent American Artists. 2 vols. New York: Appleton and Company, 1872–1874.

Butler, Judith. *Gender Trouble: Feminism and the Subversion of Identity.* New York: Routledge, 1990.

Caffey, David L. *Land of Enchantment, Land of Conflict: New Mexico in English-Language Fiction.* College Station: Texas A&M University Press, 1999.

Calderón, Héctor, and José David Saldívar, eds. *Criticism in the Borderlands: Studies in Chicano Literature, Culture, and Ideology.* Durham, NC: Duke University Press, 1991.

Cather, Charles Fectigue. Letter to Jennie Cather, October 30, 1870. Cather Family Papers, Nebraska Historical Society. (Duplicate at Love Library, University of Nebraska.)

Cather, George P. Letter to Jennie Cather Ayre, March 17, 1876. Nebraska Historical Society.

Cather, Willa. Articles and Reviews. See Curtin, William M.

Cather, Willa. "The Bohemian Girl." *McClure's* 39 (August 1912): 420–43.

Cather, Willa. *Willa Cather's Collected Short Fiction, 1892–1912.* Edited by Virginia Faulkner. Lincoln: University of Nebraska Press, 1965.

Cather, Willa. *Death Comes for the Archbishop.* 1927. Scholarly ed. Historical essay and explanatory notes by John J. Murphy. Textual editing by Charles W. Mignon with Frederick M. Link and Kari A. Ronning. Lincoln: University of Nebraska Press, 1999.

Cather, Willa. *Death Comes for the Archbishop.* 2nd ed. Illustrated by Harold von Schmidt. New York: Knopf, 1929.

Cather, Willa. "The Enchanted Bluff." *Harper's* 118 (April 1909): 774–81.

Cather, Willa. Interviews, Speeches, and Letters. See Bohlke, L. Brent.

Cather, Willa. Letter to Edith Lewis, October 4, 1936. Willa Cather Pioneer Memorial, Red Cloud, Nebraska.

Cather, Willa. Letter to Florence Pearl England, September 10, 1896. Casperson Collection, Drew University, Madison, NJ.

Cather, Willa. Letters to Ferris Greenslet. Houghton Library, Harvard University, Cambridge, MA.

Cather, Willa. *A Lost Lady.* 1923. Scholarly ed. Historical essay by Susan J. Rosowski with Kari A. Ronning. Explanatory notes by Kari R. Ronning. Textual editing by Charles W. Mignon and Frederick M. Link with Kari A. Ronning. Lincoln: University of Nebraska Press, 1997.

Cather, Willa. *Lucy Gayheart.* 1935. Reprint, New York: Vintage, 1995.

Cather, Willa. *My Ántonia.* 1918. Scholarly ed. Edited by Charles Mignon, with Kari Ronning. Historical essay by James Woodress, with Kari Ronning, Kathleen Danker, and Emily Levine. Lincoln: University of Nebraska Press, 1994.

Cather, Willa. *One of Ours.* 1922. Reprint, New York: Vintage, 1991.

Cather, Willa. *On Writing.* Foreword by Stephen Tennant. 1949. Reprint, Lincoln: University of Nebraska Press, 1988.

Cather, Willa. *O Pioneers!* 1913. Scholarly ed. Edited by Susan J. Rosowski and Charles W. Mignon with Kathleen Danker. Historical essay and explanatory notes by David Stouck. Lincoln: University of Nebraska Press, 1992.

Cather, Willa. *The Professor's House.* 1925. Scholarly ed. Historical essay by James Woodress. Explanatory notes by James Woodress with Kari A. Ronning. Textual editing by Frederick M. Link. Lincoln: University of Nebraska Press, 2002.

Cather, Willa. *The Song of the Lark.* 1915. Reprint, New York: Bantam Books, 1991.

Cather, Willa. *Stories, Poems, and Other Writings.* Edited by Sharon O'Brien. New York: Library of America, 1992.

Coke, Van Deren. *Photography in New Mexico: From the Daguerrotype to the Present.* Albuquerque: University of New Mexico Press, 1979.

Collection and notes on paintings of the Amon Carter Museum, Fort Worth, Texas.

Collection of the Thomas Gilcrease Institute of American History and Art, Tulsa, Oklahoma.

Comer, Krista. *Landscapes of the New West: Gender and Geography in Contemporary Women's Writing.* Chapel Hill: University of North Carolina Press, 1999.

Cooper, James Fenimore. *The Prairie.* 1827. Edited by and introduction by James P.

Elliott. Albany: State University Press of New York, 1985.

Cristy, Raphael James. *Charles M. Russell: The Storyteller's Art.* Albuquerque: University of New Mexico Press, 2004.

Corbin Henderson, Alice. *Red Earth: Poems of New Mexico.* Chicago: Ralph Fletcher Seymour, 1920.

Curtin, William M., ed. *The World and the Parish: Willa Cather's Articles and Reviews, 1893–1902.* 2 vols. Lincoln: University of Nebraska Press, 1970.

Daniels, Stephen. *Fields of Vision: Landscape Imagery and National Identity in England and the United States.* Princeton, NJ: Princeton University Press, 1993.

Danly, Susan, and Leo Marx, eds. *The Railroad in American Art.* Cambridge: Massachusetts Institute of Technology Press, 1988.

Danly, Walther, ed. *The Railroad in the American Landscape 1850–1950.* Wellesley, MA: Wellesley College Museum, 1981.

Deacon, Desley. *Elsie Clews Parsons: Inventing Modern Life.* Chicago: University of Chicago Press, 1997.

Delpar, Helen. *The Enormous Vogue of Things Mexican: Cultural Relations between the United States and Mexico, 1920–1935.* Tuscaloosa: University of Alabama Press, 1992.

D'Emilio, Sandra, and Suzan Campbell. *Visions and Visionaries: The Art and Artists of the Santa Fe Railway.* Salt Lake City: Peregrine Smith Books, 1991.

D'Emilio, Sandra, and Sharyn Udall. "Inner Voices, Outward Forms: Women Painters in New Mexico." In *Independent Spirits,* edited by Trenton, 153–81.

Dickson, Carol E. "'Recounting' the Land: Mary Austin and Early Twentieth-Century Narratives of Nature." In *Such News of the Land,* edited by Edwards and DeWolfe, 47–58.

Drinnon, Richard. *Facing West: The Metaphysics of Indian-Hating and Empire-Building.* 1980. Reprint, Norman: University of Oklahoma Press, 1997.

Duvert, Elizabeth. "With Stone, Star, and Earth: The Presence of the Archaic in the Landscape Visions of Georgia O'Keeffe, Nancy Holt, and Michelle Stuart." In *The Desert Is No Lady,* edited by Norwood and Monk, 197–222.

Edwards, Thomas S., and Elizabeth A. De Wolfe, eds. *Such News of the Land: U.S. Women Nature Writers.* Hanover, NH: University Press of New England, 2001.

Eisler, Benita. *O'Keeffe and Stieglitz: An American Romance.* New York: Doubleday, 1991.

Engel, Leonard, ed. *The Big Empty: Essays in Western Landscapes as Narrative.* Albuquerque: University of New Mexico Press, 1994.

Etulain, Richard W. *Re-Imagining the Modern American West: A Century of Fiction,*

History, and Art. Tucson: University of Arizona Press, 1996.

Evernden, Neil. "Beauty and Nothingness: Prairie as Failed Resource." *Landscape* 27, no. 3 (1983): 1–20.

Evers, Larry. Introduction to *The Land of Journeys' Ending,* by Mary Austin. 1924. Reprint, Tucson: University of Arizona Press, 1983.

Farrar Hyde, Anne. *An American Vision: Far Western Landscape and National Culture, 1820–1920.* New York: New York University Press, 1990.

Faulkner, Virginia, with Frederick C. Luebke, eds. *Vision and Refuge: Essays on the Literature of the Great Plains.* Lincoln: University of Nebraska Press, 1982.

Faulkner, Virginia, ed. *Willa Cather's Collected Short Fiction.* See Cather.

Fetterley, Judith, and Marjorie Pryse. *Writing out of Place: Regionalism, Women, and American Literary Criticism.* Urbana: University of Illinois Press, 2003.

Fink, Augusta. *I-Mary: A Biography of Mary Austin.* Tucson: University of Arizona Press, 1983.

Fischer, Mike. "Pastoralism and Its Discontents: Willa Cather and the Burden of Imperialism." *Mosaic* 23 (1990): 31–44.

Francaviglia, Richard, and David Narrett, eds. *Essays on the Changing Images of the Southwest.* College Station: Texas A&M University Press, 1994.

Fryer, Judith. "Desert, Rock, Shelter, Legend: Willa Cather's Novels of the Southwest." In *The Desert Is No Lady,* edited by Norwood and Monk, 27–46.

Garland, Hamlin. *The Book of the American Indian.* 1923. Edited by Keith Newlin. Acton, MA: Copley Publishing Group, 2002.

Garland, Hamlin. *The Moccasin Ranch: A Story of Dakota.* New York: Harper and Brothers, 1909.

Gelfant, Blanche H. *Women Writing in America: Voices in Collage.* Hanover, NH: University Press of New England, 1984.

Gibson, Arrell M. *Santa Fe Collection of Southwestern Art: An Exhibition at Gilcrease Museum, Tulsa, Oklahoma, 26 September–21 November 1983.* Foreword by Fred A. Meyers. Chicago: Santa Fe Railroad, 1983.

Gilpin, Laura. *The Enduring Navajo.* 1968. Reprint, Austin: University of Texas Press, 1994.

Glanz, Dawn. *How the West Was Drawn: American Art and the Settling of the Frontier.* Ann Arbor, MI: UMI Research Press, 1982.

Goetzmann, William H., and William N. Goetzmann. *The West of the Imagination.* New York: W. W. Norton, 1986.

Goodman, Audrey. *Translating Southwestern Landscapes: The Making of an Anglo Literary Region.* Tucson: University of Arizona Press, 2002.

Graulich, Melody. Afterword to *Cactus Thorn,* by Mary Austin. Reno: University of Nevada Press, 1988.

Graulich, Melody. Afterword to *Earth Horizon,* by Mary Austin. 1932. Albuquerque: University of New Mexico Press, 1991.

Graulich, Melody. Introduction to *The Land of Journeys' Ending,* by Mary Austin. 1924. Urbana: University of Illinois Press, 2003.

Graulich, Melody. Introduction to *Western Trails: A Collection of Short Stories by Mary Austin.* Reno: University of Nevada Press, 1987.

Graulich, Melody, and Elizabeth Klimasmith, eds. *Exploring Lost Borders: Critical Essays on Mary Austin.* Reno: University of Nevada Press, 1999.

Gregg, Andrew K. *New Mexico in the Nineteenth Century: A Pictorial History.* Albuquerque: University of New Mexico Press, 1968.

Gruber, Laura Katherine. "'The Naturalistic Impulse': Limitations of Gender and Landscape in Mary Hallock Foote's Idaho Stories." *Western American Literature* 38 (2004): 353–73.

Hall, Sharlot M. "God's Country—the Desert." *Out West* 29, no. 1 (July 1908): 3–26.

Hart, E. Richard, ed. *That Awesome Space: Human Interaction with the Intermountain Landscape.* Salt Lake City, UT: Westwater Press, 1981.

Hassrick, Peter H. With essays by Donna Davies, Bradley A. Finson, and Stephanie Foster Rahill. *The American West: Out of Myth, into Reality.* Washington, DC: Trust for Museum Exhibitions, 2000.

Hegeman, Susan. "Landscapes, Indians, and Photography in the Age of Scientific Exploration." In *The Big Empty,* edited by Engel, 49–74.

Henderson, Alice Corbin. *See* Corbin Henderson, Alice.

Hutchinson, Elizabeth. "Many Wests: Photographic Images of Western Peoples." *Western American Literature* (Fall 2004): 334–46.

Jackson, Bruce. "That Awesome Space." In *That Awesome Space,* edited by Hart, 3–8.

Jackson, Helen Hunt. *Ramona.* [Illustrated by Henry Sandman.] 1884. Reprint, Boston: Little, Brown, 1912.

Jackson, John Brinckerhoff. *A Sense of Place, a Sense of Time.* New Haven, CT: Yale University Press, 1997.

Jacobs, Margaret D. *Engendered Encounters: Feminism and Pueblo Cultures, 1879–1934.* Lincoln: University of Nebraska Press, 1999.

James, Edwin. *Account of an Expedition from Pittsburgh to the Rocky Mountains, performed in the Years 1819, 1820. By Order of the Hon. J. C. Calhoun, Secretary of*

War, Under the Command of Maj. S. H. Long, of the U. S. Top. Engineers. 3 vols. Philadelphia: H. C. Lea, 1822–1823.

Jaycox, Faith. "Regeneration through Liberation: Mary Austin's 'The Walking Woman' and Western Narrative Formula." *Legacy* 6 (1989): 5–12.

Jeffrey, Julie Roy. "'There is Some Splendid Scenery': Women's Responses to the Great Plains Landscape." *Great Plains Quarterly* 8 (Spring 1988): 69–78.

Jordan, David, ed. *Regionalism Reconsidered: New Approaches to the Field.* New York: Garland Publishing, 1994.

Kingman, Lee, ed. *The Illustrator's Notebook.* Boston: The Horn Book, 1978.

Kinsey, Joni L. *Plain Pictures: Images of the American Prairie.* Washington, DC: Smithsonian Institution Press, for the University of Iowa Museum of Art, 1996.

Kolodny, Annette. *The Land Before Her: Fantasy and Experience of the American Frontiers, 1630–1860.* Chapel Hill: University of North Carolina Press, 1984.

Kolodny, Annette. *The Lay of the Land: Metaphor as Experience and History in American Life and Letters.* Chapel Hill: University of North Carolina Press, 1975.

Kovinick, Phil. *The Woman Artist in the American West, 1860–1960.* Exhibition Catalog. Fullerton, CA: Muckenthaler Cultural Center, 1976.

Lamar, Howard. "Seeing More than Earth and Sky: The Rise of a Great Plains Aesthetic." *Great Plains Quarterly* 9 (Spring 1989): 69–77.

The Land of Sunshine [magazine], 1892–1901; continued as *Out West,* 1901–1916. Edited by Charles F. Lummis until 1910, when new series of volume numbers begins.

Langlois, Karen S. "Marketing the American Indian: Mary Austin and the Business of Writing." In *A Living of Words: American Women in Print Culture,* edited by Susan Albertine, 151–68. Knoxville: University of Tennessee Press, 1995.

Langlois, Karen S. "Mary Austin and Lincoln Steffens." *Huntington Library Quarterly* 49 (1986): 357–84.

Lanigan Stineman, Esther. *Mary Austin: Song of a Maverick.* New Haven, CT: Yale University Press, 1989.

Larson, Judy L. *American Illustration, 1890–1925: Romance, Adventure and Suspense.* Calgary, AB (Canada): Glenbow Museum, 1986.

Lawrence, Karen R. *Penelope Voyages: Women and Travel in the British Literary Tradition.* Ithaca, NY: Cornell University Press, 1988.

Lewis, Edith. *Willa Cather Living.* New York: Knopf, 1953.

Limerick, Patricia. *Desert Passages: Encounters with the American Deserts.*

Albuquerque: University of New Mexico Press, 1985.

Limerick, Patricia. "Haunted by Rhyolite: Learning from the Landscape of Failure." With photographs by Mark Klett. In *The Big Empty,* edited by Engel, 27–48.

Limerick, Patricia. *Legacy of Conquest: The Unbroken Past of the American West.* New York: Norton, 1987.

Luhan, Mabel Dodge. *Edge of Taos Desert: An Escape to Reality.* New York: Harcourt, Brace, 1937.

Luhan, Mabel Dodge. Letters to Elsie Clews Parsons. Parsons Papers, American Philosophical Society, Philadelphia.

Luhan, Mabel Dodge. *Taos and Its Artists.* New York: Duell, Sloan and Pearce, 1947.

[Lummis, Charles F.] "Kit Carson: An Interview with Jessie Benton Frémont." *The Land of Sunshine* 6, no. 3 (February 1897): 97–103.

Lummis, Charles F. *The Land of Poco Tiempo.* New York: Charles Scribner's Sons, 1893.

Lummis, Charles F. *Mesa, Cañon and Pueblo.* New York: Century, 1925.

Lummis, Charles F. Review of Mary Austin, *The Land of Little Rain. Out West* 19, no. 6 (December 1903): 679–80. [Inclusive page numbers of the full review article in which the review is featured as the lead item in Lummis's regular column, "That Which Is Written," are 679–90.]

Lummis, Charles F. *Some Strange Corners of Our Country.* 1892. Reprint, Tucson: University of Arizona Press, 1989.

March, John. *A Reader's Companion to the Fiction of Willa Cather.* Edited by Marilyn Arnold, with Debra Lynn Thornton. Westport, CT: Greenwood Press, 1993.

Marx, Leo. *The Machine in the Garden: Technology and the Pastoral Ideal in America.* New York: Oxford University Press, 1964.

May, Antoinette. *Helen Hunt Jackson: A Lonely Voice of Conscience.* San Francisco: Chronicle Books, 1987.

McClure's Magazine, 1906–1912.

McMurtry, Larry. *In a Narrow Grave: Essays on Texas.* Albuquerque: University of New Mexico Press, 1968.

Meldrum, Barbara Howard, ed. *Under the Sun: Myth and Realism in Western American Literature.* Troy, NY: Whitston Publishing, 1985.

Michaels, Walter Benn. *Our America: Nativism, Modernism, and Pluralism.* Durham, NC: Duke University Press, 1995.

Middleton, Jo Ann. *Willa Cather's Modernism: A Study of Style and Technique.* Cranbury, NJ: Associated University Presses, 1990.

Mignon, Charles. "Cather's Copy of *Death Comes for the Archbishop.*" In *Cather Studies 4,* edited by Thacker and Peterman, 172–86.

Mignon, Charles. Textual Commentary. In Cather, *My Ántonia.* Scholarly ed., 481–521.

Mignon, Charles. Textual Essay. In Cather, *Death Comes for the Archbishop.* Scholarly ed., 515–65.

Mignon, Charles. "Willa Cather's Archbishop: The Legible Forms of Spirituality." In *Willa Cather and the Culture of Belief,* edited by Murphy, 139–66.

Mignon, Charles. "Willa Cather's Process of Composing." *Resources for American Literary Study* 29 (2003–2004): 165–84.

Miller, Darlis A. *Mary Hallock Foote: Author-Illustrator of the American West.* Norman: University of Oklahoma Press, 2002.

Moers, Ellen. *Literary Women.* Garden City, NY: Doubleday, 1976.

Moore, Sarah J. "No Woman's Land: Arizona Adventurers." In *Independent Spirits,* edited by Trenton, 131–51.

Morgan, N. Wayne. "Main Currents in Twentieth-Century Western Art." In *The Twentieth-Century West,* edited by Nash and Etulain, 383–406.

Moseley, Ann. "The Creative Ecology of Walnut Canyon: From the Sinagua to Thea Kronborg." In *Willa Cather's Ecological Imagination,* edited by Rosowski, 216–36.

Murphy, John J. "Holy Cities, Poor Savages, and the Science Culture: Positioning *The Professor's House.*" In *Willa Cather and the American Southwest,* edited by Swift and Urgo, 55–70.

Murphy, John J., ed. *Willa Cather and the Culture of Belief: A Collection of Essays.* Provo, UT: Brigham Young University Press, 2002.

Naef, Weston J., and James N. Wood. *The Era of Exploration: The Rise of Landscape Photography in the American West, 1860–1885.* Buffalo and New York: Albright-Knox Gallery and Metropolitan Museum of Art, 1975.

Nash, Gerald D., and Richard W. Etulain, eds. *The Twentieth-Century West: Historical Interpretations.* Albuquerque: University of New Mexico Press, 1989.

Nelson, Barney. Afterword to *The Flock,* by Mary Austin. Reno: University of Nevada Press, 2001.

Nelson, Barney. *The Wild and the Domestic: Animal Representation, Ecocriticism, and Western American Literature.* Reno: University of Nevada Press, 2000.

Newlin, Keith. Introduction to *The Book of the American Indian,* by Hamlin Garland. Acton, MA: Copley Publishing Group, 2002.

Nilowski, Carol Porterfield. "Revisioning the American Frontier: Mary Hallock

Foote, Mary Austin, Willa Cather, and the Western Narrative." Ph.D. diss., Indiana University of Pennsylvania, 1996.

Norwood, Vera. "Crazy-Quilt Lives: Frontier Sources for Southwestern Women's Literature." In *The Desert Is No Lady,* edited by Norwood and Monk, 74–95.

Norwood, Vera. "The Photographer and the Naturalist: Laura Gilpin and Mary Austin in the Southwest." *Journal of American Culture* 5 (1982): 1–28.

Norwood, Vera, and Janice Monk, eds. *The Desert Is No Lady: Southwestern Landscapes in Women's Writing and Art.* Tucson: University of Arizona Press, 1987.

O'Keeffe, Georgia. *Georgia O'Keeffe.* New York: Viking Press, 1976.

Padget, Martin. *Indian Country: Travels in the American Southwest, 1840–1935.* Albuquerque: University of New Mexico Press, in cooperation with the William P. Clements Center for Southwest Studies, Southern Methodist University, 2004.

Padget, Martin. "Travel, Exoticism, and the Writing of Region: Charles Fletcher Lummis and the 'Creation' of the Southwest." *Journal of the Southwest* 37, no. 3 (1995): 421–49.

Parsons, Elsie Clews. Letters to Mabel Dodge Luhan. Parsons Papers, American Philosophical Society, Philadelphia.

Pearce, T. M., ed. *Literary America, 1903–1934: The Mary Austin Letters.* Westport, CT: Greenwood Press, 1979.

Pearce, T. M. *Mary Hunter Austin.* New York: Twayne, 1965.

Pells, Richard H. *Radical Visions and American Dreams: Culture and Social Thought in the Depression Years.* 2nd ed. Middletown, CT: Wesleyan University Press, 1984.

Pennell, Joseph. *Modern Illustration.* London: George Bell and Sons, 1895.

Pennell, Joseph. *Pen Drawing and Pen Draughtsmen.* New York: Macmillan, 1920.

Pitz, Henry C. *The Practice of Illustration.* New York: Watson-Guptil, 1947.

Porter, David H. "Cather on Cather: Two Early Self-Sketches." *Willa Cather Newsletter and Review* 45, no. 3 (Winter/Spring 2002): 55–60.

Porter, David H. "Cather on Cather II: Two Recent Acquisitions at Drew University." *Willa Cather Newsletter and Review* 46, no. 3 (Winter/Spring 2003): 49, 53–58.

Porter, Nancy. Afterword to *A Woman of Genius,* by Mary Austin. Old Westbury, NY: Feminist Press, 1985.

Pratt, Mary Louise. *Imperial Eyes: Travel Writing and Transculturation.* London: Routledge, 1992.

Pryse, Marjorie, ed. *Stories from the Country of Lost Borders,* by Mary Austin. New Brunswick, NJ: Rutgers University Press, 1987.

Putzi, Jennifer. "Capturing Identity in Ink: The Captivities of Olive Oatman." *Western American Literature* 39, no. 2 (Summer 2004): 176–97.

Raine, Anne. "'The Man at the Sources': Gender, Capital, and the Conservationist Landscape in Mary Austin's *The Ford.*" In *Exploring Lost Borders,* edited by Graulich and Klimasmith, 343–66.

Rainey, Sue. *Creating* Picturesque America: *Monument to the Natural and Cultural Landscape.* Nashville, TN: Vanderbilt University Press, 1994.

Randall, Margaret. *Dancing with the Doe: New and Selected Poems, 1986–91.* Albuquerque, NM: West End Press, 1992.

Randall, Margaret, and Barbara Byers. *Into Another Time: Grand Canyon Reflections.* Albuquerque, NM: West End Press, 2004.

Reed, Walt. *Harold von Schmidt Draws and Paints the Old West.* Flagstaff, AZ: Northland, 1972.

Reynolds, Guy. "Modernist Space: Willa Cather's Environmental Imagination in Context." In *Willa Cather's Ecological Imagination,* edited by Rosowski, 173–89.

Riis, Jacob. *The Old Town.* Illustrated by W. T. Benda. New York: Macmillan, 1909.

Ringe, Donald A. *The Pictorial Mode: Space and Time in the Art of Bryant, Irving and Cooper.* Lexington: University Press of Kentucky, 1971.

Rosowski, Susan J. *Birthing a Nation: Gender, Creativity, and the West in American Literature.* Lincoln: University of Nebraska Press, 1999.

Rosowski, Susan J. "Willa Cather's Female Landscapes: *The Song of the Lark* and *Lucy Gayheart.*" *Women's Studies* 11 (1984): 233–46.

Rosowski, Susan J., and Bernice Slote. "Willa Cather's 1916 Mesa Verde Essay: The Genesis of *The Professor's House.*" *Prairie Schooner* 52 (1984): 91–92.

Rosowski, Susan J., ed. *Cather Studies 3.* Lincoln: University of Nebraska Press, 1996.

Rosowski, Susan J., ed. *Cather Studies 5: Willa Cather's Ecological Imagination.* Lincoln: University of Nebraska Press, 2003.

Rosowski, Susan J., with Kari A. Ronning. Historical essay. In *A Lost Lady,* by Willa Cather. Scholarly ed. Lincoln: University of Nebraska Press, 1997.

Rossi, Paul A., and David C. Hunt. *The Art of the Old West: From the Collection of the Gilcrease Institute.* New York: Knopf, 1971.

Rothman, Hal K., ed. *Reopening the American West.* Tucson: University of Arizona Press, 1998.

Rudnick, Lois. Introduction to *Edge of Taos Desert,* by Mabel Dodge Luhan. 1937.

Albuquerque: University of New Mexico Press, 1987.

Rudnick, Lois. "Re-Naming the Land: Anglo Expatriate Women in the Southwest." In *The Desert Is No Lady,* edited by Norwood and Monk, 10–26.

Runte, Alfred. "The Artist and the Environment: The Role of Romanticism in Saving the American West." In *That Awesome Space,* edited by Hart, 32–34.

Ruppert, James. "Discovering America: Mary Austin and Imagism." In *Studies in American Indian Literature,* edited by Allen, 243–58.

Ryder, Mary R. "Willa Cather as Nature Writer: A Cry in the Wilderness." In *Such News of the Land,* edited by Edwards and DeWolfe, 75–84.

Sandweiss, Martha A. "Laura Gilpin and the Tradition of American Landscape Photography." In *The Desert Is No Lady,* edited by Norwood and Monk, 62–73.

Scharff, Virginia. "Introduction: Women Envision the West, 1890–1945." In *Independent Spirits,* edited by Trenton, 1–7.

Scheick, William J. "Mary Austin's Disfigurement of the Southwest in *The Land of Little Rain.*" *Western American Literature* 27 (1992): 37–46.

Schlenz, Mark. "Rhetorics of Region in *Starry Adventure* and *Death Comes for the Archbishop.*" In *Regionalism Reconsidered,* edited by Jordan, 65–85.

Schwarz, Ted. "The Santa Fe Railway and Early Southwest Artists." *The American West* (October 1982): 32–41.

Schwind, Jean. "The Benda Illustrations to *My Ántonia:* Cather's 'Silent' Supplement to Jim Burden's Narrative." *PMLA* 100 (1985): 51–67.

Sergeant, Elizabeth Shepley. *Willa Cather: A Memoir.* 1953. Reprint, Athens: Ohio University Press, 1992.

Silko, Leslie Marmon. *Storyteller.* New York: Arcade, 1981.

Sivils, Matthew Wynn. "Willa Cather's 'River of Silver Sound': Woman as Ecosystem in *The Song of the Lark.*" *Southwestern American Literature* 30, no. 1 (Fall 2004): 9–21.

Slote, Bernice. "Willa Cather and Plains Culture." In *Vision and Refuge,* edited by Faulkner and Luebke, 93–105.

Smith, E. Boyd. Letters to and from the Houghton Mifflin Company. Houghton Library, Harvard University, Cambridge, MA.

Smith, Sherry L. *Reimagining Indians: Native Americans through Anglo Eyes, 1880–1940.* Oxford: Oxford University Press, 2000.

Solnit, Rebecca. *As Eve Said to the Serpent: On Landscape, Gender, and Art.* Athens: University of Georgia Press, 2001.

Spicer, Edward H. *Cycles of Conquest: The Impact of Spain, Mexico, and the United States on the Indians of the Southwest, 1533–1960.* Tucson: University of Arizona Press, 1962.

Staples, Joe. "'Discovering' New Talent: Charles F. Lummis's Conflicted Mentorship of Sui Sin Far, Sharlot Hall, and Mary Austin." *Western American Literature* 40, no. 2 (2005): 175–205.

Stineman, Esther Lanigan. *See* Lanigan.

Stoller, Marianne L. "Peregrinas with Many Visions: Hispanic Women Artists of New Mexico, Southern Colorado, and Texas." In *The Desert Is No Lady,* edited by Norwood and Monk, 125–45.

Stouck, David. "Mary Austin and Willa Cather." *Willa Cather Pioneer Memorial Newsletter* 23, no. 2 (1979): n.p.

Stout, Janis P. "Brown and White at the Dance: Another Word on Cather and Race." *Willa Cather Newsletter and Review* 49, no. 2 (Fall 2005): 37–39.

Stout, Janis P. "The Observant Eye, the Art of Illustration, and Willa Cather's *My Ántonia.*" In *Cather Studies 5,* edited by Rosowski, 128–52.

Stout, Janis P. "'Poor Caliban': Willa Cather and the Song of the Racial Other." *Willa Cather Newsletter and Review* 47 (2003): 29–32, 42.

Stout, Janis P. "Seeing and Believing: Willa Cather's Realism." *American Literary Realism* 33 (Winter 2001): 168–80.

Stout, Janis P. *Through the Window, Out the Door: Women's Narratives of Departure, from Austin and Cather to Tyler, Morrison, and Didion.* Tuscaloosa: University of Alabama Press, 1998.

Stout, Janis P. "Willa Cather and Mary Austin: Intersections and Influence." *Southwestern American Literature* 21 (1996): 39–60.

Stout, Janis P. *Willa Cather: The Writer and Her World.* Charlottesville: University Press of Virginia, 2000.

Stout, Janis P., ed. *A Calendar of the Letters of Willa Cather.* Lincoln: University of Nebraska Press, 2002.

Stratton-Porter, Gene. *A Girl of the Limberlost.* Illustrated by Wladyslaw T. Benda. 1909. Reprint, Bloomington: Indiana University Press, 1984.

Swift, John N., and Cheryl C. Swift. "Willa Cather and American Plains Ecology." *Interdisciplinary Studies in Literature and the Environment* 8, no. 2 (Summer 2001): 1–12.

Swift, John N., and Joseph R. Urgo, eds. *Willa Cather and the American Southwest.* Lincoln: University of Nebraska Press, 2002.

Taft, Robert. *Artists and Illustrators of the Old West, 1850–1900.* New York: Scribner's, 1953.

Taylor, Cynthia. "Claiming Female Space: Mary Austin's Western Landscape." In *The Big Empty,* edited by Engel, 119–32.

Teague, David W. *The Southwest in American Literature and Art: The Rise of a Desert*

Aesthetic. Tucson: University of Arizona Press, 1997.

Thacker, Robert. *The Great Prairie Fact and Literary Imagination.* Albuquerque: University of New Mexico Press, 1989.

Thacker, Robert, and Michael A. Peterman, eds. *Cather Studies 4: Willa Cather's Canadian and Old World Connections.* Lincoln: University of Nebraska Press, 2001.

Thomson, David. *Silver Light.* New York: Knopf, 1990.

Tompkins, Jane. *West of Everything: The Inner Life of Westerns.* New York: Oxford University Press, 1992.

Trenton, Patricia, ed. *Independent Spirits: Women Painters of the American West, 1890–1945.* Los Angeles: Autry Museum of Western Heritage and Berkeley: University of California Press, 1995.

Truettner, William H. *Art in New Mexico, 1900–1945: Paths to Taos and Santa Fe.* Washington, DC: National Museum of American Art, 1986.

Truettner, William H., ed. *The West as America: Reinterpreting Images of the Frontier, 1820–1920.* Washington, DC: Smithsonian Institution Press, 1991.

Urgo, Joseph R. "'Dock Burs in Yo' Pants': Reading Cather through *Sapphira and the Slave Girl.*" In *Willa Cather's Southern Connections: New Essays on Cather and the South,* edited by Ann Romines, 24–37. Charlottesville: University Press of Virginia, 2000.

Walther, Susan Danly. See Danly.

Weigle, Marta. "From Desert to Disney World: The Santa Fe Railway and the Fred Harvey Company Display the Indian Southwest." *Journal of Anthropological Research* 45 (1989): 115–37.

Weigle, Marta. "Southwest Lures: Innocence Detoured, Incensed, Determined." *Journal of the Southwest* 32, no. 4 (1990): 499–540.

Weigle, Marta, and Kyle Fiore. *Santa Fe and Taos: The Writer's Era, 1916–1941.* Santa Fe: Ancient City Press, 1994.

Weitenkampf, Frank. *The Illustrated Book.* Cambridge, MA: Harvard University Press, 1938.

Welty, Eudora. "The House of Willa Cather." In *The Art of Willa Cather,* edited by Bernice Slote and Virginia Faulkner, 3–20. Lincoln: University of Nebraska Press, 1974.

Wilson, Chris. *The Myth of Santa Fe: Creating a Modern Regional Tradition.* Albuquerque: University of New Mexico Press, 1997.

Wilson, Malin. "Walking on the Desert in the Sky: Nancy Newhall's Words and Images." In *The Desert Is No Lady,* edited by Norwood and Monk, 47–61.

Woodress, James. *Willa Cather: A Literary Life.* Lincoln: University of Nebraska Press, 1987.

Wyatt, David. "Mary Austin: Nature and Nurturance." In *The Fall into Eden: Landscape and Imagination in California,* by Wyatt. New York: Cambridge University Press, 1986.

Wynn, Dudley. "Mary Austin, Woman Alone." *Virginia Quarterly Review* 13 (1937): 243–56.

Zwinger, Ann H., ed. *Writing the Western Landscape: Mary Austin and John Muir.* Boston: Beacon Press, 1994.

INDEX

Index

Index

INDEX

Index

INDEX